About Island Press

Since 1984, the nonprofit Island Press has been stimulating, shaping, and communicating the ideas that are essential for solving environmental problems worldwide. With more than 800 titles in print and some 40 new releases each year, we are the nation's leading publisher on environmental issues. We identify innovative thinkers and emerging trends in the environmental field. We work with world-renowned experts and authors to develop cross-disciplinary solutions to environmental challenges.

Island Press designs and implements coordinated book publication campaigns in order to communicate our critical messages in print, in person, and online using the latest technologies, programs, and the media. Our goal: to reach targeted audiences—scientists, policymakers, environmental advocates, the media, and concerned citizens—who can and will take action to protect the plants and animals that enrich our world, the ecosystems we need to survive, the water we drink, and the air we breathe.

Island Press gratefully acknowledges the support of its work by the Agua Fund, Inc., The Margaret A. Cargill Foundation, Betsy and Jesse Fink Foundation, The William and Flora Hewlett Foundation, The Kresge Foundation, The Forrest and Frances Lattner Foundation, The Andrew W. Mellon Foundation, The Curtis and Edith Munson Foundation, The Overbrook Foundation, The David and Lucile Packard Foundation, The Summit Foundation, Trust for Architectural Easements, The Winslow Foundation, and other generous donors.

The opinions expressed in this book are those of the author(s) and do not necessarily reflect the views of our donors.

Green Cities
of Europe

Edited by
Timothy Beatley

Green Cities
of Europe

Global Lessons on Green Urbanism

Edited by
Timothy Beatley

 ISLANDPRESS

WASHINGTON | COVELO | LONDON

ISLAND PRESS is a trademark of the Center for Resource Economics.

Library of Congress Cataloging-in-Publication Data

Beatley, Timothy, 1957-
    Green cities of Europe : global lessons on green urbanism / edited by Timothy Beatley.
        p.   cm.
    Includes bibliographical references and index.
    ISBN 978-1-59726-974-2 (cloth : alk. paper)
    ISBN 1-59726-974-3 (cloth : alk. paper)
    ISBN 978-1-59726-975-9 (pbk. : alk. paper)
    ISBN 1-59726-975-1 (pbk. : alk. paper)   1. Urban ecology (Sociology)—Europe—
Case studies. 2. Urbanization—Environmental aspects—Europe—Case studies.
3. Sustainable urban development—Europe—Case studies. 4. Environmental policy—
Europe—Case studies. I. Title.
    HT243.E85B43 2012
    307.76094—dc23   2011041660

Text design by Paul Hotvedt
Typesetting by Blue Heron Typesetters, Inc.
Printed on recycled, acid-free paper ♲

Manufactured in the United States of America
10   9   8   7   6   5   4   3   2   1

Keywords: Aalborg Charter; Agenda 21; bicycle infrastructure; bike share; biodiversity; biophilic cities; climate change; community garden; congestion pricing; Copenhagen; eco-city; environmental policy; Freiburg, Germany; green building; green governance; green roofs; green urbanism; greenhouse gas emissions; greenway planning; floodplain management; Helsinki; London; Paris; pedestrian infrastructure; renewable energy; Rieselfeld, Germany; stormwater management; sustainable mobility; transit; urban metabolism; Vauban, Germany; Vélib'; Venice; Vitoria-Gasteiz, Spain.

Contents

Chapter 1   Introduction: Why Study European Cities?   1
Timothy Beatley

Chapter 2   Paris, France: A 21st-Century Eco-City   29
Lucie Laurian

Chapter 3   Freiburg, Germany: Germany's Eco-Capital   65
Dale Medearis and Wulf Daseking

Chapter 4   Copenhagen, Denmark: Green City amid the
Finger Metropolis   83
Michaela Brüel

Chapter 5   Helsinki, Finland: Greenness and Urban Form   109
Maria Jaakkola

Chapter 6   Venice, Italy: Balancing Antiquity and
Sustainability   129
Marta Moretti

Chapter 7   Vitoria-Gasteiz, Spain: From Urban Greenbelt
to Regional Green Infrastructure   155
Luis Andrés Orive and Rebeca Dios Lema

Chapter 8   London, England: A Global and Sustainable
Capital City   181
Camilla Ween

Chapter 9   **Conclusion: Green Cities of Europe as
             Compelling Models**   215
             Timothy Beatley

             Contributors   225
             Index   227

1

Introduction: Why Study European Cities?

Timothy Beatley

We are living on an increasingly urban planet. In 2008 we passed the half-way mark—50% of the world's population now live in cities, and that percentage is projected to increase to 70% by 2050. There is no turning back the urban trend. Yet ironically we have as a species yet to successfully design and plan cities that will accommodate our economic and demographic needs while uplifting and elevating us, and protect, restore, and nurture the planet and its natural systems. That we need new models of urbanization—that is, sustainable urbanization—is especially clear here in the U.S. Where to look for new models is always a question, and as this book argues, European cities remain a powerful source of potent ideas and inspiring practice. The chapters to follow, chosen to highlight the practices of some of these most innovative European urban exemplars, are written by experts and local planners who know these cities well.

Where we look first should be determined by a combination of those places with basic similarities—cultural, economic, political—and places employing a rich array of innovative tools, strategies, and ideas. And of course we should also look at cities that have already been successful at bringing about, and maintaining over a long period of time, the urban qualities and conditions we admire.

This is an especially promising time to think about and promote the environmental role of cities. There has been considerable attention paid in the last decade to how notions of sustainability begin to apply at local and regional levels. Many communities around the U.S. (and the world) are struggling to develop and implement a wide variety of initiatives and programs to make their communities more sustainable and livable. While the global (and local) problems faced are daunting, never has there been more attention paid to, and more faith expressed in, the ultimate sustainability of cities. In UN meetings, such as the 2006 UN World Urban Forum in Vancouver, which I attended (and the two subsequent world urban forums in Nanjing and Rio, respectively), nations across the globe have embraced the concepts of sustainable urbanization and sustainable communities as central to any real progress toward solving world environmental and social problems on an increasingly urban planet.[1]

In the face of absent federal leadership on climate change, mayors and other local government leaders have shown significant leadership. The Mayors Climate Change Agreement, an initiative of former Seattle mayor Greg Nickels, has been signed by some 1,054 cities (as of July 2011), committing them to meet, and ideally exceed, the greenhouse emission targets of the Kyoto Accord. Many cities have embraced the goals and vision of sustainability, but are not entirely sure how to reach them and are hungry for new ideas, tools, methods, and models.

Cities and metropolitan regions are the newest and perhaps most important venues in tackling sustainability and in advancing a green agenda. It is at this level that many things are possible, that creative and innovative practice can find expression, that committed citizens and organizations can exert pressure and make a difference. The promise of the local is great indeed, and its stock is on the rise.

Over the last several decades, many American cities and local governments have developed and implemented sustainability initiatives, from Chicago to Cleveland to Santa Monica. Many of these communities have attempted to become fundamentally greener and have made significant and impressive strides. Yet, despite good progress in many communities, these initiatives are still very much in their formative stages, especially when compared with their European counterparts. In few other parts of the world is there as much interest in urban sustainability and urban greening policy as in Europe, especially northern and northwestern Europe.

I have been studying green initiatives in European cities for nearly twenty years (see *Green Urbanism: Learning from European Cities*).[2] One of my first observations from this work was that sustainability appeared to be much more commonly applied and pursued at the local or municipal level in Europe, and this is especially true for the cities included in this book. "Sustainable cities" resonates well and has important political meaning and significance in these locales, and on the European urban scene generally.

Europe has indeed been a pioneer in the area of sustainable cities. Fifteen years ago, the EU funded the start-up of a critical initiative, the Sustainable Cities and Towns Campaign, which became an important network of communities pursuing common sustainability goals. Participating cities approved the so-called Aalborg Charter (from Aalborg, Denmark, the site of the first campaign conference). As of 2011, more than 2,500 cities and towns had signed the charter.[3] In addition to connecting cities and providing information about sustainability initiatives, this organization gives out a European Sustainable City Award (the first was issued in 1996), something that has become highly coveted and valued by politicians and city officials. I had the chance to visit the mayor of Albertslund, Denmark, a winner of this award, and will not forget the pride with which the mayor held up the award for us to photograph; he clearly viewed this as a significant accomplishment, and as a credit to the value (political and popular) placed on all matters green and sustainable.

Europeans have found many similar ways to inspire, encourage, and provide positive support for cities pursuing sustainability. Cities can now compete for the designation of Green Capital City, for instance. This program was created by the European Commission to recognize cities that have a "consistent record of achieving high environmental standards," and are "committed to ongoing and ambitious goals for further environmental improvement and sustainable development." Cities are also chosen to serve as role models for other cities, and to inspire other cities in a bit of friendly competition.[4]

European cities represent important sources of ideas and inspiration about green urban development and policies. The chapters that follow attempt to go well beyond the brief descriptions and anecdotal materials currently available about these cities, to understand, document, and describe much more thoroughly these innovative local (and regional) European green efforts. The result will be an extremely important and valuable resource for the hundreds of communities in the U.S. aiming to become more sustainable.

It is important to recognize and acknowledge the special role that Europe, and European cities, have played in the development of American cities. The most famous U.S. planners, designers, and landscape architects have visited prized European cities, gardens, and landscapes as a way of stoking their creative fires. This was true for luminaries and design greats such as Frederick Law Olmsted, Daniel Burnham, and Clarence Stein, among many others. And some of our most important planning ideas and tools can trace their origins directly to Europe. Zoning, for instance, was pioneered in German cities and brought to New York City by Edward Bassett.

While innovation transfers and learning have gone in both directions, examples from European cities have been especially fruitful for American cities. For several decades, beginning in the 1970s, groups like the German Marshall Fund sponsored study trips to Europe for mayors, and other local officials, with remarkable results. From waste-to-energy, to public transit, to urban design and efforts at pedestrianizing urban centers, American visitors take away important lessons and inspiration from these visits. Sometimes they fall flat (consider congestion pricing in New York City), but for the most part these innovations have taken hold.

Ironically, the antiquity of European cities (compared with American cities) is sometimes offered as an important difference that makes them less relevant to the American scene. But a strong case can be made that there is much to be learned from human settlements that have endured shocks of many kinds, that have grown and contracted, that have survived through war and famine and every other disruption. John Gallagher, a writer for the *Detroit Free Press*, makes the point that even shrinking American cities can learn from Europe. While decline in population in American cities like Detroit and Cleveland is met here with "civic panic," in Europe the perspective is of a longer arc: "The ebb and flow of population over time has given Europeans a more relaxed view of shrinkage," Gallagher argues.[5]

There are now many different, sometimes competing, ecological city-building models out there, and which ones are most useful or relevant remains an open question. There is no single model (nor should there be). Our imaginations have been captured by the hi-tech, tabula rasa projects like the eco-city Dongtan in China (now scratched) and Masdar City (under construction) in Abu Dhabi. There is a strong argument to be made that our best examples are ones that build onto and improve the existing conditions of already present cities, suggesting the importance of London or Vienna or Lyon, not Masdar (though I do believe there are things to learn from this new town as well). The journalist Chris Turner writes, "In a place like Masdar, you might find some fascinating future-tense technologies, but if you're looking for the state of the art in complete street design, mixed-use development and multimodal transit—in urban sustainability, that is—then Copenhagen's the place to go."[6]

One of the qualities that makes these European cities so important to understand is the creative blending of the new and the old, the importance of seeing long-term sustainability as necessarily embedded in a deeper span of history and commitment to place. Creatively balancing the new and the technological with the old and human is something that planners and designers in the U.S. and around the world are still attempting to work out, and there are many examples to follow in European cities—from the creative insertion of photovoltaic solar panels in central Copenhagen to the sensitive design of a tram system that fits well and works within the context of the narrow streets and historic buildings of Edinburgh.[7]

For many Americans (though certainly not all), these times of economic crisis and family belt-tightening have led to some questioning of the merits of the so-called American Dream. Large houses and cars, profligate spending, a commitment to the personal and individual realm, all those qualities that seem distinctly part of the American psyche and sensibility are in flux. In 2005 the social theorist Jeremy Rifkin wrote an informative, thought-provoking book called *The European Dream*,[8] in which he compared and contrasted these cross-Atlantic value systems, arguing that the Europeans in many ways have their priorities in better order. Table 1.1 compares these two perspectives on life. According to Rifkin, the American Dream "puts an emphasis on economic growth, personal wealth, and independence. The new European Dream focuses more on sustainable development, quality of life, and interdependence."[9] While the American Dream is, Rifkin believes, "deeply personal and little concerned with the rest of humanity," the European version is "more expansive and systemic in nature and, therefore, more bound to the welfare of the planet."[10] Rifkin may be exaggerating these differences but there seems to be much truth to the comparison, which further supports the utility of learning from European practices.

Opinion surveys suggest a shift in the direction of smaller housing units, and a desire and intention to become more embedded in neighborhood and place.[11] The trends suggest that the attributes of the European Dream described by Rifkin are increasingly attractive to many Americans. Perhaps more important is to recognize that from a sustainability perspective, and from a perspective of planetary health, the European Dream is a better model. I should not overstate the shifts in American lifestyle and consumption; Americans will still be highly consumptive, highly individualistic in their outlook, eschew the public for the private, and (at least in the short term) be very dependent on cars. Nevertheless, we seem unusually poised for change, and looking at European urban innovations and planning seems especially timely indeed.

Table 1.1   Comparing the U.S. and Europe

U.S.	Europe
Autonomy	Embeddedness
Self-reliance	Inclusive relationships
Risk-takers	Risk-averse
Personal wealth	Quality of life
Private property	Collective responsibility
Nature: to be conquered	Nature: "indivisible web of life"
Economic growth	Sustainable development
Emphasis on work	"Leisure and deep play"

Source: Summary from Rifkin, *The European Dream.*

On top of the concerns about the high fiscal and infrastructural costs associated with prevailing urban sprawl, are the costs associated with rising obesity rates among children and adults and the health care and other costs associated with our sedentary, mostly car-dependent lifestyles. Americans are not getting much exercise, and individual and community health are in no small measure an outcome of unsustainable land use patterns. It is time to search for new and healthier models of urban development. Figuring out how to design places and communities that propel us forward as pedestrians, that allow a natural integration of physical exercise and activity into our daily lives, that help to make us healthy is a major goal, and European cities again provide inspiration and hope.

The Global Model of European Cities

Another way to answer the question "Why study European cities?" is perhaps a more substantive angle: they possess, or a great many of them do anyway, many of the essential qualities of sustainable place-making and urban sustainability that we aspire to in the U.S. What is it that recommends European cities as exemplars for the emerging urban age?

While European cities have been experiencing considerable decentralization pressures, they are typically much more compact and dense than American cities. And while sprawl has been happening in Europe, there are still many more positive and compelling examples of cities maintaining and even growing dense urban cores. In Oslo, for instance, as a result of explicit planning policy, the city and region have densified. According to a University of Oslo study, in less than a decade Oslo has experienced an 11% increase in persons per hectare,[12] and in the process has protected an immense surrounding forest ecosystem (what the Norwegians affectionately refer to as the *marka*). The study notes the strong support for compact cities among Norwegian spatial planners, described as now having a "hegemonic status as a model for sustainable urban development."[13] It may not be surprising that planners are in such strong support, but elected officials and politicians in Oslo also understand its importance as a guiding paradigm for future growth and development.

In Freiburg, Germany (see chapter 3), a set of principles has been created—the Freiburg Charter for Sustainable Urbanism, with compact urban form at the center. Box 1.1 summarizes these twelve guiding principles, which are evidenced in Freiburg but would apply to many other European cities as well.[14]

These characteristics of urban form make many other dimensions of local sustainability more feasible (e.g., public transit, walkable places, energy efficiency). There are many factors that explain this urban form, including a historic pattern of compact villages and cities, a limited land base in many countries, and different cultural attitudes about land. Nevertheless, in the cities covered in this book (Copenhagen, Freiburg, Helsinki, London, Paris, and Vitoria-Gasteiz), there are conscious policies aimed at strengthening a tight urban core. And importance has been placed, in cities like Freiburg and Copenhagen, on maintaining populations living in the very center of these cities; unlike cities succumbing to sprawl, they are twenty-four-hour metropolises.

Major new growth areas in European cities tend to be located in more sustainable locations—adjacent to existing developed areas—and typically are designed at relatively high densities. New growth areas, furthermore, typically include and design-in a wide range of ecological design and planning concepts. From solar and wind energy, to community food production, to natural drainage, these new development areas and urban neighborhoods demonstrate convincingly that *ecological* and *urban* can go together. Many good examples of this compact green growth can be seen in the new development and redevelopment areas in many of the cities described in this book, from Vauban in Freiburg, to the Thames Gateway in London.

Sustainable Mobility

Rethinking the role of the car in cities (and society more generally) remains a major challenge for contemporary planners in the U.S. In the face of rising global demand for oil, and declining supplies (peak oil), many of us believe something must change (and will). While there is much work

Box 1.1
The Freiburg Charter for Sustainable Urbanism

Quo Vadis Civitas?
The future model for new settlements should be the Compact City. This is a city concept consisting of independently functioning units, in which the aspects of everyday life can be laid out and accessed within walking distance by all members of society. The City of the Future is a city of social and functional integration, cultural diversity, accessible education, resource conservation and regional dialogue. When outward growth is unavoidable or imperative for economic or cultural reasons, that growth should follow the principle of the Compact City. The following 12 principles are intended to provide the point of departure for the Compact City and as such serve as the foundation for the Sustainable City. They should be applied to all new development.

The 12 Guiding Principles
Spatial
    I. Diversity, Safety & Tolerance
    II. City of Neighborhoods
    III. City of Short Distances
    IV. Public Transport & Density
Content
    V. Education, Science & Culture
    VI. Industry & Jobs
    VII. Nature & Environment
    VIII. Design Quality
Process
    IX. Long-Term Vision
    X. Communication & Participation
    XI. Reliability, Obligation & Fairness
    XII. Co-operation & Partnership

Source: Academy of Urbanism, 2010.

in redefining the nature of the car itself (the move toward hybrids, and electric cars such as the Mitsu or the GM Volt), and some creative work in imagining a fleet of ultra-light urban automobiles,[15] the larger challenge will be to invest in the urban form and non-auto infrastructures that will increasingly permit urbanites to wean themselves from car dependence.

In the cities described in this book, a high level of priority is given to building and maintaining fast, comfortable, and reliable systems of public transport. Regional and national train systems are fully integrated with local transit. It is easy to shift from one mode to another. And with the continuing commitment to the development of a European high-speed rail network, modal integration is becoming even greater. Cities like Freiburg, which never gave up on its municipal trams, or Paris, which plans to dramatically expand its metro system in years ahead, show how we can address the future of urban mobility.

Very good train service, and the continued expansion and improvement of Europe's high-speed rail network, are important aspects of quality of life there. Especially impressive has been the expansion of high-speed rail into countries and parts of Europe where it did not formerly exist, such as Spain and Italy, and the transformative effects it is already having. As we struggle to understand why high-speed rail is so controversial in the U.S., Europeans continue to set high goals for the future. For example, Spain plans to provide ten thousand kilometers by 2020 and to put 90% of the country's population within thirty minutes of a high-speed rail station. Already the high-speed link from Barcelona to Madrid has shifted much travel away from air transport, with significant reductions in carbon emissions (a passenger traveling by high-speed train consumes an estimated one-fifth the carbon emissions of someone traveling by plane). A key message from Europe is that creating the conditions for car-free or car-reduced urban lives will require these kinds of inter-city rail investments.

Importantly, these investments complement, and are coordinated with, major land use decisions. Virtually all the major new growth areas identified have good public transit service as a basic, underlying assumption. The new community growth areas of Rieselfeld and Vauban, in Freiburg, for instance, both had new tramlines installed before the projects were fully built (both projects are described in chapter 3). Similarly, in the dense redevelopment of Hammarby Sjöstad, a fast tram runs down the spine of the neighborhood, providing unusually quick mobility, and from the start an attractive alternative to the car. There is recognition in these cities of the importance of giving options to new residents, establishing sustainable mobility patterns early, and integrating the investments in transit with high-density housing, as in the case of Hammarby.

Europeans have innovated and brought to scale many of our best sustainable mobility ideas. Car sharing, for instance, was pioneered in Zurich and other European cities, and has become a viable and increasingly popular option. Car sharing in North America has grown from a few hundred members in a handful of cities in the 1990s to more than half a million members, using more than ten thousand vehicles available in numerous cities.[16] Cities like Paris are extending further the idea of a network of small urban cars, available for short-term use. Paris recently unveiled its Autolib scheme, a network of electric-powered blue cars (also referred to as bubble cars), to be available at some one thousand dispersing locations around the city.[17]

Rates of car ownership in European cities (and countries), though on the rise, remain significantly lower than their American counterparts, and the relatively successful efforts of cities like Copenhagen, a result of the combination of providing walkable urban living conditions and investing in excellent alternatives to the car (e.g., transit, bicycles), show that significantly reducing dependence on cars is possible indeed. Few would argue that the quality of life is lower in Copenhagen because of the reduced dependence on cars (in fact, just the opposite).

Bicycles are one of the more ubiquitous and important mobility options in green European cities, those in the Netherlands, Germany, and northern Europe in particular. There are some eight hundred kilometers of bike lanes in Berlin, for instance, and Vienna has more than doubled its bicycle network since the late 1980s. Copenhagen now has a policy of installing bike lanes along all major streets, and bicycle use in that city has risen substantially. Forty percent of home-to-work trips in Copenhagen are made by bike, and the city is aspiring to go higher. Its new Green Cycle Routes initiative is creating new bicycle commuting routes into the city through and alongside parks and green areas. And even cities like London, where bicycles have been less important, are making significant and impressive strikes, creating there a series of Cycle Superhighways (discussed in chapter 8).[18]

In addition to expanding and enhancing their bicycle infrastructure, these cities have been the trailblazers and innovators in the area of public bikes. European cities have been responsible for pioneering the first, second, and third generations of public bikes, arguably beginning with the ideas of the Dutch activist Luud Schimmelpennink for a network of White

Bikes in Amsterdam, free for use by anyone who needed one. More innovations followed, including the still-impressive City Bikes programs operated in Scandinavian cities such as Copenhagen and Helsinki. In the case of Copenhagen, some 2,500 public bicycles have been made available throughout the center of the city. Few cities have been as bold in their support of public bicycles as Paris, under its new Vélib' bike system (an amalgam of the words *vélo*, bike in French, and *liberté*) (see chapter 2 and figure 1.1). Now the largest such system in the world, there are some 20,000 public bikes available from some 1,400 Vélib' docking stations scattered around the city, as of 2011.[19] These European systems have helped along a small but increasing number of North American cities now establishing similar shared bike systems (e.g., Denver, Washington, Boston, New York, Montreal).

Walking Cities

Getting people out of their cars also requires creating urban places and spaces that delight, that bring people in contact with one another and with interesting objects, events, and environments. Whether Barcelona's

Figure 1.1 The Vélib' shared bike system in Paris. European cities have led the way with innovative bicycle mobility programs. Credit: Timothy Beatley.

Ramblas or Copenhagen's Strøget, Bologna's arcaded sidewalks or Paris's pathways along the Seine, European cities provide countless examples of what is possible in the public realm.

While European cities have experienced a rise in automobility, their core urban form remains remarkably pedestrian. It is hard to overstate the value and importance of walkable streets, and indeed walkable cities. Providing physical exercise, opportunities to socialize, connections to place and nature, and enjoyment and fun, walking is an essential element of a green city. Spending time in cities like Vitoria-Gasteiz, it is almost impossible not to be an avid pedestrian; it is indeed the best way to get around (see chapter 7). Nearly half the trips made in Vitoria-Gasteiz are by foot, and no wonder, as it is a city of short distances, where emphasis has been placed on creating functional and beautiful pedestrian connections. The city puts walking front and center in its plans.

The concept of shared space and shared streets was pioneered in the Netherlands, with their concept of the *woonerf*, but has now been extended in many other creative ways.[20] The Dutch and the Danish have been leaders in applying the notion of naked streets and intersections—taking away car-oriented signage, lighting, and so forth as a technique for slowing cars and sending the psychological message that streets are public and pedestrian spaces as well. In London, and other cities in the UK, similar shifts toward shared space have occurred, including the designation of so-called home zones, and more recently experimentation with DIY street reclaiming. As the London chapter makes clear (see chapter 8), new approaches to way-finding will also be necessary.

Biophilic Cities

How to achieve compactness and density, but also ensure that urban inhabitants have adequate access to parks, trees, waterfronts, and nature, remains another key challenge and another way in which European cities lead the way. In many American cities (and certainly many European cities as well), the prevailing living (and working) environments are largely of concrete and asphalt, not especially green or natural despite the acknowledged need for such elements in our lives. E. O. Wilson's concept of biophilia suggests that we have coevolved as a species to need nature, that it is not optional but rather essential for emotional (and physical) health and well-being.[21]

Schools without natural daylight, workplaces with little or no connection to the outside (and lower worker productivity as a result), and urban neighborhoods with few trees, green areas, or elements of nature around them are common. It is perhaps not surprising that Americans are inside so much of the day when conventional city and urban design pays such little attention to celebrating, restoring, and integrating nature and natural systems into our communities. One outcome is what the journalist Richard Louv has called Nature Deficit Disorder—a particular concern that children today are suffering from growing up in denatured neighborhoods and communities.[22]

Many European cities have an extensive greenbelt and regional open space structure, with a considerable amount of natural land actually owned by the cities. Extensive tracts of forest and open lands are owned by cities such as Vienna, Berlin, and Graz (among many others).

Cities such as Helsinki and Copenhagen are spatially structured so that large wedges of green nearly penetrate the centers of these municipalities. Helsinki's large Keskuspuisto central park is a good example. It extends in an almost unbroken wedge from the center to an area of old-growth forest to the north of city, some one thousand hectares in area and eleven kilometers long (see chapter 5).[23] In addition, the city has developed an extensive, integrated network of green spaces. In Stockholm, there are an estimated one thousand parks and seven relatively large nature reserves, together constituting about 40% of the city's land area. Included here is Stockholm's large Ekopark very close to the city's center, where it is a short walk for thousands of urbanites to ancient oaks and diverse flora and fauna. And in cities like Copenhagen and Stockholm, there are many beaches and bathing areas, even places along the Copenhagen Harbor where, as a result of efforts at improving water quality over a number for years, urban residents are encouraged to swim (see chapter 4).

There is an important trend in the direction of creating and strengthening ecological networks within and between urban centers, another area where European cities have been leading the way. This has been most evident in Dutch cities, where national and provincial governments have focused on creating and protecting ecological networks. The Dutch government's innovative Nature Policy Plan created a national ecological network consisting of core areas, nature development areas, and corridors. This network is then further delineated at the provincial level, and cities in turn are tiering this network and building on it. Such networks at the city level can consist of ecological waterways (e.g., canals), tree corridors, and green connections between parks and open space systems. At the other end of the scale are efforts to connect together these national ecological networks to create a very ambitious European-wide ecological network.

European green cities have also been leaders in integrating regional climate and weather considerations into their local plans, with climatic elements common in German and Austrian plans, for instance. Cities like Freiburg have identified important corridors for airflows and breezes and placed height and building limitations in these areas (more in chapter 3). Similarly cities such as Stuttgart are notable for the designation of "ventilation corridors," or cool air movement zones intended similarly to ensure that cool breezes through that city are preserved.[24] Another important aspect of a biophilic city, exemplified by many of these cities, is an appreciation for and celebration of the unique climatic conditions and weather that prevail.

Oslo is a remarkable example of a green and biophilic city, with a compact and, as mentioned above, densifying urban form. Two-thirds of the land within the city's boundaries is actually owned by the city and maintained as protected forests that flank the city to the north. And nature in other forms surrounds to the south, with extensive natural shorelines and the Oslo fjord. Oslo's vision for its future, as expressed in its green plan, is "the blue and green and the city in between."[25] The city's emphasis on containing growth, in combination with protecting and setting aside such large expanses of green space, mean that urbanites there are never very far from nature. Indeed, it is estimated that some 94% of the population of Oslo lives within three hundred meters of a park or green area.[26] In Vitoria-Gasteiz, the percentage is nearly 100% (see chapter 7). In both cities, compactness permits this proximity to nature, rather than working against it.

Even more impressive are the green and natural qualities that cities like Oslo are envisioning for its future. Oslo has set the goal of daylighting (bringing back to the surface) and restoring all eight rivers that run through the city from the north to the Oslo fjord.[27] One of these, the Akerselva, has already been mostly restored, providing a remarkable green corridor, with trails and parks and abundant wildflowers, and the experience of the sound of several waterfalls in the middle of the city (see figure 1.2).

Vitoria-Gasteiz, like Oslo, has protected an unusual amount of habitat and natural land, almost half the land in this municipality. The city's greenbelt consists of a network of connected, encircling parks that serve

Figure 1.2 Oslo has given priority to restoring the rivers that run through the city. The Akerselva, shown here, is a major green amenity to urban residents and a popular place to walk, bicycle, and picnic. Credit: Timothy Beatley.

as a biological corridor connecting major ecosystems of the Zadorra River and the Vitoria Hills.

European cities have been pioneers in the areas of urban ecology and urban greening, with many instituting impressive programs to support, encourage, and plan for green, ecological elements. Many European cities either mandate or subsidize green features in new urban developments and in the retrofitting of existing urban areas. The installation of ecological or green rooftops has been a common practice, for example, the result of a mix of incentives and mandates. In many Dutch, German, and Austrian cities there have been long-standing green rooftop programs. In Linz, Austria, for instance, one of the most extensive green roof programs in Europe, the city often requires building plans to compensate for the loss of green space taken by a new development, and the green roof has been one common response. This city, like many others in Europe, also provides a subsidy for retrofitting existing rooftops with a green roof—paying up to 35% of the cost of an installation. The programs have been quite successful with hundreds of green roofs scattered throughout the city. Green roofs have been shown to provide a number of important environmental benefits, and to accommodate a surprising amount of biological diversity. Many other innovative urban greening strategies can be found in these cities, from green streets, to green bridges, to urban stream daylighting.

Integrating such green features into city building can take many creative forms. Green walls offer similar ecological benefits to green rooftops, and here as well Europeans have been leading the way. These structures cool the urban environment, retain stormwater, reduce energy consumption, and provide important habitats for birds and invertebrates. And depending on their location, they may be more visible and serve to enhance the greenness of cities.

Some of the cities discussed in this book, including Paris, are home to spectacular examples of green features. Patrick Blanc is a Parisian botanist who has designed amazing organic or green walls, for both interior and exterior spaces. Blanc's exterior vertical gardens, or *le mur vegetal* (plant wall) as he prefers to call them, offer one special way by which nature, albeit a highly artificial form, can find expression in an dense city. The green wall that graces the edge of the Musée du Quai Branly in Paris, a few blocks from the Eiffel Tower, is perhaps the most famous of his designs (with its 15,000 habitat plants, representing some 170 different species). And Paris has become a kind of epicenter of green walls, with more than two hundred installed or in some stage of planning (see chapter 3).

But green walls are popping up all over Europe. They include the magnificent wall at the CaixaForum Museum in Madrid, boasting some 250 different species of plants on this spectacular vertical garden, and they are beginning to find their way to American cities, from San Francisco to Portland. European cities have been leaders in programs and projects that demonstrate that nature and urban density can coexist. Examples include, for instance, Blanc's green wall design for the eight-story Hotel Athenaeum in London, and the new Bosco Verticale residential towers, now under construction in Milan, Italy, that will boast some 730 trees (and thousands of shrubs and plants), which will wrap the exterior of these twenty-seven-story towers with a blanket of green. Dubbed the "world's first forest in the sky," and designed by Stefano Boeri, this Milan project is emblematic of the European sensibility that cities can, if creatively planned and designed, integrate closeness to the natural world.[28]

Hammarby Sjöstad in Stockholm and Vauban in Freiburg are exemplary designs that create conditions where kids have connected spaces, away from the dangers of cars, and where moving from small green areas around one's home to larger green parks and landscapes in the city is possible. Greenwich Millennium Village in London is another positive example, and distinctive in its creative combination of high-density sustainable housing with impressive access to nature, including a new ecology park. This design provides residents with unusual visual and pedestrian access to a restored riparian wetland system, and a series of elevated boardwalks, bird blinds, and a nature center and viewing structure. Residents routinely watch nesting birds and aquatic life, in an area of the Thames River ecosystem previously defined by industrial development (see chapter 8).

There are many other exemplary projects to cite, too many for this short book. In Malmo, Sweden, the Western Harbor district (Vastra Hamnen) has been an international exemplar of an ecological brownfield redevelopment, and one that incorporates the natural world as a key design priority from the beginning. Builders working on projects here must satisfy a minimum green spaces factor (a formula stipulating a minimum level of greenery), as well as a system of green points. Builders have also included in their projects a variety of green and biophilic elements, such as nesting boxes for birds or bat boxes, butterfly courtyards, fruit trees, and green rooftops.[29] Green courtyards, native vegetation, and a vegetated water channel meandering throughout are a few of the more prominent and important green features there.

Climate Change and Renewable Energy

Energy and climate change are very much on the planning agenda, and these exemplary European cities are taking a host of serious measures to lower greenhouse gas (GHG) emissions, conserve energy, and promote renewable sources. European cities (and nations) have been early adopters and supporters of renewable energy and distributed energy techniques (energy production integrated into neighborhoods and urban communities).

The heavy use of combined heat and power generation along with district heating, especially in northern European cities, is one reason for typically lower per capita levels of CO_2 production. Helsinki, for instance, has one of the most extensive district heating systems, connecting more than 91% of the city's buildings. The result is a substantial increase in fuel efficiency and significant reductions in pollution emissions. District heating combined with decentralized combined heat and power plants are now commonly integrated into new housing districts in these cities.

Many cities, including Heidelberg, Freiburg, and Vienna, have set ambitious maximum energy consumption standards for new construction projects. Heidelberg sponsored a low-energy social housing project to demonstrate the feasibility of such designs, and in many cities there have been efforts to evaluate and reduce energy consumption in schools and other public buildings. Incentive programs have been established that allow schools to keep a certain percentage of the savings from energy conservation and retrofitting investments (e.g., Heidelberg's innovative system of performance contracts).

The idea of the "passive house"—which through careful design and passive solar and climate features uses even less energy (on the order of 15 kWh/year/m²)—has been pioneered in German and Austrian cities and is already widely discussed in the U.S. In addition, cities like Freiburg and Berlin have been competing for the label "Solar City," with each providing significant subsidies for solar installations. In Malmo, the Western Harbor project set a high standard with its goal of providing 100% of the energy needs for this redeveloped urban district from local renewable energy. This goal was in fact achieved through a mix of strategies and technologies, including a wind turbine, roof- and facade-mounted solar hot water heating panels, as well as the use of seawater and deep aquifer water for heating and cooling. Barcelona remains one of the few cities to have mandated solar energy: it now requires all new major construction and renovation to meet a minimum percentage of hot water needs (65%) from solar hot water heating, resulting in a dramatic rise in the amount of installed thermal solar in that city.

Cities can significantly support and underwrite the solar energy and renewable energy sectors, as many European municipalities have done. In these ways, cities can directly contribute to the economic viability of solar technologies (reducing the cost of photovoltaic panels, for instance), stimulate further private investment, and raise the public visibility of energy issues and options.

The vision of positive-energy buildings—buildings as power plants that produce more power than they need—is no longer a pipe dream, but a concept that is being put into practice in many places. One example, often cited by Jeremy Rifkin, is the GM factory in Aragon, Spain, which produces energy sufficient for some 4,600 homes from its rooftop array of photovoltaic panels.

When it comes to positive-energy office buildings, the Elithis Tower in Dijon, France, is purported to be the world's first (see figure 1.3). The fifty-four-thousand-square-foot building, completed in 2009, was designed to use a minuscule amount of energy compared with conventional office buildings (only about 20 KWh per square meter, about one-twentieth the

Figure 1.3 The Elithis Tower, in Dijon, France, is purported to be the world's first positive-energy office building. Credit: Tropism Communication.

French average). It was designed to produce more energy than it needs to operate, thus having a "positive" energy balance. By 2012 all new buildings in France must meet the low standard of 50 kWh per square meter per year of energy usage, and by 2020 all new buildings in the country are to be positive-energy.

Europe's greenest cities continue to push the envelope on climate change and renewable energy. Germany has shown the importance of feed-in tariffs, for instance, and creative financial instruments such as green mortgages that help home buyers to produce power. Copenhagen made a splash by declaring its intention of becoming the world's first carbon-neutral capital city.[30] And many European cities, from Vienna to London, have set high greenhouse emission targets. London's Climate Change Action Plan, for instance, sets the ambitious target of a 60% reduction by 2025 (double the target set by the UK national government).[31] The London Plan identifies a number of specific programs and actions, with many, such as congestion pricing, already in use. The Paris Climate Plan similarly sets a goal of 75% reduction in GHG emissions by 2050, and a similar range of energy and climate initiatives (including extensive use of geothermal energy, for instance, as described in chapter 3).

Per capita carbon emissions in these green European cities are already substantially lower than in American cities, and through many of the kinds of efforts described here are actually projected to decline. Stockholm's carbon emissions per capita were, for instance, a modest 3.4 tons per person in 2009 (down from 5.4 in 1990), and projected to decline to 2.8 tons by 2015, as a result of a variety of new green energy measures.[32]

New and impressive strategies for adapting to climate change impacts have also been adopted in many European cities, for instance Paris's steps to prepare for future heat waves (by designing buildings to enhance natural cooling and shading, and instituting a registry of vulnerable citizens who would be contacted and checked on during such events). Many coastal cities, such as Rotterdam and Hamburg, have developed innovative strategies for adapting to long-term sea level rise.

Sustainable Urban Metabolism: Cities as Systems of Material and Resource Flows

I have often argued that cities should be understood as living organisms with a complex and interconnected metabolism.[33] Cities rely on many inputs (food, energy, building materials) and produce many outputs (air and water pollution, solid waste). Our urban planning and management regimes usually don't take account of these flows, at least in any systemic way. One important notion of a sustainable city, however, is one that reenvisions and reimagines its metabolism, understanding it as a complex system, and looking for ways to, at once, reduce the size of the flows (e.g., the amounts of energy consumed by buildings, the amount of solid waste generated), shorten the supply lines by which these resources are delivered (e.g., growing more food locally and regionally, developing local and regional sources of wood and timber), and close the resource loops. The latter goal, especially, is about shifting from a linear urban metabolism to a circular urban metabolism, where waste flows are redefined as productive inputs to other urban activities. European cities have in many ways led the way in this new thinking and practice.

Cities like Stockholm and London have taken important steps to better understand and support these urban flows. Stockholm was one of the earliest cities to begin to develop strategies for closing resource loops, even reorganizing its governmental structure to ensure that different departments and sectors began to adopt a more "eco-cycles" perspective.[34]

The view of cities as complex sets of metabolic flows might also help to guide us in dealing with those situations (especially in the shorter term) where some degree of reliance on resources and energy from other regions and parts of the world still occurs. Understanding that food transported to large American cities will still occur, despite great efforts to promote local and regional production, suggests that efforts should be made to mitigate or compensate for the energy consumed and carbon emitted in this process. Perhaps that means contributions to a fund by which either solar and renewable energy projects or carbon-sequestration initiatives are supported in these regions and countries.

Perhaps this view of cities suggests the need to forge new sustainable (and equitable) relationships between and among regions in the world, and where cities strive for new sustainable relationships with their (international) hinterlands (e.g., through mechanisms such as sustainable sourcing agreements, region-to-region trade agreements, urban procurement systems based on green certification standards, among others). Embracing a metabolic view of cities and metropolitan areas takes us in some interesting and potentially very useful directions.

London is one place where there has been impressive new work to understand the metabolism of that city, especially through the report "City Limits: A Resource Flow and Ecological Footprint Analysis of Greater

London," commissioned by the Greater London Authority (GLA). This study presents one of the few comprehensive snapshots of a large city's metabolism—its flows and resource demands. The findings show that London requires immense flows of resource inputs, for instance, and requires a land area three hundred times its spatial boundaries to supply these goods and resources. The study has served as an important call to arms and a critical lens through which to understand and guide many policy and planning endeavors in that city, from food to energy (see chapter 8).

Few cities, however, have advanced further in rethinking urban metabolism than the Scandinavian ones. Swedish cities, and especially Stockholm, have led the way. Stockholm has worked hard to overcome the usual divisions that exist in local government, and to bring together its different municipal departments and agencies to coordinate their work and adopt a more holistic perspective on material and resource flows in the city. The most prominent outcome of this new approach has been the new urban ecological district Hammarby Sjöstad, which has emerged as a demonstration or pilot of what a circular urban metabolism might look like in practice. Now commonly referred to as the "Hammarby model," it serves as a key example of how this metabolic flows view can manifest in a new approach to urban design and building in a dense urban neighborhood. From the beginning of the planning of this new district, efforts were made to think systematically and holistically, to understand the inputs, outputs, and resources that would be needed and that would result. One example can be seen in the treatment of organic household waste: Biogas is extracted from it and returned to the neighborhood to be used as a cooking fuel in many natural gas stoves. A waste output, understood before as a problem, becomes redefined as a valuable asset.

Food production is another important opportunity to shorten supply lines and reform urban metabolism. European cities have a long and rich history of providing allotment gardens, and cities such as Copenhagen, Freiburg, Paris, and Vitoria-Gasteiz all have extensive gardens available in and near urban settings. Vienna has been able to retain a significant amount of agriculture within its municipal boundaries (some five thousand hectares, or about twelve thousand acres)—an advantage and function of compact urban form—and provides financial subsidies for local farmers producing organically. Copenhagen has set goals for how much of the food sold in city restaurants is to be organic, and cities like London have developed action plans for promoting local farms and producers and increasing opportunities for growing (and selling and processing) food in the city. Northern European cities have also led the way in separating, collecting, and composting food waste from restaurants and households. And on a host of innovative community food topics, from community-supported agriculture to agritourism to slow food, Europe has led the way.

This new paradigm of sustainable urban metabolism will require profound changes in the ways we conceptualize cities and metropolitan regions (seeing them as complex systems of metabolic flows), as well as in the ways we plan and manage them. New forms of cooperation and collaboration between municipal agencies and various urban actors and stakeholder groups will be required (e.g., municipal departments will need to formulate and implement integrated resource flows strategies). New organizational and governance structures will likely be necessary (e.g., every city with a foreign policy minister?) as well as new planning tools and methods (e.g., mapping the resource flows of a city and region will become a standard part of preparing a comprehensive plan).

Green Cities, Green Governance

European cities have also been leaders in taking steps to reduce their own environmental impacts—to walk the talk, if you will, by putting into place innovative governance structures that support their sustainability plans. American cities have made progress here as well, but still lag behind the efforts of Europeans. The European approach often begins with an emphasis on understanding ecological impacts and taking steps to reduce the direct effects of their own purchasing decisions, infrastructure investments, and delivery of services. Green audits are common and many cities have gone through one or more environmental management systems (and gained certification under schemes such as the EU's Eco-Management and Audit Scheme). Cities like Oslo, London, The Hague, and Vienna have prepared, or commissioned the preparation of, ecological footprint studies that assess the extent of the environmental resource demands placed on the planet from the residents and businesses in those cities (as expressed in terms of land area required). These footprint studies show how resource-efficient European cities tend to be, compared with American cities. The ecological footprint for Vienna, for example, has been estimated at 3.9 hectares per person, half to a third the size of most American cities.[35]

European cities have experimented with new ways of taking into account these sustainability goals in their decisions. Heidelberg, for instance, was one of the early pioneers in the development of the concept of eco-budgeting, as a way of helping elected officials understand and compensate for environmental damage. A number of Danish cities, including Copenhagen, have developed and are using some form of "green accounts" to track annual consumption of energy, greenhouse gas emissions, and so forth (see chapter 4). Many European cities have developed some form of environmental indicators, often through EU funding and support.

Shifting municipal fleets (buses, trucks, etc.) to greener fuels has been an increasingly common strategy undertaken by European cities, again reflecting a recognition of the need for local governments to set a good example and to serve as sustainability leaders. Few cities have done as much as Stockholm, where the city now runs some four hundred ethanol buses and a rail system powered by electricity from renewable sources. The city's goal is to reach a point in 2025 where the entire public transit system will be "fossil-fuel free."[36]

Working with local companies and businesses to help them become more sustainable is another hallmark of European green cities. A notable example is Vienna's EcoBusiness Plan, which has provided some six hundred local businesses (since 1998) with advice and guidance about energy efficiency and other strategies for reducing ecological impacts (and in turn enhancing profits).[37]

I have also always been impressed with the extent to which many European green cities have developed initiatives and programs to reach out to other parts of the world, often the developing world, to support sustainability initiatives, out of a sense of respect for and obligation to others living more humbly. *Glocalism* (a merging of the global and the local) is a word I often now use to describe this simultaneous emphasis on local economy and environment, and on responsible globalism, the recognition that cities have opportunities to uplift and improve living conditions and ecological protections in places thousands of miles away.[38] Whether in the form of support for fair trade (the first so-called fair trade town is found in the UK), or programs for sharing urban innovations, or assisting in the building of needed infrastructure in less-developed cities, European cities are often at the fore.

Models for the Future

European cities are facing many of the same serious problems and trends that are working against sustainability in American cities: a dramatic rise in auto ownership and use, a continuing pattern of deconcentration of people and commerce, and a lack of affordable housing. European cities exert a tremendous ecological footprint on the world, as do American cities (although European cities produce about half the per capita carbon emissions of American cities). Yet, despite these trends, European cities still represent a much more compelling model for the times we live in: at once more energy- and resource-efficient, more supportive of innovative green projects, more demanding of the environmental performance of buildings and cityscapes, and generally more reflective of a priority given to sustainability.

There are certainly many differences between the American and European contexts—social, political, economic—that help explain why green city ideas have had greater application and currency in Europe. These include a more limited land and resource base, a long history of urban living, a stronger planning and regulatory system, a parliamentary political system that often gives greater representation to green concerns, and stronger cultural support for a variety of green city ideas (e.g., public transit, pedestrian environments, energy conservation). Nevertheless, these compelling European examples will and must find ever-greater currency on the American scene, as the environmental challenges we face become ever more serious (e.g., climate change, declining oil supplies, severe water shortages), and the inherent merits of these forms of green urban living become ever more obvious.

The case studies in this book show that it is possible to apply virtually every green or ecological strategy or technique, from solar and wind energy to graywater recycling to food production, in very compact urban settings. These cases show that cities (and municipal governments) can do much to help bring these ideas about, nurture them, and financially and politically support them—from making parking spaces available for car sharing companies, to financially subsidizing the installation of green rooftops, to instituting incentives for the production of renewable energy in the city, to mandating certain green elements and features.

The "how" includes understanding the importance of partnerships and collaboration between different parties with an interest in sustainability. It includes integrating sustainability into municipal decision-making structures, and changing the economic and other incentive structures to support green options. It means getting different municipal departments to talk to one another and to work together (e.g., as they do in Stockholm), and getting different public and private actors to join in common initiatives that demonstrate that green urban ideas are possible and desirable.

For many reasons, then, European cities inspire and inform, and generally set the standard for green and sustainable efforts around the world. What follows here is a series of detailed cases of arguably the leading cities in Europe. Each chapter tells the story of an urban exemplar pushing the limits and boundaries and forging new conceptions of the green city. More specifically, the chapter objectives are as follows:

> To provide compelling examples of what is possible in American cities and metropolitan areas, especially in the face of declining global oil, climate change, and other challenges that will make business as usual very difficult or impossible; to show hopeful examples of how cities can both profoundly reduce their ecological footprints and also create beautiful, vibrant, highly livable, enduring urban environments.

> To provide the first detailed set of case studies and detailed descriptions of the most innovative green cities in Europe; to identify and describe the most exemplary and cutting-edge cities, and to provide detailed and in-depth descriptions of these efforts, written by local experts who know the programs and initiatives well.

> To identify political, social, and other factors and ingredients that help to explain successful development and implementation of green city initiatives; and to extract and discuss the important lessons for American cities learned in each place.

> To identify trends and future directions in green cities in Europe and the U.S., and to provide recommendations for how state and federal governments might facilitate and strengthen the development of such exemplary local efforts.

The emphasis in what follows is on learning from local (in-country) authors what is special about what their city is doing, how in practice its green and sustainable policies and planning are working, and whatever insights or lessons might be useful in redirecting American city policy.

As the British green author Herbert Girardet is fond of saying, "There can be no sustainable future without sustainable cities."[39] American cities, especially, must take this admonition to heart, and no better stock of ideas and inspiration can be found than those in the green cities of Europe.

Notes

1. See, for example, United Nations, World Urban Forum, "Report of the Fifth Session of the World Urban Forum," Rio, 2010, 42.

2. Timothy Beatley, *Green Urbanism: Learning from European Cities*, Washington, DC: Island Press, 2000.

3. European Sustainable Cities and Towns Campaign, "The Campaign," accessed May 4, 2011, http://sustainable-cities.eu/.

4. European Green Capital, "About the Award," accessed May 9, 2010, http://ec.europa.eu/.

5. John Gallagher, *Re-imagining Detroit: Opportunities for Redefining an American City*, Detroit: Wayne State University Press, 2010, 6.

6. Chris Turner, "Forget Sci-Fi Cities: Street-Level Livability Is a Better Way to Urban Sustainability," April 1, 2011, accessed May 4, 2011, http://www.mnn.com/.

7. See, for example, "Present Meets Past in Edinburgh," *Parsons Brinckerhoff Magazine*, First Quarter, 2011, 11.

8. Jeremy Rifkin, *The European Dream*, New York: Jeremy P. Tarcher/Penguin, 2005.

9. Ibid., 13–14.

10. Ibid., 14.

11. See, for example, National Homebuilders Association, "Characteristics of Single-Family Homes Started in 2009," October 7, 2010, accessed August 7, 2011, http://www.nahb.org/.

12. A shift from 37.9 in 2000 to 42.3 in 2009. See Institute of Transport Economics, "The Challenge of Sustainable Mobility in Urban Planning and Development in Oslo Metropolitan Area," Norwegian Centre for Transport Research, July 2009.

13. Ibid., i.

14. Academy of Urbanism, "The Freiburg Charter for Sustainable Urbanism," 2010.

15. See William Mitchell, Chris Borroni-Bird, and Lawrence D. Burns, *Reinventing the Automobile*, Cambridge: MIT Press, 2009.

16. "What Is Car Sharing," accessed May 6, 2011, http://www.carsharing.net/.

17. Kim Willshen, "Paris to Introduce Self Service Electric Car Scheme," *Guardian*, December 16, 2010.

18. See Transport for London, "Barclays Cycle Superhighways, FAQs," accessed December 22, 2011, http://www.tfl.gov.uk/.

19. See http://www.velib.paris.fr/.

20. For a discussion of the concept of the woonerf, see Beatley, *Green Urbanism*.

21. See E. O. Wilson, *Biophilia*, Cambridge: Harvard University Press, 1984. See also Timothy Beatley, *Biophilic Cities: Integrating Nature into Urban Design and Planning*, Washington, DC: Island Press, 2010.

22. Richard Louv, *Last Child in the Woods: Saving Our Children from Nature Deficit Disorder*, Chapel Hill, NC: Algonquin, 2008.

23. Beatley, *Green Urbanism*.

24. "Stuttgart: Cool City," accessed December 21, 2011, http://sustainablecities.dk/.

25. City of Oslo, *Oslo Green Plan*, 2007. See also Timothy Beatley, "Biophilic Oslo," forthcoming in Mark Luccarelli and Per Gunnar Roe, eds., *Green Oslo*, Surrey, UK: Ashgate.

26. City of Oslo, *Oslo Green Plan*.

27. Ibid.

28. "Towers of Trees: Vertical Forests in the Sky Are the Height of Green Living," *Daily Mail*, October 28, 2011.

29. See, for example, Timothy Beatley, *Native to Nowhere*, Washington, DC: Island Press, 2005.

30. See Timothy Beatley, *Low-Carbon Copenhagen*, report prepared for Timelines Engineering, 2010.

31. Greater London Authority, 2007.

32. European Green Capital, "Stockholm: European Green Capital, 2010," 2010, 30.

33. What follows draws heavily on earlier reports written by the author, such as *Sustainable Cities in the Southeastern U.S.: Trends and Future Directions*, prepared for Department of Defense Sustainable Ranges Initiative, 2009. See also "Green Regions, Green Regionalism," in Ethan Seltzer and Armando Carbonell, eds., *Regional Planning in America*, Cambridge, MA: Lincoln Institute of Land Policy, 2011.

34. Beatley, *Green Urbanism*.

35. See, for example, "The Ecological Footprint of the City of Vienna," Stadt Vienna, accessed December 15, 2011, http://www.wien.gv.at/.

36. European Green City, "Stockholm," 32.

37. City of Vienna, "Vienna Environment Report," 2006/2007, 90.

38. For more discussion of this idea, see Beatley, *Native to Nowhere*.

39. Herbert Girardet, *Creating Sustainable Cities*, Dartington, UK: Green Books, 1999.

2

Paris, France:
A 21st-Century Eco-City

Lucie Laurian

Paris, with a population of 2.2 million, is the capital of and largest city in France, a nation of 64.7 million (INSEE 2010a,b). Paris is regularly ranked among the great world cities, and its history, economy, culture, and iconic landmarks make it the most visited city in the world. In 2010 it was third on the Global Power City Index (IUS 2010), fourth on the Global Cities Index (*Foreign Policy* 2010), the seventh most livable city (*Monocle* 2010), and third on the World City Survey—second for quality of life and fourth for economic activity (Knight Frank 2010).

Paris entered the 21st century with a new administration and a strong commitment to sustainability. Perhaps most visibly, since 2001 Paris increased the proportion of urban space devoted to public transit, pedestrians, and bikes, and launched a rapid bus transit system and public bikes program. High-speed car lanes give way to bikers and roller-skaters on Sundays and become beaches in the summer. New electric tramway lines are replacing overcrowded bus lines. Biodiversity is increasing on land and in the Seine, and bee colonies are thriving. The city is also increasing renewable energy production. Many of these changes stem from a less visible paradigm shift in the environmental priorities of the city administration.

Paris faces challenges common to all megacities. Reports of political corruption are not unusual. Many lower- and middle-class households struggle to find adequate and affordable housing despite substantial subsidized housing provision. Traffic congestion generates long and stressful commutes and poor air quality, particularly along major transportation axes.

What is unique about Paris is not the problems it faces, but the strategies it implements to address them. I here focus on innovations, recent achievements, and ongoing projects addressing environmental sustainability.[1] I briefly discuss the socioeconomic and historical context of urban and sustainable development in Paris, as well as key features of the French environmental policy context. The unique political tensions between the city and the national government are particularly relevant to understanding sustainability strategies, especially in the area of public transportation. In light of this context, I present Paris's current environmental sustainability policies and strategies. I organize the discussion around the central tenets of the Paris Climate Plan: adaptation to climate change, energy (buildings' energy use and renewable energy production), transportation (transit and nonmotorized), and nature (green spaces and biodiversity).

Geographic, Socioeconomic, and Environmental Policy Context

Paris is located in northern France along the River Seine in a sedimentary basin. Its key topographic features are two islands in the city center (Saint-Louis and Cité) and three hills (Montmartre, Télégraphe, Sainte-Geneviève). Paris benefits from a mild oceanic climate, with temperatures between 15 and 25 degrees Celsius in summer and generally above freezing in winter.

Paris is located in the Île-de-France region. The Paris urbanized area counts 11.7 million residents, or 18% of the country's population, and is one of the largest metropolitan areas in Europe (INSEE 2010c). The land area of the city proper is 105 km² (41 mi²)—only 87 km² (34 mi²) when excluding the two woodlands under its jurisdiction but outside its physical boundaries (Ville de Paris 2010a). Given its population and small land area, Paris is one of the densest cities in the world. Excluding the woodlands from its land base, Paris has about 25,200 residents/km² (65,300/mi²). Within the city, the densest neighborhoods are in the historically working-class northern and eastern districts, with up to 41,700 residents/km² (108,000/mi²) in the 11th district (Ville de Paris 2010b).

The French population, historically Caucasian and Catholic, is increasingly diverse, with 3.68 million foreigners (5.6% of the population) and 5.25 million immigrants, naturalized or not (8.1% of the population; see INSEE 2010d). Paris is multicultural, with one of the largest concentrations of immigrants in Europe. About 18% of residents in the Paris urban area were born outside metropolitan France, and four out of ten immigrants in France live in the Paris region (Borrel 2005). The history of immigration in Paris goes back thousands of years. Most recently, 19th-century immigration waves brought to Paris Germans, Italians, central Europeans, and Russians. Colonial citizens immigrated during World War I, and Spaniards, Italians, Portuguese, and North Africans between the 1950s and 1970s. North and sub-Saharan Africans, Asians, and eastern Europeans have comprised the bulk of the migration since the 1980s.

Paris is a leading world city on many socioeconomic indicators. Its region hosts thirty-eight Fortune Global 500 companies and international organizations such as UNESCO and the OECD. It is an international center for education, science, culture, arts, and entertainment. Paris has some thirteen public universities with strong humanities and sciences programs, several medical, law, and business schools, and the most prestigious public elite schools for engineering, science, management, and government. It has two opera houses, dozens of major performance venues, more than 150 museums (including twenty-nine national and fifteen municipal ones), dozens of monuments, hundreds of art galleries, and more than ten thousand restaurants and cafés. In any given week, Paris theaters show about one hundred plays and two hundred films.

In 2009, Paris and its region produced a GDP of €552.1 billion (US$768.9 billion), 29% of the national GDP (INSEE 2010e), ranking it the sixth highest in GDP among the world's urban areas (PricewaterhouseCoopers 2009). The economy of Paris's metropolitan area is mainly reliant on service industries and high-tech manufacturing. Of Paris's 1.7 million jobs, 55% are in the service sector, 26% in administration, 10% commercial, 7% industrial, and 2% in the construction sector (Préfecture de Paris 2004). With about twenty-seven million visitors per year, tourism-related jobs employ 6.2% of the city's workforce and 3.6% of all workers in the region, for a total economic impact of about €8 billion (Ville de Paris 2007a).

Wealth is not equally distributed in Paris's urban landscape. Housing values ranged in 2010 from about €8,000 to €12,000/m^2 in the center and western districts, €6,000 to €8,000/m^2 in outlying areas, and under €6,000/m^2 in the northeastern districts.

Politically, France is a bicameral republic with a multiparty electoral system, a directly elected president, and appointed ministers. France is currently in its Fifth Republic, characterized by strong presidential powers and economic and political centralization.[2] The country is divided into twenty-six regions, one hundred departments, and about thirty-six thousand municipalities. Although the regions were created in 1982 to decentralize decision making, central government powers remain strong. Understanding sustainability initiatives in Paris thus requires a discussion of the national policy context and the relations between Paris and central government.

The 17th-century Parisian rebellion "la Fronde" is the iconic precursor of the tensions between Paris and central government. Under Louis XIII, Richelieu diminished the powers of the nobility and Parliament. When the Parliament of Paris refused to approve royal taxes in 1648, civil war followed with a blockade of Paris in 1649. The Fronde sought to limit the constitutional power of the monarchy and, for the first time, made explicit the conflicts of interests between Paris, the royal central government, and the parliamentary process. While it did not change the regime, the people of Paris played a central role in these fights and became seen as a threat to the monarchy.

Louis XIV moved the court away from Paris to Versailles in 1682. The 1789 French Revolution recalled Louis XVI to Paris and overthrew the monarchy, creating the First Republic in 1792. After this, Paris remained the center of national political shifts, especially during the 1848 and 1871 uprisings.[3]

The Industrial Revolution brought to Paris a flow of rural migrants in search of manufacturing jobs. Early in the Second Empire, in 1853, Napoleon III appointed Baron Haussmann as prefect of the Seine Department. Haussmann spearheaded Paris's major urban and sanitation works. He ordered the demolition of entire residential blocks and narrow medieval streets to widen existing boulevards and create about twenty-five new straight, wide, tree-lined boulevards and avenues. He generalized the homogeneous neoclassical facades and five-story building elevation, which are still hallmarks of Paris's architectural identity. This program sought urban beautification and sanitation, and easier police operations during reoccurring social uprisings. In 1860 Paris also annexed surrounding villages, setting the city's current boundaries.

The siege of Paris that followed the French surrender in the 1870/71 Franco-Prussian War again demonstrates the intense conflict between Paris and the national government. A Parisian rebellion, "the Commune," resisted both the surrender and the foreign occupation. After fights in the northeast of Paris (Montmartre and the working-class 11th and 20th districts), national troops brutally suppressed the Commune, with about twenty thousand executions.

Technological and industrial advances marked the last decades of the 19th century. Two Universal Expositions grandly displayed this progress, one in 1889 with the inauguration of the Eiffel Tower, and one in 1900 with the inauguration of the underground Métro.

During World War I, German invasion was avoided with the victory at Marne in 1914 when, famously, Paris taxi drivers brought soldiers to combat zones. Between the wars, Paris became known for its modern artistic and intellectual communities. The Nazis occupied the city between 1940 and 1944. The city was not physically damaged, but the human costs were tremendous. Under Vichy orders, police forces deported tens of thousands of Parisians.

The post–World War II era saw the first major suburban expansion of the city. Within the city, eight- to ten-story residential buildings were constructed, both private and subsidized. Massive subsidized housing projects (cités) were built in nearby towns, especially to the north and east of Paris. The large-scale La Défense business district was built to the west of Paris. Métro lines were added in- and outside the city, and a new suburban commuter train network, the RER, was created to serve nearby and distant suburbs. The freeway system was enlarged. The Boulevard Périphérique expressway ring road was built around Paris, marking the city's physical boundaries.

The post-1970s era saw the deindustrialization of northern and eastern suburbs. The subsidized housing cités became ghettos for immigrants and the unemployed, while the center of Paris and the western and southern suburbs shifted their economies toward services and high-tech industries. In the mid-1980s, riots started to occur in these suburban ghettos, where unemployment is often upward of 20% (*Le Parisien* 2010). In 2009, about 30% of youths between fifteen and twenty-nine years old in these zones were unemployed (Chevalier 2010).

In addition to affordable housing and enhanced transportation networks, urban development in the 1980s and 1990s focused on great projects, most selected by sitting presidents, such as the Great Arch at La Défense, the Louvre pyramid, the Bastille Opera, and the National Library.

Administratively, Paris is divided into twenty districts (*arrondissements*),[4] each with its own city hall and directly elected council, which elects a district mayor. Selected members from each district council form the Paris City Council (Conseil de Paris), which elects the mayor of Paris.[5] Paris's administrative and political situation stems from an eventful history.

Paris became an independent municipality in 1790 when the French Revolution created municipal entities throughout the territory. The Revolution, however, framed Paris's political independence as a national threat. While municipal structures remained everywhere else, the office of mayor of Paris and the Paris Municipal Council were abolished in 1795. They were only briefly reformed in 1834, 1848, and 1870–71. Paris therefore did not have a mayor or independent government between 1871 and 1977. For a century, it remained under the control of state-appointed prefects of the Seine Department (e.g., Haussmann) and prefects of police. Paris obtained a permanent, independent, and elected mayor and council in 1977, but its police force is still under state control.

Before he was elected president, Jacques Chirac was the mayor of Paris between 1977 and 1995. Jean Tibéri, also a central conservative, took office between 1995 and 2001. Bertrand Delanoë, elected in 2001 and reelected in 2008, is Paris's first Socialist mayor. All the activities related to sustainable development described in this chapter are direct outcomes of his administration.

National Environmental Policy and Relevant Planning Frameworks

France adopted its Charter for the Environment in 2005. It is integrated into the preamble to the Constitution and establishes people's rights to live in a "balanced environment" with due respect for health. This constitutional right is on par with the human rights of 1789 and the welfare rights of 1946. It positions sustainable development at the core of all French laws. It creates the notion of duty (for individuals and public authorities) to preserve the environment, and establishes the centrality of ecological responsibility and of the precautionary principle.

The most recent and comprehensive effort to modernize France's environmental law and policies is President Nicolas Sarkozy's Grenelle de l'Environment. The Grenelle sets national environmental policy orientations and action plans. Sarkozy presented it in 2007 as the Ecological New Deal, a revolutionary emphasis on environmental concerns. Grenelle 1 sets general national goals: to reduce greenhouse gas (GHG) emissions, prepare for climate change impacts, anticipate declining natural and energy resources and increasing fuel prices, and promote "sober" and sustainable growth with energy efficiency and renewable energies. Developed through an extensive collaborative process, Grenelle 1 was adopted quasi-unanimously in October 2008.

The Grenelle 2 law, adopted in July 2010, implements the Grenelle 1 goals. It sets specific objectives, strategies, incentives, and regulations. In practice, however, it fails to fully implement Grenelle 1. Many argue that Grenelle was "killed," as the application of the law was weakened by lobbying interest groups. *Le Monde* ran articles in May 2010 titled "How Grenelle II Was Undone" and "Have Deputies Betrayed the Grenelle?" The left and the Greens voted against Grenelle 2, and some NGOs exited the participatory process entirely.

Political and economic crises forced the government to abandon the carbon tax project at the end of 2009.[6] While Grenelle 1 called for increasing the national renewable energy portfolio to 20% by 2020, amendments make it difficult to install wind turbines and favor large wind farms over distributed generation.[7] The government backtracked on calls to reduce the use of pesticides in agriculture (a major source of water contamination). Several other measures were postponed, including plans to reduce the value added tax on products that meet sustainability criteria.

Despite these implementation gaps, Grenelle has significant implications for sustainable development. Debates leading to the Grenelle laws put environmental sustainability high on the national political agenda between 2007 and 2009, building knowledge and commitment among elected officials and bureaucrats. Grenelle also had several tangible outcomes:

> Large grocery chains agreed to inform consumers about the environmental impacts of their purchases. In 2008, labels indicating the carbon emitted during the life cycle of three hundred common products were introduced. Leclerc and Casino (among the largest chains) introduced carbon labels on one thousand products, along with their price tags and receipts—the first experimentation of this kind in France.

> Real estate professionals provide information about buildings' energy performance in all advertisements. Informing buyers and renters about energy performance has been compulsory since 2006 and 2007, respectively.

> The new notion of Green and Blue Networks (Trame verte et bleue) emphasizes the protection of ecological corridors.

The Sustainable Cities Plan (Plan Ville durable), launched in October 2008, supports green urban development projects (EcoQuartiers, EcoCités) through national competitions and awards. As part of the Sustainable Cities Plan, the government released the "Plan to Restore Nature in the City" in November 2010. It addresses stormwater runoff, energy, climate change adaptation, biodiversity, sanitation, and the use of toxic products. It relies on voluntary actions by municipalities and focuses on the development of about one thousand biodiversity inventories, Green and Blue Networks, and wetland restoration.

The French legal framework for sustainability initiatives and urban and regional planning is relatively centralized. Grenelle 2 uses this feature to support compact urban forms, energy efficiency, and public transportation. This is implemented through nationally mandated Regional Planning Schemes (Shémas de cohérence territoriale, SCOTs) that coordinate regional urban growth and development. Grenelle 2 mandates that SCOTs be developed for the whole territory by 2017.

Regional planning is controlled via Regional Planning Directives (Directives territoriale d'aménagement, DTAs, created in 1995 and since renamed Regional Planning and Sustainable Development Directives, or Directives territoriale d'aménagement et de développement durable, DTADDs). Through the DTADDs, the national government can impose regional goals and strategies for land development anywhere in France. The DTADDs can impose goals and strategies concerning urban form, housing, transportation, telecommunications, economic development, public spaces, natural areas, agricultural and forest lands, energy use, greenhouse gas emissions, and so forth. Between 2003 and 2007, the national government developed and approved six DTADDs.

All local plans[8] and SCOTs must be compatible with DTADDs. For twelve years following the adoption of a DTADD, the national government can deem any project that implements it a Public Interest Project (Projet d'interet général, PIG). These PIGs become enforceable and cannot be legally challenged. Through the DTADDs and the PIGs, the national government can thus exert power over urban and regional planning and require localities to implement infrastructure programs deemed of national significance.[9] In addition, Grenelle 2 mandates that by 2012 regions adopt Regional Air, Climate, and Energy Plans (Schéma régional climat air énergie, SRCAEs), and that all municipalities over fifty thousand residents adopt Local Climate and Energy Plans (Plans climat énergie territorial, PCET, which must be consistent with the SRCAEs).

The New, Greener Paris

In this context of strong national powers and tensions between the capital and the government, of strongly stated but weakly implemented national environmental policies, and of local planning mandates regarding climate change, Paris stands out as a very distinct municipality. A Socialist–Green municipal administration has transformed Paris urban development since 2001, demonstrating strong commitment and capacity to implement ambitious sustainable development initiatives. The remainder of this chapter focuses on Paris's most recent and innovative strategies concerning climate change, energy use and production, transit and nonmotorized transportation, and green space and biodiversity protection.

Climate Planning: Adaptation, Energy Efficiency, and Renewable Energy

The European Union signed the Kyoto Protocol as a unit, committing to reduce emissions of GHGs by 8% by 2010 (from 1990 levels). France has fairly low GHG emissions given its reliance on nuclear energy, and is only required to freeze emissions. Between 1990 and 2003, French per capita CO_2 emissions decreased. Industry reduced emissions by 22% and energy generators by 10%. Yet transportation emissions rose 23% and buildings emissions increased by 14% (ADEME 2010).

France also needs to contribute to the EU 20-20-20 goals (reducing GHG emissions by 20% and increasing energy efficiency and renewable energy production by 20% by 2020). France seeks to boost renewable energy production by 23% by 2020. Energy efficiency and renewable energies are thus high on the national agenda.

The first French National Plan to Combat Climate Change (Programme national de lutte contre le changement climatique, PNLCC) was adopted in 2000. The climate plans of 2004 and 2006 set specific goals, and the 2004 plan supports the adoption of local climate plans. Local plans must focus on buildings and fleet efficiency, on decentralized energy production where possible, and on changing the behaviors of all economic actors. The current national objective, "Factor 4," is to decrease carbon emissions from 8 to 2 teqCO$_2$ per person by 2050.[10]

The Paris Climate Plan (Plan climat de Paris, PCP; see Ville de Paris 2007d) was adopted in October 2007 after a wide public consultation in 2006.[11] It is consistent with the Paris Urbanism Plan (Plan local d'urbanisme, PLU) and with the Paris Transportation Plan (Plan de déplacements de Paris, PDP). Although 2008 was the first year of implementation of the PCP, Paris had already put in place climate-relevant initiatives, reducing road traffic and lowering the energy use of public buildings. Paris began its systematic GHG emission audits in 2005 with a pilot Carbon Audit (Bilan carbone) followed by a citywide analysis of GHG emissions, including transportation, heating, and consumption sources (Ville de Paris 2007b).[12]

The Paris Climate Plan is based on these studies. Paris buildings use about 35,000 GWh of energy (the production of four nuclear plants) and produce 1.75 million teqC (6.5 million teqCO$_2$) per year—mainly because Paris's old housing stock is poorly insulated. The transport of persons is estimated to produce about 1.75 million teqC, despite a dense public transit system that emits only 100,000 teqC for 3 billion passengers per year (taxis included). The transport of goods and merchandise is also estimated at about 1.75 million teqC. Waste and consumption account for about 1.3 million teqC. Paris has very little industry, but tourism is a major source of emissions, at 4.4 million teqC, due to tourists' air travel (Ville de Paris 2007c).

The Paris Climate Plan addresses adaptation to climate change, buildings' energy efficiency, and renewable energy. Another part of the PCP, transportation and green spaces, will be discussed in the next sections.

ADAPTATION TO CLIMATE CHANGE

The Paris Climate Plan seeks to adapt to climate change by mitigating the risks of heat waves and flooding. The Plan for Heat Waves (Plan canicule, PC) responds to the summer 2003 event, when temperatures remained above 30°C for several weeks, with some days above 40°C (104°F). This event generated an increase of mortality of 127% in the populations of elderly and isolated persons (Ministère de l'intérieur 2007). Today, isolated persons can register in the Chalex database ("Chalex" is a combination of *chaleur*, meaning "heat," and *extrême*). During heat waves, those listed are contacted regularly by phone and are visited at home. The city also sponsors public information campaigns to encourage solidarity between generations and neighbors. The PC is very explicit about adapting to these extreme weather events *without* relying on air-conditioning. Instead, it supports increasing insulation, shutters, sun shading, ventilation, as well as cooling systems using district cooling and geothermal energy.

The PCP also seeks to mitigate flood risks. Upstream reservoirs and the elevation that separates the Seine from streets and buildings may not be sufficient to protect the city from major floods. The roads along the Seine flood most years for a few days. The last floods that affected residential buildings and service delivery occurred in 1924 and 1955, with record floods in 1658 and 1910. In the event of a 1910-level flood, about a million Parisians could lose power, heating, and drinking water (Ville de Paris 2007d). Maps of floodable areas are provided to all home buyers. The utility company Electricité de France (EDF) was asked to ensure continued service to all elevated floors in the case of a flood. Works to separate electrical circuits for basements/ground floors and higher stories will continue throughout the coming decade (Françoise 2010).

Buildings and Energy Use

The objectives of the Paris Climate Plan are to reduce GHG emissions by 25%, to consume 25% less energy, and to use 25% of the city's energy from renewable sources by 2020 compared to 2004, and to reduce emissions by 75% by 2050.[13] French buildings account for 42% of the national energy consumption, 23% of CO_2 emissions, and a third of GHG emissions (APUR 2010a). In response, Paris has launched an ambitious program to improve the energy efficiency of municipal and private buildings.

National energy-efficiency policies rely on regulations and incentives. France's old housing stock can use 250–350 kWh/m²/year.[14] Current regulations for new construction (Régulation Thermique, RT2005) impose a maximum energy use of 130 kWh/m²/year in the northern climatic zone (where Paris is located) for buildings heated with fossil fuels, and 250 kWh/m²/year for those heated electrically. RT2005 was not revised in 2010 as planned, but RT2012 (to be implemented in 2013) should impose a maximum of 60 kWh/m²/year in the Paris climate zone (MEEDDM 2010a).

Buildings that use 10% less energy than mandated by RT2005 receive the High Energy Performance label (Haute performance energétique, HPE2005). Buildings that use 20% less receive a Very High Energy Performance label (Très haute performance energétique, THPE2005). New buildings that use under 50 kWh/m²/year (65 kWh in the northern part of France), or under 80 kWh for renovations, receive the Low Energy Consumption label (Batiment basse consommation, BBC). THPE- and

BCC-rated buildings are eligible for development density bonuses (Ville de Paris 2007d; MEEDEM 2010b).

In 2008 the Paris municipality launched an energy diagnostic for all its properties. More than 50% of the Paris administration's GHGs emissions stem from municipal buildings, such as public housing, city halls, schools, and child care centers (Ville de Paris 2007d). The city plans to insulate about three thousand public structures by 2020, and it plans to meet BBC standards for all new municipal construction. The city also manages about 220,000 subsidized housing units, with an average energy consumption of about 270 kWh/m² each; it plans on renovating these units to BBC standards (Ville de Paris 2007d). Some renovations and a diagnostic campaign to identify all necessary work are under way.

In the private sector, Paris counts about 1.4 million housing units in ninety-six thousand buildings, mostly managed by condominium associations. Combined, they use 35,000 GWh and emit 6.4 million tons of CO_2 (Ville de Paris 2007d). Paris's housing stock is old: 85% of structures were built before 1975, 48% before 1915, and 25% before 1850 (Ville de Paris 2007d; APUR 2010a). Buildings constructed before the mid-1970s tend to be poorly insulated.

In 2009 the Paris Urbanism Office (Atelier Parisien d'Urbanisme, APUR) assessed energy losses of Paris buildings via an aerial thermography study of roofs and facades (APUR 2010a). The results, down to the building level, are available online.

Based on this new building-level data, the city launched its first large-scale thermal insulation program. The municipality offers free audits and decision support, and it subsidizes insulation projects for condominium associations and owners (whether they occupy or rent dwellings). Subsidies are funded by the municipality and the National Housing Agency (Agence nationale de l'habitat). They can be used to fund insulation (e.g., roof, facade, windows), efficient heating and water heating systems, ventilation, and renewable energies.

Subsidies available to owners include grants (écoprimes) of €500 to €1,500 depending on household income. Needy households qualify for €1,500 if their unit uses more than 330 kWh/m² and if renovations can reduce energy use by at least 30%. Subsidies up to €4,000 per unit are available for owners who rent their units with controlled rents, provided the work can reduce energy consumption from more than 330 to less than 230 kWh/m². For condominium associations, subsidies cover 70% of the building energy audit. Zero-interest loans (*éco-prêt*), created in 2009, can also finance insulation projects.

Renewable Energy

Currently, the main energy source for Paris is Electricité de France, which uses 14% renewable energy, mainly wind and hydro (EDF 2010). On its territory, Paris produces 817 GWh/year of renewable energy—2.5% of the city's total energy consumption. About 85% of this production is from waste incineration. To develop renewable energies, the PCP seeks to increase Paris's reliance on solar, geothermal, wind, and hydro—all currently minimal in its portfolio. Between 2008 and 2010, the city assessed in detail its potential for renewable energy production to identify ideal locations for the installation of new production sites (Ville de Paris 2010c).

Energy recovery from waste incineration generates 672 GWh/year in heat and 22 GWh/year in electricity. The municipality controls the Paris District Heating Company (Companie parisienne de chauffage urbain, CPCU), founded in 1927 to produce steam and hot water. It heats about five hundred thousand housing units via 440 kilometers of pipes, making it the second-largest district heating network in Europe (Ville de Paris 2010c). Waste incineration provides about 45% of the CPCU's energy. If 60% of its energy source was renewable (including waste/biomass), it could benefit from the 2009 National Housing Law that set the value added tax on district heating at 5.5% (down from 19.6%). The Paris Climate Plan thus mandates the CPCU to reach this 60% target by 2020 (Ville de Paris 2007d). In addition, Paris's seventy-kilometer district cooling network is the largest in Europe, with eight plants producing 290MW (Ville de Paris 2010c).

Geothermal is Paris's second source of renewable energy. Paris has thirty-eight geothermal installations—seventeen used for heating, fifteen for cooling, and six for heating and cooling—totaling 116 GWh/year. The largest planned infrastructure project is a 52 GWh production site, with two more under study for a production of 20 and 55 GWh (Lagadec 2010; Ville de Paris 2010d). With the ability to tap into the 1,800-meter-deep Dogger aquifer and recover water at 57°C, geothermal energy has strong potential in Paris.

Solar energy makes up less than 1% of Paris's renewable energy portfolio. Paris currently has 20,500 m² installed solar panels—about 12,000 m² for solar water heating at 113 sites (5.6 GWh/year), and 8,000 m² photovoltaic panels at 33 sites (807 MWh/year). Another 39,000 m² are planned by 2014 and the Climate Plan aims for 200,000 m² (Ville de Paris 2010c).

Two small wind turbines (30 MW combined) were installed to explore potential expansion, and the possibility of high-wind turbines along the Périphérique expressway is under study. The city also seeks to experiment with low-speed underwater turbines in the Seine (*hydroliennes*).[15]

Paris cannot directly mandate the use of renewable energy in private developments. Except for Planned Unit Developments projects (Zone d'aménagement concerté, ZAC), municipalities cannot impose measures that go beyond national standards and regulations. Most energy efficiency and renewable energy innovations can thus be found in ZACs:

> On the ZAC Rungis (13th district), a mixed-use development on 3.85 hectares will create three hundred housing units, office and commercial space, a day care center, and a retirement home. Energy use will come in below RT2005 standards with high-quality insulation, 4,000 m² of solar panels, solar water heating, and geothermal energy.

> On the ZAC Boucicaut (15th), a three-hectare development in a residential area will include a school, child care center, center for handicapped people, women's shelter, 350 housing units, businesses, offices, and green space. It will use low-emissivity windows, solar panels, and geothermal energy, and aims for an average energy use of 65 KWh/m².

> The fifty-nine-hectare redevelopment project Clichy-Batignolles (17th) will create 3,500 housing units, businesses, and public services. Via building design (e.g., insulation, passive solar), it plans for energy consumption to come in under 38 KWh/m². It includes energy production with geothermal and solar panels.

> The ZAC Pajol (18th) redevelops 3.4 hectares along railroad tracks for public structures (sports and cultural facilities, a library, a youth hostel, a middle school, and a university unit). It will feature 3,500 m² of PV panels and 200 m² of solar water heater panels, making it the largest urban PV unit in France.

> The ZAC Claude-Bernard (19th) plans for 330 housing units, a school, a child care center, a retirement home, 40,000 m² of office space, and 8,000 m² for businesses. It seeks to provide enough renewable energy to cover at least 25% of all the energy used on-site.

The Frequel-Fontarabie (20th) project plans for the rehabilitation of insalubrious structures to reach 65 kWh/m²/year, and for new constructions to meet the German Passivhaus standard (under 15 kWh/m²/year). This is the most ambitious project in Paris for low-energy consumption. For these innovations, it received the prize EcoQuartier (part of the EcoQuartier program created under Grenelle 2) from the Ministry of Ecology and Sustainable Development.

While we have yet to see the long-term effects of Paris's energy efficiency subsidies, these projects will be completed in the next few years and will soon provide models and economic and environmental performance data for future developments and renovation projects.

Transit and Nonmotorized Transportation

The Paris Climate Plan seeks to reduce GHG emissions from transportation sources, favoring transit and nonmotorized transportation modes. Before this focus on climate change, the 1996 Law on Air and Energy Efficiency (Loi sur l'air et l'utilisation rationnelle de l'énergie) required that all French metropolitan areas with more than one hundred thousand residents adopt urban transportation plans (Plans de déplacements urbains, PDUs) to reduce automobile dependence and encourage nonmotorized transportation.[16]

The Paris Transportation Plan (Plan de déplacements de Paris, PDP), adopted in February 2007, is consistent with the Paris Climate Plan. Overall, the PDP focuses on extending the already dense public transit systems and facilitating walking and biking (Ville de Paris 2007e). It seeks to reduce transportation-related GHG emissions by 25% by 2013 and 60% by 2020 (compared to 2004 levels), mainly by reducing car use.[17] It seeks to increase transit services 20% by 2013, reduce car traffic by 26% by 2013 and by 40% by 2020, and increase the number of trips made by bike by 300% by 2020. In fact, automobile traffic in Paris was on the decline before the adoption of the plan. Between 2001 and 2007, car traffic declined by 17%, and it further decreased by 2% between 2007 and 2008 (Ville de Paris 2007e, 2009a).

Improvements to park-and-ride facilities are planned, as well as more multimodal transfer points. The PDP also supports the use of low-emissions vehicles with recharge stations and lower parking rates for small and electric vehicles. Paris currently has eighty-four recharge stations for a total recharge capacity of 221 cars, 64 motorcycles/mopeds, and 4 trucks (see Ville de Paris 2010e for an updated map online).

The most significant development to support electric vehicle use is the new car-sharing program Autolib', launched in late 2011. In December 2010 the City of Paris and forty participating municipalities contracted with the firm Bolloré to install electric "Blue Cars" and their charging stations for public use throughout the region. The program was inaugurated in December 2011 with 250 stations and 250 cars. When fully implemented, it will provide three thousand electric cars for short-term use at a thousand stations, including seven hundred in Paris. Cars will be available for a subscription of €144 per year, €15 per week or €10 per day, plus €5 for the first half hour of use, €4 for the next half hour, and €6 for each subsequent half hour. This will make Paris and the participating municipalities the first European center to provide public electric cars on this scale (Verdevoye 2010).

The PDP also addresses merchandise transport and tourism, which account for a large part of traffic-related GHG emissions. About 90% of the €32 million of goods that enter and leave the city yearly are transported by road. The PDP promotes freight and the use of barges. It also seeks to change delivery regulations, such as increasing delivery hours for low-emissions vehicles. Tourism-related air transport is a very significant source of GHGs emissions (4 million TEC/year). While this is not under the direct control of the municipality, the PDP seeks to inform tourism professionals and propose new regulations on tourist buses' emissions and parking. The city also entered discussions with the two airports to diminish or compensate for the impact of tourism-related air travel.

URBAN AND REGIONAL TRANSIT SYSTEMS

In practice, the bulk of the PDP strategies revolve around transit provision and facilitating nonmotorized transportation. Paris already has a dense transit network and is already highly compact, mixed-use, and walkable. The changes under way thus constitute a new, "second generation" approach to transit and nonmotorized travel.

Paris transit system.[18] Paris's first regular public transit system (horse-drawn omnibuses) dates back to 1828. Motorized bus lines opened in 1906 and bus transit has grown ever since. About one billion trips are made on the sixty-four bus lines in Paris and about two hundred suburban lines every year (about a third in Paris and two-thirds in suburbs). Paris operates about 4,580 buses, including 537 "double" buses, 62 electric narrow midi-buses servicing the Montmartre area, and 103 minibuses on designated neighborhood lines (the *traverses*). Noctilien buses operate throughout the night. Buses run on 190 kilometers of dedicated bus lanes, shared with taxis and bicycles, including 68 kilometers of lanes that are physically separated from cars (Ville de Paris 2009a; Lefebvre 2010).

The major change in the last few years is the transformation of Paris's busiest bus lines into a bus rapid transit system, Mobilien (see figure 2.1). This program, launched in 2008, comprises 17 lines in Paris (13 are already restructured, 4 are in process) and about 130 more in the region. Mobilien buses drive on separated lanes (which double as bike lanes). Some are located between traffic and sidewalks, others in the center lanes of wide avenues. They provide wider sidewalks, islands for loading areas, and narrower pedestrian crossings (Ville de Paris 2010f). Each stop provides real-time information about the arrival time of upcoming buses. Mobilien lines thus allocate more space to buses, pedestrians, and bikes to the detriment of car lanes, and have improved the speed and comfort of service.

Figure 2.1 Paris's Mobilien, or bus rapid transit, runs buses on seventeen separated bus lanes in the city, improving speed and comfort. Credit: Lucie Laurian.

The Métro is Paris's underground subway system. Inaugurated in 1900, it has fourteen major lines with 214 kilometers (133 miles) of rail, and three hundred stations, sixty-two of which are transfer points. It is a very dense network, with about two to five minutes waiting time between trains, two minutes between stops onboard, and ten-minute walks between stops on the surface. About 3.9 million passengers use the Métro daily (for 1.473 billion trips in 2008). Paris is extending Métro lines within and outside city limits. The most recent line (#14), inaugurated in 1998 and extended in 2003 and 2007, is entirely automated (RATP 2011).

The RER is a suburban train system created in the 1960s to connect Paris and its nearby and distant suburbs. The five RER lines, with 257 stops and 587 kilometers (365 miles) of rails, connect with key Métro, bus, and train stops. The RER served 451 million passengers in 2006.[19]

In recent years, Paris and its suburban neighbors added four new electric tramway lines. Three tramway lines opened in nearby suburbs in 1992, 1997, and 2006. In Paris proper, the overburdened bus lines on the ring road around Paris (Petite Ceinture), with their sixteen million passengers per year, are being replaced by tramway lines. The first segment opened in December 2006, covering about a third of the city's perimeter. Construction for the second segment started in 2009. It will add twenty-five stops over 14.5 kilometers and connect with two RER lines, forty-three bus lines, and ten Métro lines (for an estimated 155,000 passengers per day) (RATP 2011).

In addition, Paris is developing a river shuttle boat line, Voguéo. The city inaugurated the service mid-2008 with five stops on the both sides of the Seine in the east of Paris. The experiment, which ended in June 2011, will be replaced by three different river shuttle boat lines (one in the city center, one serving the east of the city and the eastern suburbs, and one serving the west of the city and western suburbs) in 2013 (Voguéo 2011).

Regional transportation: National versus regional plans. Public transit in the Paris region is currently an area of intense political tension between the city, the region, and the national government. About 70% of trips in the Paris region are suburb-to-suburb. The national government and the region independently (and uncooperatively) are calling for circular transit systems around the capital.

In 2004 Paris and the region began a joint, deliberative regional transportation planning process. A €18.6 billion regional transportation plan was approved in 2008 (Plan de mobilisation pour les transports en

Île-de-France). This plan seeks to add, by 2020, 300 kilometers of bus lines, 120 kilometers of tramway lines, 105 kilometers of tram or train, 20 kilometers of RER lines, 13 new multimodal nodes, and 80 kilometers of Métro, including a 60-kilometer Arc Express line circling Paris in its densest residential suburbs (Région Île-de-France 2009). Arc Express would be expected to serve fifteen thousand passengers per peak hour for a total investment of €5 billion. About twenty-five of these extension projects are under way.

Without consultation or cooperation with Paris or the region, President Sarkozy proposed an alternative Grand Paris plan, framed as a matter of national interest. In 2008 he created a new office of the "Secretary of State for the Development of the Capital Region" and launched an international design competition for the "post-Kyoto" Paris. Sarkozy's Grand Paris plan also sought an administrative reorganization of Paris and its immediate suburbs into a new metropolitan authority (presumably headed by one of his appointees), but this attempt was abandoned in light of the local elected officials' strong opposition.

The most substantial element of the Grand Paris plan is a high-speed, automatic, double-loop Métro system linking nine regional economic centers further out from Paris than the region envisioned. Of the €35 billion Grand Paris project, €21 billion would be allocated to this new Métro system, expected to serve six thousand passengers per peak hour—far fewer than the region's plan. Initially, the Grand Paris also sought national control over all development and taxation[20] within 1.5 kilometers of all forty new stops. The region and mayors strongly oppose this plan, seen as national imposition in local matters. In addition, the national government created the Société du Grand Paris in 2010, a nonelected and nationally controlled body charged with implementing the project, and granted the right to expropriate land and preempt development. This project, in direct competition with the preexisting regional plan and the wishes of local elected officials, is the latest development in the historical power struggle between Paris (here allied with the region) and the national government (Subra 2010; Blanc 2009).

Sarkozy's Grand Paris project was adopted as law in May 2010. It grants national control over development in a four-hundred-meter radius around each new stop and increases taxes on properties within eight hundred meters of stops (CNDP 2010c). The national government cannot fund the Grand Paris scheme without regional support, and the law requires that both the Grand Paris and the Arc Express project be submitted to public debate. The first of at least seventy public meetings took place in

September 2010 (CNDP 2010a,b). In mid-November 2010, both the region and the Grand Paris architects proposed alternative plans merging
elements from each set of projects, along with a new concept of an elevated
Métro over existing highways (AIGP 2010; CRIF 2010; Ramnoux 2010).
It appears likely that a compromise between the two plans will be reached
and that the lines the region envisioned will be built, but the debates are
ongoing.

NONMOTORIZED TRANSPORTATION

By its sheer density and urban form (e.g., narrow medieval streets, tree-
lined avenues), Paris is a highly walkable city. It takes about two hours to
walk across the city from east to west or north to south. Almost any location in the city is within a five- or ten-minute walk from Métro and bus
stops, schools, parks, grocery stores, and one of Paris's eighty-two fresh
produce markets. About 10.5 million trips are taken daily in Paris, 56% of
which are nonmotorized (54% by foot, 2% by bike), 29% by transit, and
14% by car and motorcycle (Ville de Paris 2007e; DREIF 2004).

Walking. To improve pedestrian safety and quality of life, the municipality created quiet neighborhoods (*quartiers tranquiles*) in 1990 and green
neighborhoods (*quartiers verts*) after 2001. Both limit driving speed to
30 kmh, often include wider sidewalks, speed bumps, elevated pedestrian
crossings, bike lanes, tree plantings, and favor residential parking. Today,
71 of these 30-kmh zones cover 18.2 km², or 21% of the total Paris area
(Lefebvre 2010).

Beyond these neighborhoods, and without creating strictly pedestrian
areas (the only pedestrian area is around Les Halles), the current administration has pursued strong programs to improve pedestrian safety and
comfort. It has actively transformed public space by widening sidewalks
and improving pedestrian crossings in high traffic areas. Between 2001 and
2009, the total area devoted to streets declined by 5% and the total sidewalk area increased by 13% (Lefebvre 2010).

The renovation of the Place de la République illustrates this approach.
One of the largest in Paris (280 m by 120 m), this traffic-dominated mega-
intersection connects seven major traffic axes, five Métro lines, and four
bus lines. With its central statue of the République, it is a key gathering
site for political and musical events. The place has not changed since its
creation during the Second Empire and is now overtaken by cars, which
occupy 60% of its area. The square will undergo a major transformation

with a large, open central area, 50% more space for pedestrian use, 30% more trees, and only half the current area devoted to car traffic. The roundabout around the statue will be entirely eliminated. Project completion is planned for 2013. A similar transformation of the car-saturated intersection Place de Clichy was recently unveiled, also with more space for pedestrians, bikes, and bus lanes.

Paris has also developed unique road-sharing practices that occur over time rather than space. Since 2002 the operation Paris Breathes (Paris respire) closes high-speed roads along the Seine to traffic every Sunday and holiday from 9 to 5. These roads are open to pedestrians, roller-skaters, and cyclists. This program has since been extended to fifteen neighborhoods. The Paris Beach (Paris Plages) operation, also launched in 2002, entirely closes high-speed lanes along the Seine from mid-July to mid-August to create a beach promenade. The first "beach" spanned 2.8 kilometers on the right bank between the Louvre and the Pont de Sully. In 2006 Paris Plages added another location, with 1.5 kilometers of "beach" on the Bassin de la Villette in the northeast. Each features sand, beach chairs, palm trees, and in recent years swimming pools, sports and games, refreshment areas, and a temporary library. Each year Paris Plages counts about four million visitors.

Biking. Also emblematic of Paris's commitment to nonmotorized transportation, biking amenities have dramatically improved in the last decade. Since 2001 the municipality created 440 kilometers of bike lanes, for a total of 640 kilometers by the end of 2010 (Lefebvre 2010; Ville de Paris 2010g).

A 2008 national decree on road safety creates new regulations for urban slow traffic zones (30-kmh *zones de circulation apaisée*, peaceful circulation), which Paris is authorizing as well (although this idea was originally proposed in Paris in 2005). Two-way biking is now allowed on one-way streets in 30-kmh zones. This program has been implemented on a thousand streets in sixty-five neighborhoods, creating shorter and more direct cycling routes. By 2014 two-way biking will be allowed on all streets in 30-kmh zones. This will add 700 kilometers of bike lanes in Paris, including two major paths crossing the entire city, expanding Paris's bike path network by 30% (Baïze 2010; Ville de Paris 2010g).

The 2008 decree on road safety also created very slow traffic zones (20-kmh *zones de rencontre*, interaction zones) where pedestrians have priority over other road users. Paris created three interaction zones since 2008, in the 17th, 11th, and 20th districts. This is a direct, albeit so far limited, application of the Dutch and British *woonerf* or *home zone* models (see the new signage indicating entrance to these zones in figure 2.2).

Also highly publicized, Paris launched its public bike program Vélib' in July 2007. It offers about 20,000 public bicycles at 1,450 docking stations (one every three hundred meters). Anyone with a subscription (costing €1/day, €5/week, or €29/year) can use a bike for free for the first thirty minutes of any trip, with an unlimited numbers of trips. Longer trips cost €1 to €4 for each additional thirty minutes. By 2008 Vélib' had about fifty thousand uses per day and bike use had increased by a third (Ville de Paris 2009a). Vélib' is funded via a private–public partnership whereby the company JCDecaux incurs the costs of the program in exchange for free advertisement space on municipal structures (e.g., bus stops).

The municipality is also considering transforming the high-speed lanes along the Seine to facilitate pedestrian access to the river. This would involve slowing down traffic on the Right Bank and closing 2.3 kilometers of these lanes entirely on the Left Bank. Impacts would involve slower traffic and redistribution of through traffic to the Péripherique expressway. The prefect of police, who controls transportation on these high-speed lanes, expressed concerns about congestion at the July 2010 meeting of the Paris City Council, and public consultation on these projects began in the fall of 2010. They will likely occur incrementally (Ville de Paris 2010h).

Green Spaces and Biodiversity

Paris is relatively green, with about five hundred thousand trees along streets and in open spaces—one hundred thousand along streets, three hundred thousand in the woodlands, thirty-six thousand in parks and gardens, thirty-four thousand in cemeteries, eight thousand along the Péripherique expressway, and ten thousand in schools and sports facilities (Ville de Paris 2009b). I focus here on green spaces and biodiversity in parks and on paved surfaces.

Green Spaces

Paris has 478 public green spaces: two large woodlands outside Paris's physical boundaries, 16 large parks, hundreds of gardens and neighborhood parks, and 14 cemeteries, including the forty-four-hectare Père-Lachaise.[21] The Bois de Vincennes and Boulogne woodlands cover, respectively, 995 hectares and 846 hectares—each more than twice the size of New York's Central Park. Excluding these woodlands, which are outside Paris's physical

Figure 2.2 Signage indicates a zone in which pedestrians have priority over other modes of travel. Credit: Lucie Laurian.

boundaries, green spaces in the city make up a total of 553 hectares (i.e., 6.4% of Paris's land area; see DEVE 2010).

The oldest and most iconic public gardens are the Tuileries, created in the 16th century for the Louvre Palace; the Luxembourg Garden, created for Marie de Medici's 1612 castle (now the Senate); and the Jardin des Plantes, Paris's first public garden, created by Louis XIII and devoted to natural sciences. In the Second Empire, Napoleon III and Baron Haussmann added parks on annexed lands, including Parcs Montsouris, des Buttes Chaumont, and Monceau, as well as the woodlands.

In the mid-1980s and 1990s, the municipality created large parks on derelict industrial sites. The thirty-three-hectare Parc de la Villette (1984) is on the site of former slaughterhouses. The Parc de Belleville (1988) sits on a previously insalubrious area. The Parc André Citroën (1992) is on the site of a car manufacturing plant. The 3.5-hectare Jardin Atlantique (1994) was created above the Montparnasse railroad tracks. The Parc de Bercy (1997) replaced abandoned wine warehouses. The elevated 4.5-kilometer Promenade plantée (2000) runs on a corridor of unused railroad tracks and inspired similar projects in Europe and the U.S. (e.g., the High Line in New York City).

The Paris Climate Plan calls for increasing vegetation, not for the carbon sink it provides (its effect is only significant for the woodlands) but to promote shading and cooling, to absorb sound, to reduce particulate matter, and to enhance quality of life. The municipality's commitment and ability to continue to add green space is astounding given the city's density, property values, and development pressure. Between 2001 and 2008 the current city administration added thirty-two hectares of green spaces within city limits—ten hectares by opening existing green spaces to the public (at museums, foundations, agronomy gardens, etc.), and adding twenty-two more via forty new parks and gardens. These additions range from large parks, such as the Jardins d'Eole (4.22 hectares) and Clichy-Batignoles (4.4 hectares), to park extensions and small community gardens. For instance, the central turf at the Auteuil racetrack was converted to a six-hectare public park. Inaugurated in July 2010, the 1.4-hectare Serge Gainsbourg Garden is on a slab built in 2007 to cover the Périphérique expressway near Porte des Lilas, in order to abate noise and nuisance. It features hills, a prairie with wildflower plantings, and a community garden. The administration plans to add another thirty hectares between 2008 and 2014 (Moricou 2010). The large-scale urban redevelopment project Paris Rive Gauche around the National Library should add ten hectares of green spaces. Les Halles, undergoing major renovations, will feature a 4.3-hectare garden.

A recent trend in Paris is the creation of community gardens. There are now more than fifty, managed by neighborhood nonprofit organizations. They are federated by the Green Hand Network (Réseau Main Verte) and supported by the city's Office of Green Spaces (Direction des Espaces verts et de l'Environnement, DEVE). Gardening groups are encouraged to sign the Main Verte Charter, created in 2003 to promote organic gardening practices. In the 20th district only, fifty abandoned areas were identified for potential garden sites and fifty have been planted. Residents' involvement is encouraged to enhance social life, sense of place, and social insertion, and many gardens provide activities for children and social, educational, and cultural events.

Paris's parks and gardens are managed by the DEVE, with a staff of four thousand and a budget of €33 million in 2009. The municipality owns and manages a forty-hectare plant nursery outside Paris with large greenhouses and hundreds of plant species, including forty thousand trees—four thousand of which are harvested yearly. Parks and gardens management emphasizes environmentally sensitive practices. The use of chemical herbicides and pesticides diminished by 90% over the last fifteen years, and about 70% of the fertilizers used are nonchemical (DEVE 2010). To promote sustainable practices, the DEVE is expanding the certification of parks and gardens under an ecological label, which considers water management, soil quality, integrated pest management, biological pesticides, and locally adapted species.[22] About eighty parks have received the label and the DEVE plans expand it to all others (DEVE 2010; Ville de Paris 2010i). These changes are consistent with a national effort to reduce the use of toxic pesticides in nonagricultural areas.[23] Independently, the Bois de Vincennes has begun its ISO 14001 certification process (ISO 14001 is the international standard for environmental management systems).

Biodiversity

This new approach to the management of green spaces supports urban biodiversity. Paris's biodiversity is increasingly well documented and protected. Paris has over 160 species of trees. It is home to 600 wild animal species, including 10 amphibian, 174 bird, 3 reptile, 33 mammal, and 36 fish species (e.g., sponges, jellyfish, snails, mussels, dragonflies, stag beetles, crayfish, pikes, trout, eels, frogs, toads, newts, lizards, slowworms, common kestrels—about fifty pairs nest on Notre Dame, the Eiffel Tower, and high rises—peregrine falcons, tawny owls, bats, and hedgehogs). Paris is also host to about one thousand insect species and two thousand species of wild plants and mushrooms. Paris has several nationally protected species, including lizards, common midwife toads, marsh frogs, tawny owls, grey herons, red foxes, white-legged damselflies, and great capricorn beetles, also protected at the EU level (see table 2.1). Most of these reside in parks and woodlands and use Paris's green corridors, such as the Canal de l'Ourcq and the unused circular railroad track Petite Ceinture (Vaquin 2006; Ville de Paris 2010j).

Biodiversity in Paris is not limited to parks and gardens. The humid microclimate of the Seine banks creates biodiversity hot spots, with mosses, gypsywort, spotted ladysthumb, lichens, and ferns. While former mayor Jacques Chirac's promise that the Seine would be clean enough to swim in the mid-1990s remains unfulfilled, improvements in water quality over the last decades have made the aquatic environment favorable to a diversity of plants, ducks (mallards, coots, wagtails), and fish species. In the 1960s the Seine in Paris had only four or five fish species. Today it hosts about twenty species with large populations and ten less common species (e.g., roaches, tenches, gudgeons, bleaks, perchs, pikes, eels). The water is clean enough for trout to reproduce downtown, but the fish remain too contaminated for human consumption, mainly by PCBs accumulated in soil and sediments.[24]

Paris signed the Regional Charter for Biodiversity in 2004. The planning process for Paris's Biodiversity Plan was launched in 2010, starting with an inventory of wild flora and fauna in public parks and gardens. A white paper on the preservation and restoration of biodiversity was published in October 2010. It emphasizes knowledge gathering and public information, the sustainable management of green spaces (public and private), supporting the creation of green roofs and walls, the protection of ecological corridors, and regional cooperation. The Biodiversity Plan, based on this draft, was adopted by the Paris City Council in November 2011 (APUR 2010b; Ville de Paris 2010i).

The rehabilitation and construction of ponds (*mares*) is an important element of biodiversity-protection efforts. There are twenty ponds in Paris as of 2011 (twelve of them created since 2001). They range from 10 m^2 to 2,500 m^2 and are typically 80 centimeters to 1.5 meters deep to support aquatic fauna and flora. Four additional ponds are planned in future garden projects.

Table 2.1 Wild and protected animal species in Paris

	In Paris		In France
Type	Number of species	Number of nationally protected species	Number of species
Insects	1,038	1 (10 regionally protected)	40,280
Amphibians	9	7	40
Reptiles	3	2	41
Birds	166 (including 51 nesting, 17 occasionally present)	119	545
Mammals	32	11	229
Total	1,249	149	41,135

Source: Ville de Paris, "Espèces protégées et remarquables," Feb. 2, 2010, http://www.paris.fr/.

Not limited to green spaces, vegetation and biodiversity are also found on roofs, walls, and sidewalks. Many EU cities are creating green surfaces on rooftops. Despite the innovative sixty-nine-thousand-square-foot sloping green roof on the 1984 landmark sports and concerts arena Palais Omnisports de Bercy, the proportion of green roofs in Paris remains limited and Paris is lagging compared to other European cities. Ninety public buildings are covered with green roofs, totaling 36,000 m² (Lagedec 2010). About 20,000 m² of these were added between 2007 and 2009, and ten additional projects are planned. A census of the roofs that *could* be planted estimates Paris's green roof capacity to be 314 hectares—that is, 1.15% of suitable roofs are planted (Ville de Paris 2010c).[25]

On the other hand, Paris is becoming a leader in green walls. In 2006 Paris had about 55 exterior green walls, with 174 planned by the end of 2007 and 90 under study. About 40 were installed in 2007 and 17 in 2009. The city plans to add 30 green facades by 2014 (Lagedec 2010). Two of the best-known green walls in Paris were designed by Patrick Blanc for the Museum of Primitive Arts and the BHV store (see figure 2.3). Some green walls are on exterior facades, while others are in courtyards and parking lots.

In addition to green roofs and walls, vegetation and biodiversity are also increasing on Paris's sidewalks. On the formal end of the spectrum, the planting of street trees dates back to the late 16th century. Paris had thirty-eight thousand trees along boulevards and avenues in 1855. By the end of the 19th century, Paris had eighty-eight thousand street trees, albeit of relatively few species. Different species were introduced in the 20th

Figure 2.3 A Patrick Blanc–designed green wall on the facade of the department store BHV. Credit: Timothy Beatley.

century, but the number of trees only increased by 3% between 1895 and 1995. Since the late 1990s, the number of street trees increased dramatically, reaching over one hundred thousand today. About 2,400 trees are planted yearly—1,500 replacement trees and 900 additional ones (Ville de Paris 2008).

On the informal end of the spectrum, Guerilla Gardening (a U.S.- and British-based eco-rebellious movement) plants seeds anywhere and everywhere. The Paris and regional administrations recently supported this movement. The regional-scale operation Let It Grow (Laissons pousser) is sponsored by the region's Naturparif organization, the Regional Agency for Nature and Biodiversity, and by about fifteen municipalities. In spring 2010, Let It Grow distributed twenty thousand bags of wild flower and grass seeds to residents and associations to be planted anywhere (e.g., at the base of trees, in sidewalk cracks, on roundabouts, at the base of buildings). Consistent with this approach to "let it grow," the city now voluntarily lets wild grasses and plants grow at the base of trees, along sidewalks, and between cobblestones. Public information campaigns specify that this is not negligence but a new way to promote biodiversity.

Finally, it is important to mention the place of bees in the Paris environment. Essential for the pollination of most plants, bees pollinate about seven hundred flowers a day within three kilometers of their hives. While bee colonies in western Europe are struggling, Paris bees are doing well, perhaps due to the general environmental conditions in the city with higher temperatures (2°C higher than the region on average), high plant diversity, a long flowering season in parks and gardens, green spaces managed without chemical fertilizers or insecticides, and plantations on terraces and balconies.

About four hundred beehives are dispersed throughout the city, some with educational functions. All hives are reported to and supervised by the National Union of French Apiculture (Union Nationale de l'Apiculture Française, UNAF). The UNAF launched the campaign "Bees, Sentinels of the Environment" in 2005, and dramatically increased the visibility of bees as a key species, resulting in the installation of additional beehives. Recent studies found that honey production in beehives in Paris and the industrial suburb of Saint-Denis is much more abundant and diverse in pollens than the production of rural beehives (Ministère de l'environnement 2010; Doré 2010). The association Parti Poétique installs beehives and sells "concrete honey" (*miel béton*) to support awareness of the importance of urban bees (Banque du miel 2010). This led the *BBC News* to run the headline

"Paris Fast Becoming Queen Bee of the Urban Apiary World" in the summer of 2010 (Schofield 2010).

The Luxembourg Garden has hosted the Paris apiculture school and its
beehives since 1856 (figure 2.4), but most of Paris's beehives were installed
in the last thirty years. The roof of the Garnier Opera has been home to
bees since 1982. The Parc George Brassens, opened in 1986, has about fifteen beehives. The beehives at the Maison Paris Nature (Park Floral) were
installed in 1996. About fifty beehives were installed in the Bois de Vin-
cenne and Boulogne in the last ten years. There are six beehives in the Parc
Kellerman, two in the Parc Monceau, seven at the Jardin d'Acclimatation,
ten at the Aqueduc Community Garden, and several more in the 19th and
20th districts. In 2010, ten beehives were installed on the roof of the 4th
district City Hall and at other major public and nonprofit sites.[26] If bees
are a relevant indicator species (as many experts believe; see Paxton 2000),
then they suggest that Paris is indeed on a path toward improved environmental quality.

Conclusion

In this chapter, I chose to emphasize areas of progress and success in environmental policy and practice in Paris. A complete report on the state of
the environment in Paris would also highlight ongoing areas of concern.
Air quality in Paris is relatively poor, largely due to traffic-related emissions. Despite transit alternatives and long commute times, many subur-
banites still find it more convenient to drive into the city. The planned
regional transit systems and additional park-and-ride structures might al-
leviate urban traffic in the coming decades.

Efforts to increase the energy efficiency of buildings are under way,
but Paris's old housing stock will make this transition long and costly.
With the exception of the energy produced through waste incineration,
Paris is only now starting to develop its renewable energy infrastructure.
The potential of geothermal energy production is high, but it will take
decades before locally produced renewable energy amounts to a significant
portion of energy use. The municipality has nonetheless set the city on
this path.

Areas of more visible success are Paris's bus rapid transit and biking
infrastructure. The city is eliminating car lanes to make space for bus and
bike lanes, wider sidewalks, and larger pedestrian areas. The ratio of urban space devoted to transit, pedestrians, and bikes versus cars is steadily

Figure 2.4 The beehives at the Luxembourg Garden in Paris. There are now four hundred beehives throughout the city. Credit: Lucie Laurian.

increasing, which, in the long run, may be a key indicator of sustainability. Public bikes and the temporary closing of high-traffic roads for bike and pedestrian uses are some of the most innovative and successful programs to promote nonmotorized transportation. It remains to be seen whether the upcoming shared electric cars program will significantly decrease the number of cars in the city and their emissions.

Finally, the municipality is continuing to increase the amount of green spaces in the city. Adding green areas and successfully promoting biodiversity in one of the densest cities in the West speaks to the commitment of Paris to remain a livable city and continue on a path toward environmental sustainability. Thriving fish and bee populations may be the best indicator of this success so far.

References

ADEME. 2010. Changement climatique, chiffres clefs. http://www.ademe.fr/.
AIGP (Atelier international du Grand Paris). 2010. Vers un grand système métropolitain: Un scénario évolutif proposé par l'atelier international du Grand Paris. http://www.ateliergrandparis.com/.

APUR (Atelier Parisien d'Urbanisme). 2010a. Thermographie des immeubles parisiens. Jan. http://www.apur.org/.

———. 2010b. Situation et perspectives de la place de la nature à Paris. Rapport d'étape, June. http://www.apur.org/.

Baïze, C. 2010. Les vélos autorisés à rouler à contresens dans les rues de Paris. Le Monde. July 16.

Banque du miel. 2010. http://www.banquedumiel.org/.

Blanc, C. 2009. L'ambition nationale du Grand Paris. Le Monde. Nov. 23.

Borrel, C. 2005. Enquêtes annuelles de recensement 2004 et 2005. http://www.insee.fr/.

Chevalier, L. 2010. Près de 30% des jeunes issus des ZUS au chômage en 2009. Feb. 11. http://www.emploi-pro.fr/.

CNDP (Commission nationale du débat public). 2010a. Débat publique Arc Express. http://www.debatpublic-arcexpress.org/.

———. 2010b. Débat publique Grand Paris. http://www.debatpublic-reseau-grand paris.org/.

———. 2010c. Les contrats de developpement territorial. http://www.debatpublic -reseau-grandparis.org/.

CRIF (Conseil regional d'Île-de-France). 2010. Arc Express/Grand Paris: La base d'un rapprochement. Nov. 15. http://www.iledefrance.fr/.

DEVE (Direction des Espaces verts et de l'Environnement). 2010. Rapport d'activité 2009 de la direction des Espaces verts et de l'Environnement. http://www.paris.fr/.

Doré, M. 2010. Apiculture urbaine: Les abeilles font fureur à Paris. La Presse. Aug. 16.

DREIF (Direction régionale de l'Equipement de l'Île-de-France). 2004. Les déplacements de Franciliens en 2001–2002: Enquête globale de transport. http:// www.ile-de-france.equipement.gouv.fr/.

EDF (Electricité de France). 2010. Accueil. http://energie.edf.com/.

Foreign Policy. 2010. The 2010 global cities index. In "Metropolis Now," special section of Foreign Policy 181, Sept./Oct.: 119–52.

Françoise, Y., Climate-Energy Division Director, Paris City Hall. 2010. E-mail exchange. Dec. 24.

INSEE (Institut National de la Statistique et des Études Économiques). 2001. Île-de-France a la page: Les zones urbaines sensibles en Île-de-France. http://www .insee.fr/.

———. 2010a. Recensement de la population. http://www.insee.fr/.

———. 2010b. Population totale. http://www.insee.fr/.

———. 2010c. Populations de 1975 à 2030: Comparaisons regionals. http://www .insee.fr/.

———. 2010d. Évolution et structure de la population, recensement 2007. http:// www.insee.fr/.

———. 2010e. Produits intérieurs bruts régionaux et valeurs ajoutées régionales de 1990 à 2009. http://www.insee.fr/.

IUS (Institute for Urban Strategies, at the Mori Memorial Foundation). 2010. Global power city index, 2010. http://www.mori-m-foundation.or.jp/.

Kamin, B. 2010. Ten years of green roofs in Chicago: Mayor Daley's green thumb and iron fist have produced impressive gains, but the movement remains in its infancy. Chicago Tribune. April 20.

Knight Frank. Wealth report: World cities survey, 2010. http://www.knightfrank
.com/.

Lagadec, E., Strategy of Sustainable Development Division Director, Paris Agency of
Urban Ecology. 2010. E-mail correspondence, Dec. 3.

Le Monde. 2010a. Comment le projet de loi Grenelle II a été détricoté. May 4.

———. 2010b. Ca vous regarde: Les deputes ont-ils trahi le Grenelle? May 11.

Le Parisien. 2010. Val-de-Marne: Les cités du département minées par le chômage.
March 4.

Lefebvre, P., Head Engineer and Scientific and Technical Adviser to the City of Paris
Streets and Transportation Division. 2010. E-mail exchange. Dec. 6.

MEEDEM (Ministère de l'écologie, de l'énergie, du développement durable et de la
mer). 2010a. Réglementation thermique "Grenelle Environnement, 2012." July
6. http://www.developpement-durable.gouv.fr/.

———. 2010b. Le Grenelle 2 décrypté: Articles et décrets sur le bâtiment. http://
www.plan-batiment.legrenelle-environnement.fr/.

Ministère de l'environnement. 2010. Les abeilles en ville. Sept. http://quartiers
durables.re/.

Ministère de l'intérieur. 2007. Plan départemental d'une gestion d'une canicule
(PDGC) à Paris. June. http://www.prefecturedepolice.interieur.gouv.fr/.

Monocle. 2010. Most livable cities in the world. *Monocle* 4, July. http://www.psfk
.com/.

Moricou, P., Elected Representative on the Municipal Council of the Paris 15th
District. 2010. E-mail exchange. Nov. 2.

Paxton, R. 2000. Conserving our bees. http://www.well.com/~davidu/bees.html.

Préfecture de Paris. 2004. Shema de developpement commercial de Paris. http://www
.paris.pref.gouv.fr/.

PricewaterhouseCoopers. 2009. Emerging market city economies set to rise rapidly in
global GDP rankings. http://www.pwc.com/.

Ramnoux, S. 2010. Un troisième projet de supermétro au-dessus de l'A 86. *Le
Parisien.* Oct. 1.

RATP (Régie Autonome des Transports Parisiens). 2011. Le Réseau. http://www.ratp
.fr/.

Région Île-de-France. 2009. Plan de mobilization pour les transports en Île-de-France.
http://www.aut-idf.org/.

Schofield, H. 2010 Paris fast becoming queen bee of the urban apiary world. *BBC
News.* Aug. 14.

Subra, P. 2010. Grand Paris, un bilan d'etape. *Le Monde.* June 9.

Vaquin, J.-B. 2006. *Atlas de la nature à Paris.* Paris: Le Passage.

Verdevoye, A.-G. 2010. La Blue Car de Bolloré rafle le marché Autolib' à Paris. *La
Tribune.* Dec. 17.

Ville de Paris. 2007a. Politique de tourisme. http://www.paris.fr/.

———. 2007b. Climat info carbone. Jan. 6.

———. 2007c. Diagnostic des déplacements à Paris et en Île-de-France. Jan. 12.
http://www.paris.fr/.

———. 2007d. Plan climat de Paris. Oct. 1. http://www.paris.fr/.

———. 2007e. Plan de déplacements de Paris. http://www.paris.fr/.

————. 2008. Le remplacement des arbres en milieu urbain. Sept. 22. http://www.paris.fr/.

————. 2009a. Le bilan des déplacements à Paris en 2008. http://www.paris.fr/.

————. 2009b. Les arbres en chiffres. Sept. 14. http://www.paris.fr/.

————. 2010a. Dimensions. http://www.paris.fr/.

————. 2010b. La population par arrondissement de 1990 à 2009. http://www.paris.fr/.

————. 2010c. Etude du potential d'énergies renouvelables de Paris: Rapport 1, Etat des lieux, bilan de la production des énergies renouvelables. June.

————. 2010d. Comité de pilotage de plan climat de Paris. Nov. 29.

————. 2010e. Bornes de recharge électrique. Oct. 13. http://www.paris.fr/.

————. 2010f. Le Mobilien. http://www.paris.fr/.

————. 2010g. Le double sens cyclable. http://www.paris.fr/.

————. 2010h. Berges de Seine. http://bergesdeseine.paris.fr/.

————. 2010i. Le livre blanc de la biodiversité à Paris. http://labs.paris.fr/.

————. 2010j. Biodiversité: Un plan pour Paris. http://www.paris.fr/.

Voguéo. 2011. Réseau Voguéo. http://www.vogueo.fr/.

Notes

1. I do not discuss these relevant but less innovative policy areas: drinking water (overall of high quality), food systems (municipal and private purchases of organic and local foods are increasing), and air pollution (roadside levels of NO_2, particulate matter, and ozone fail to meet European standards).

2. The First Republic was instituted during the 1789 Revolution. The second lasted from the 1848 Revolution until the reestablishment of the Empire in 1852. The Third Republic, created after the fall of Napoleon III, ended with the Vichy government in 1939. The fourth, established in 1946, was replaced by the more stable fifth in 1958.

3. Napoleon became emperor in 1804. After the 1814 defeat in Russia, the Restoration reestablished the monarchy. The July Revolution of 1830 created a constitutional monarchy, which lasted until the 1848 Revolution formed the Second Republic. In 1852 the Second Empire reestablished strongly centralized imperial powers and lasted until the 1870 defeat against Prussia.

4. Districts are numbered in a spiral pattern. Historically, working-class areas are in the north and east (11th and 18th to 20th districts), and wealthy areas are in the center and west (1st to 8th and 15th to 17th districts).

5. Paris is both a municipality and a department. The Paris City Council governs both.

6. Sarkozy's "carbon contribution" was to tax energy consumption and petroleum use, with an income-based financial compensation for low-income households (most industries would have been exempted). The tax was opposed by the right (as a tax), the left (as unjust), and the Greens (as too low). Planned to begin in January 2010, it was cancelled in December 2009.

7. Wind farms must include at least five towers and are defined as industrial or agricultural exploitations that can create risks or nuisances for neighbors' safety or health, requiring special permits.

8. Local Urbanism Plans (Plan local d'urbanisme) operate as comprehensive plans. They specify densities, bulk, and locations in detailed Land Use Plans (Plan d'occupation des sols).

9. PIG status also gives the national government and the development agency the right to expropriate land.

10. India emits under 1 teqCO$_2$/person/year, Europe 10, and North America about 20.

11. The European carbon credit market, launched in 2005, focuses on industry and energy production and does not directly affect Paris municipal climate strategies.

12. The Paris Climate Agency (Agence parisienne du climat), tasked with supporting the adoption of best practices, was created in 2011. Its activities are detailed at http://www.apc-paris.com/.

13. The municipality is to reduce by 30% its emissions and the energy consumption of public buildings, and to increase to 30% energy consumption from renewable sources by 2020.

14. These values are for m^2 of living areas. They include energy consumption for heating, cooling, water heating, and lighting but exclude buildings' embodied energy. The German Passivhaus and Swiss Minergie standards are more stringent (e.g., 38 kWh/m^2/year for Minergie).

15. Similar turbines operate in the Hudson River (New York) and the Saint Lawrence River (Canada), both with higher currents than the Seine.

16. At the national scale, Grenelle 1 and 2 promote non-road transportation. Grenelle 1 calls for the creation of new public transit lines nationwide, mainly tramway and separated bus lanes. Grenelle authorizes cities with more than three hundred thousand residents to experiment with urban road tolls, and it supports car-sharing programs and a recharging infrastructure for electric vehicles.

17. The city administration seeks to reduce the commuting and professional car use of its 6,200 employees (estimated at 46,300 teqCO$_2$/year), to reduce its fleet by 10%, and to shift its 841 garbage trucks and 3,847 cars and buses toward efficient vehicles. This could lower municipal fleet emissions by 30% (Ville de Paris 2007d).

18. Paris transit systems are operated by several agencies. The Régie Autonome des Transports Parisiens (RATP) operates bus lines, Métro and tramway lines, and sections of the RER. The Syndicat des Transports d'Île-de-France (STIF) oversees transit in the Paris region. The Société Nationale des Chemins de fer Français (SNCF) operates suburban rails, a tramway line, and sections of the RER. Optile, a consortium of private operators, manages minor bus lines.

19. Paris is also a central hub in the national and European rail networks. It is one and a half hours from Brussels, two and half from London, and three from Amsterdam. Six major railway stations serve three train networks: regular trains, high-speed lines, and the Transilien suburban rails.

20. The national government plans to overtax land around these stops to preemptively recapture property value increases that can be expected from the creation of new Métro hubs. Concerns abound about the potential for corruption as development projects would likely be granted to large-scale developers.

21. These figures exclude private gardens, relatively common at the base of high residential buildings.

22. Gardens owned by the state (the Tuileries, Luxembourg, and Elysée) are still treated with chemical fertilizers, pesticides, and herbicides.

23. A national voluntary agreement signed in September 2010 commits nonagricultural land managers to reduce the use of pesticides in parks, alongside roads and sidewalks, on sports fields, in industrial zones, and at airports.

24. In June 2010 the Ministry of Ecology, Energy, and Sustainable Development made illegal in the whole region the consumption of fish from the Seine.

25. This proportion is well below the coverage of some German cities, but much more than Chicago, well known for green roof initiative despite a coverage under 0.1% (Kamin 2010).

26. The Paris airports signed the UNAF Charter, agreeing to avoid products toxic to bees. Six beehives were installed near De Gaulle Airport. Since bees are in intense contact with plants, soil, air, and water, the honey will be studied for environmental quality surveillance.

3

Freiburg, Germany: Germany's Eco-Capital

Dale Medearis and Wulf Daseking

Nestled in the southern corner of Germany near the Swiss and French borders, the city of Freiburg has long been considered a model of sustainable development for Europe and the world (see table 3.1). Freiburg is a moderate-sized city of approximately 220,000 people, with a unique combination of topography, climate, leadership, and history that have merged to make it a pioneer in renewable energy (especially solar), nature protection, transportation, and environmental planning. Freiburg's proliferation of renewable energy industries, clearly defined landscape plans and urban forests, vibrant public transportation system, and environmentally designed housing in projects in Rieselfeld, Wiehre Bahnhof, and Vauban reflect how environmental protection, economic growth, and social inclusion policies are not mutually exclusive, but interrelated. Freiburg's success can be more appreciated when one considers that it has sustained steady and continuous population growth for over thirty years.

Freiburg is recognized as a global leader in sustainable development when measured by comprehensive energy planning, water conservation, or high transportation modal splits. The city's success in merging design, transportation, and ecology is reflected in its expanding trophy case of European and global sustainability awards, and is living proof that sustainable planning is moving from the margins to the mainstream.

General Background and Profile

Freiburg's success with environmental planning proves that ambitious environmental, energy, and nature-protection initiatives are economic

Table 3.1   Background on Freiburg

Population	220,000
Area (km²)	15,306
Percent green space/parks/nature	47.1
Hectares per capita green space/parks/nature	0.031
Percent forest cover/forest canopy	42.4
Percent trips made on public transit	18
Percent trips made walking	23
Percent trips made bicycling	27
Greenhouse gas emissions per capita	0.468
Average size of houses/flats (in m²)	74.46
Meters of bikeways per person	0.78
Meters of public transit lines per capita	0.15

development opportunities rather than insufferable obstacles. Three key elements have made Freiburg a pioneer in this realm: the city's utilization of its comparative advantage with the relatively high concentration of sunlight, its rural isolation at the base of the Black Forest, and its development of a comprehensive energy program.

1. Freiburg bathes in the highest concentration of sunshine in Germany. Solar exposure in the city exceeds more than 1,700 hours of sunshine per year. This factor contributed to Karl Albrecht University becoming the largest employer for the city and region and a key catalyst for environmental industries. For more than twenty-five years, the city and the university have worked together to place Freiburg at the center of research and development for solar energy and other environmental technologies. The solar research institutions and businesses within the city are extensive, and include the prestigious Fraunhofer Institute for Solar Energy Systems, the Solar Info Center, and the International Solar Energy Society. At present, more than 450 solar and renewable energy companies call Freiburg home (Beatley 2000).

2. Freiburg's relative lack of extractible natural resources (with the exception of biomass), combined with its proximity to the French border and German historical fears of foreign incursions, helped spare the city from the blight and scars of pre- and postwar industrialization.

3. Freiburg's international attention for its pioneering work with renewable energy actually overshadows its equally

noteworthy success with integrated energy management. The city has efficiently utilized conventional energy systems, such as cogeneration, combined heat and power, and district energy systems, in tandem with increased energy-efficiency codes for new and existing homes and buildings, the promotion of biomass, solar, wind, and other renewable energies, and an integrated transportation, spatial, and urban development planning program.

Planning Context

German land use, growth management, landscape, and transportation planning policies are legendary, but Freiburg's experiences have taken the practice to new levels. Following the devastation of Freiburg in World War II, in which over 85 % of the inner city was destroyed, land use planning in Freiburg and the surrounding region concentrated on the preservation and protection of the city's historic environmental, cultural, and architectural assets. Rebuilding Freiburg after the war was skillfully done by maintaining the scale and feel of the city center through the placement of strict conditions on redevelopment. The core focus was the preservation of the old plots and the construction of new buildings and housing with mixed designs. Redevelopment started with the preservation of the medieval center by limiting the height of new buildings and preserving the use of traditional materials and designs for the buildings and streets. Attention to cultural heritage was given high priority and reflected in the laying of the main city streets, which were built with cobblestones from the Rhine, and the extension of the medieval gutters (*Baechle*). Originally operated by the local guilds to bring water to the city from the surrounding streams, the Baechle were enhanced, expanded, and replicated in other new developments of the city. Transportation planning in Freiburg has been goal-oriented to reduce automobile dependency. In the 1970s, pedestrianizing the city center started the trend toward a pedestrian- and bike-friendly modal split. City streets were changed, but space was added for bike paths and trams, rather than cars.

Unlike many German cities, over the past decade Freiburg has planned to accommodate population growth (growing from 183,000 people in 1984 to 220,000 in 2011). The goal of this effort is to keep the growth contained within the existing built areas, without resorting to development on the greenfields. This focus on developing within the existing built area is reflected in the master plans of the city. Master planning in Freiburg has played an important role since the conclusion of the Second World War and subsequent efforts to rebuild the city. It was apparent even back then that rebuilding Freiburg was a long-term, incremental process that would require thought and interconnection.

Today the planning in Freiburg has focused on the joint efforts of infill and transit-oriented development. Freiburg has also taken a regional approach by ensuring that growth management controls do not come at the expense of either the central city core or the neighboring communities. This has meant that Freiburg also placed special emphasis on the protection of the city's environmental assets, particularly the open space of the Black Forest, the Dreisam Creek, and the Rhine River valley. Carefully defined urban boundaries mesh with the surrounding rural landscape of the Black Forest, which actually penetrates the heart of the city center. A policy of "re-densification" was pursued, which promoted the integration and mixing of functions within the city center and limited sprawl-like development. Thoughtful zoning codes (*Bebaungsplaene*) were approved that tolerated a broad range of residential, commercial, and recreational activities as well as the preservation of historic structures—often within single blocks (see figure 3.1). Freiburg's success with the redevelopment

Figure 3.1 Freiburg is a compact city with new development guided into dense, contiguous urban neighborhoods. Credit: Wulf Daseking, City of Freiburg.

and focus on commercial, ecological, and social interlinkages even led to the creation of the planning term "fresh cell therapy"—the practice of using demographic metrics to assess aging trends, and responding by rejuvenating "aged blocks" through the inclusion of families and children. Despite the presence of the university and the appearance of a youthful demographic, Freiburg has a relatively large population of senior citizens. This can be seen in the tired condition of some of the older apartments and buildings. To harmonize the fusion of the new young families moving to Freiburg with the existing senior residents, the city promotes old and new designs for the fresh cell infill strategy.

Since the 1950s, Freiburg has consistently used urban planning to form the core of sustainable development. Central to this approach has been the integration of land use and transportation policy. Parallel to this has been the inclusion of culture, social stability and inclusion (such as fresh cell therapy), education, and public outreach. Together with the Academy of Urbanism in London, the Planning Department in Freiburg has completed a "Charter of Freiburg," which sets forth twelve principles as the cornerstones of the city's future-oriented development (see box 1.1 in the introduction to this volume).

Landscape Planning

City planning in Freiburg, and other German cities, is strongly influenced by regional and local landscape planning policies. In Germany, national-level nature protection laws (*Bundesnaturschutzgesetz*) and spatial planning laws (*Bundesraumordnungsgesetz*) call on each German state to identify, classify, and plan protected areas via state-level landscape plans (*Landschaftsplaene*) and to integrate these plans into broader sets of national planning activities established by the federal Environment and Planning Ministries. Under German federal planning law, local authorities can place private lands in agricultural and forested areas into categories as nature parks, landscape protection areas, or nature reserves. This classification might preclude the landowner from using or developing the land in any way inconsistent with codes or prescriptions of the authority. In addition, German nature-protection law outlines a hierarchy of landscape planning efforts that each state must perform to identify and classify open space and protected areas, down to the local level. Each plan must contain specific assessments of the existing and anticipated outcomes of development and avoid, reduce, or eliminate adverse effects from development. In virtually every German state, building permits are issued only after the completion of an environmental assessment that defines impacts and identifies strategies for mitigation.

Protection of the urban forests around Freiburg predominates in landscape and open space planning, and attention to the natural assets of the forest is evident throughout the city. Concern about the Black Forest's health and the effects of acid rain were fundamental to the contemporary German environmental movement. As with many German cities, Freiburg owns a large percentage of the land within its borders—currently about 32% (Beatley 2000). More than half this land (51%) is under nature protection and off-limits to building (Stadt Freiburg 2001). As with other German cities, building codes in Freiburg are designed to enhance, rather than obstruct, climate and "cool airflows" (*Höllentäller*) from the Black Forest in order to cleanse the city's atmosphere (Beatley 2000). This has been a focus of the city since the 1970s, when air quality and climate change started to become serious issues for the region. The core concept is to model airflows of "clean" air from the Black Forest, and facilitate or plan its passage through the city to maximize the removal of air pollutants such as mobile source emissions, ozone, or particulates from fireplaces. Every master plan in Freiburg has incorporated this concept of "clean air corridors," which in turn affects such issues as the placement and height of buildings, the applications of green rooftops, and arrangement of streets and open spaces in order to support the flow of the air from the hills through the city. This modeling is so sophisticated that height restrictions are placed on the buildings so that none is higher than approximately 12.6 meters. The city's main train station had to have a gap between the building and the facade to facilitate the flow of the air for the district behind it. Even the majority of the city's tramlines are landscaped with grass to mitigate noise and air pollution. The flow of air also has a positive energy outcome. The clean air corridors also restrict the flow of fog from the Rhine River valley into the streets, keeping the city brighter and limiting the amount of electricity used in lighting the streets.

Water

Awareness and consideration of water as a resource permeates the design and planning of Freiburg. It starts with the carefully placed stones of the Baechle and extends to innovative incentives for on-site management of stormwater and landscape planning. Freiburg has instituted several policies and incentives that have led to the application of such techniques as green roofs, bioswales, and other stormwater management features to promote natural, permeable surfaces. Freiburg, like over 40% of German cities, has instituted billing systems based on the volume of stormwater removed from individual properties (Keeley 2007). Split-rate water billing systems have replaced unified billing systems, and metrics have been established for stormwater fees based on the volume of impermeable property and estimated rainfalls at residential and commercial sites. In all zoning plans, stormwater must be managed on-site via low-impact development practices (e.g., bioswales, green roofs, rain gardens).

Transportation

Freiburg's approach to sustainable transportation planning puts biking and pedestrians on equal footing with cars (see figure 3.2). Not only are cars banned within the center city, but a 30-kmh speed limit is imposed on all residential streets (with exceptions for the main roads). As a result, 30% of all trips in Freiburg are done on bike and 15% on foot. Moreover, the city has developed more than 152 miles of bituminized and 103 miles of gravel bike paths (Buehler and Pucher 2011). The demand for bike parking has been so great that Freiburg has constructed more than 5,000 new bicycle parking spaces in the city center alone. Approximately 1,500 parking spaces for bikes have been made available at the railway station to enable train passengers a direct transfer to bicycles. Evidence emerges regularly about Freiburg's sustainable transportation programs and how biking has successfully reduced car traffic and improved air quality. Between 1982 and 1999, motor vehicle traffic throughout the city fell from 38% to 32%. Currently, the city's ratio of cars to residents is approximately 430 to 1,000, compared to the national German average of 550 to 1,000. In Vauban there are 85 cars to every 1,000 inhabitants (see the case study on page 76).

A second cornerstone of Freiburg's transportation system is public transportation—particularly light rail (see figure 3.3). Since the decision by the city in the 1960s to enhance the tram system, more than 17 miles of light rail and 168 miles of bus network have been developed. It is estimated that over 72% of all commuters in Freiburg use the tram system. Zoning and residential planning has been carefully coordinated with the development of the tram so that most of the population is within a half kilometer of a station. The lines are quick and trains run approximately every eight minutes, and approximately every four minutes during rush hour. High

Figure 3.2 Freiburg is a very pedestrian- and bicycle-friendly city, and major efforts have been made to restrict car mobility in favor of these more sustainable modes of transport. Credit: Wulf Daseking, City of Freiburg.

Figure 3.3 A key element of Freiburg's mobility system is its network of trams, which make it easy to travel to any part of the city. Credit: Wulf Daseking, City of Freiburg.

ridership within Freiburg also has been attributed to the single-fare system in which one pass (Öko-Ticket), introduced in 1991, is valid for all transit within the city and is transferable to other members of a single family. In addition, the regional transportation authority, the RVF, recognizes the Öko-Ticket on its three-thousand-kilometer system of transit lines. The local public transport authority is financially solvent and recovers more than 89% of costs from the operation of the tram—among the highest in the Federal Republic of Germany. This was only possible given decades of dedication to integrating transit into the city's planning processes. Public transit is the backbone of the city, and the tram system will continue to be extended over the next decade. The City Council has already approved plans to connect a higher percentage of the population to light rail beyond the current 70% within five hundred meters of a tram stop.

Energy and Climate

Since the 1970s, the city's leadership led efforts to halt construction of a nuclear power plant at the nearby village of Wyhl. History and the city's fate with renewable energy collided again in 1986 with the Chernobyl disaster, which moved Freiburg to consider legitimate alternatives to nuclear power and to implement practical renewable energy policies. In 1992 the city developed its first long-term energy plan. Energy conservation, renewable energy, and the development of environmentally friendly technologies and transportation formed the three pillars of Freiburg's energy and climate strategy. Solar, wind, hydro, and biomass were the core components of the city's efforts to reduce energy consumption by 10%. In 1996 Freiburg's energy policy added a new goal of reducing CO_2 emissions by 25% below 1992 levels by 2010.

Recognizing Freiburg's research and intellectual assets, the city endeavored to link its energy strategy to the city's economic development initiatives, particularly solar technology research and development. Energy and economic development policies were coupled, building on the presence of the university, and leading to a proliferation of renewable energy and solar research institutions, including the Fraunhofer Institute for Solar Energy Systems. Freiburg also hired a full-time "solar manager" to coordinate its economic development activities, and it made available, rent-free, a city-owned building to house the International Solar Energy Society. Freiburg also constructed a solar information desk in the city center to inform and broadcast solar and other environmental information. Freiburg's solar synergies have become a model of industrial ecology. The 450 renewable energy and solar companies housed in Freiburg employ more than ten thousand people (Beatley 2000, 271).

Freiburg's experiment with industrial ecology also is reflected in the "Solar Region Freiburg," a long-term vision to promote the region's renewable energy programs and innovation. The regional public utility, Badenova, of which the city of Freiburg and neighboring authorities are majority shareholders, offers "solar investment subsidies" to residents and businesses that install solar panels. Badenova has also introduced a number of innovative, cost-effective energy savings programs, including the introduction of linear time-variable electricity charges, which use meters that gauge usage according to three different time zones, and for which consumers are charged accordingly. Badenova also invests the income from the difference between the standard rate and the slightly higher regional electricity rates into biomass, photovoltaic, hydropower, and other forms of renewable energy.

Freiburg's work with solar and renewable energy seems destined to become more robust. Under the German federal government's 2001 Renewable Energy Law and recent amendments, energy companies and utilities must reimburse distributed generation of solar photovoltaic at a guaranteed and subsidized price. The current rate of €0.45 per kilowatt hour (compared to a standard electricity rate of €0.15–€0.20) is guaranteed for twenty years. The goal of the policy is to increase renewable energy's share in the electricity market, from 5% to 20% by 2020 (Daseking 2011). Photovoltaic systems are generally affordable, and installation costs €5,000–€8,000/kW. The electricity output expected in Freiburg should cover the investment costs within approximately fifteen years. In 2010 Freiburg produced more than 15 megawatts of solar photovoltaic. The local soccer stadium alone produces more than 190 kilowatts and the central train station's facade produces 55 kilowatts.

Freiburg's focus on energy policies is also oriented toward enhancing existing energy systems, such as combined heat and power. Projects such as Vauban and Rieselfeld (see below) rely on large-scale district energy systems in dense, transit-oriented developments, and have been organized around the efficient movement of heat and electricity produced via cogeneration (see figures 3.4 and 3.5). The city also has relied on the construction of advanced, energy-efficient buildings, such as "passive

Figure 3.4 The new neighborhood Vauban, a former army barracks, is designed to be car-free and incorporates a number of sustainability features, including energy-plus homes that produce more energy than they require. Credit: Wulf Daseking, City of Freiburg.

Figure 3.5 Another growth area in Freiburg, Rieselfeld also promotes walking, bicycling, and travel by tram. Credit: Wulf Daseking, City of Freiburg.

homes" (*Passivbau*). To be certified as a passive home, primary energy consumption cannot exceed 15 kW/h/m²—a staggering level of efficiency. Freiburg's experiences with pilot projects in energy-efficient housing have pointed to cost increases of no less than 5%–8% from conventional practices. The data have also pointed to energy costs and CO_2 emissions that are 30% less than average (Wörner).

In the realm of building retrofits, housing from the 1960s and 1970s presents some of the most pressing challenges. In addition to mandating that all housing since January 2011 must be built to passive standards, the city is piloting the application of passive building standards for several retrofit projects, including the seventy-year-old skyscraper in the Weingarten district.

Case Studies

Vauban

Vauban is perhaps the most recognized planned urban environmental project in Freiburg. Vauban is an urban village built on a former French

Army compound, and is designed to host and service 5,500 inhabitants. In 1992 the city purchased forty-two hectares from the German federal government and administered the development and implementation of the master plan after an international town-planning competition. The city developed clear environmental, transportation, and energy guidelines for the master plan. The creation of the plan was completed and administered within a structured and disciplined outreach and public participation process—the "Forum Vauban." Under the motto "Planning That Learns," Freiburg employed between five and seven full-time staff to oversee development of the master plan—including the hosting of more than fifty distinct public meetings and outreach events to solicit public input during the master plan's development.

The Vauban master plan calls for a car-free development of dense, mixed-use, single-family, and row-house units serviced by a new tram-line connecting to the city center and main rail station. Car ownership and parking are permitted, but only in specific and carefully managed sections at the margins of the district. Traffic calming is prioritized, implemented by the construction of "traffic pillows" and the restriction of access to most automobile through-traffic. The goal of Vauban was to maintain fewer than 150 cars per 1,000 residents by eliminating individual garages or parking for each housing unit. A single, communal "solar" garage (producing 89 kilowatts) built at the edge of the development services those residents dependent on access to automobiles. Since the completion of the project, approximately 35% of the residents have abstained from driving a car.

Since the city owned the Vauban property (it purchased the site from the state of Baden-Wuerttemberg), it had the liberty of creating site-specific purchase agreements for the sales of the homes and buildings (proffers). That is, since financing for the planning and development, particularly the infrastructure, emanated from the Baden-Wuerttemberg Development Agency (LEG), the LEG's investments could be repaid from the sale of the individual homes and buildings. Vauban is evolving into a community for young families, due the excellent light rail connections (the source of Freiburg's fame as the "City of Short Distances"), the different types of housing available, the open space and forests, and the access to multiple governmental agencies as well as shops and commerce. It is an understatement to say that Vauban is among the most popular neighborhoods.

Energy efficiency and land conservation permeates all planning aspects of Vauban. The Vauban master plan promoted mixed uses for housing, shopping, recreation, and education. A broad diversity of designs have been applied for residential and commercial properties. Housing comprises a range of market-priced and affordable "subsidized" housing units, including cohousing for more than 1,200 residents. Preservation of open space was strengthened, as reflected in the extensive network of Rigolden-Mulden stormwater systems that channel rainwater into on-site retention systems. All residential housing at Vauban has been constructed to meet Germany's new low-energy standards for buildings, 65 kW/h/m². Vauban is also host to approximately 150 passive housing units. Sixty-five percent of the electricity is produced from either the combined heat and power fueled by biomass or photovoltaic units (Sperling 2002). Heating for residential and commercial units is supplied by a district heat and power plant.

Rieselfeld

In response to continuing population growth in Freiburg and the surrounding region during the late 1980s and early 1990s, Freiburg experimented with a second large-scale, ecologically planned village at Rieselfeld (see figure 3.6). Rieselfeld is built on seventy-eight hectares of a former city-owned sludge farm at the western edge of the municipality. Freiburg wanted to accommodate 12,500 new residents and 1,500 new jobs, and, like Vauban, restrict urban sprawl by promoting thoughtfully planned, dense environmental housing. A floor-to-space ratio of 1.2 for the more than 4,800 residential and commercial units was to be realized through multistory residential buildings with a five-story limit. Density and livability were merged by developing small plots to accommodate a wide range of building functions to host shops, medical offices, schools, kindergartens, and religious buildings. Like in Vauban, tram access was paramount and car dependence was designed to be minimized by including additional bike lanes, confining parking to garages below each housing unit, and limiting the speed of cars to 30 kmh. When completed in 2011, more nine thousand inhabitants lived in Rieselfeld (Stadt Freiburg 2011).

In 1991 the city of Freiburg formed a special, public–private development agency to coordinate financing, planning, and development at Rieselfeld. Implementation of Rieselfeld was carried out in four stages spread out over two-year intervals to ensure environmental, social, and economic balance. Like many urban environmental planning projects, social inclusion and input by the public was central. The development features a mix of privately financed and socially subsidized housing. Particular

Stadt Freiburg im Breisgau, Stadtteil Rieselfeld   04. Juni 2010

Figure 3.6 Rieselfeld also demonstrates Freiburg's emphasis on dense, compact neighborhoods well served by transit. Credit: Wulf Daseking, City of Freiburg.

consideration was given to the needs of women, families, the aged, and the handicapped. A comprehensive concept for public participation was developed and carried out parallel to the town-planning process. For more on social outreach, see box 3.1 on the Rieselfeld KIOSK. The dialogue with the public resulted in the development of new, thoughtfully designed elementary and primary schools, playgrounds, recreation centers, youth and cultural centers, and an ecumenical church center that dually serviced Catholic and Protestant denominations. The demographic makeup of Rieselfeld is remarkable, and a testimony to anti-sprawl efforts.

Like Vauban, Rieselfeld is driven by ecological considerations. More than 240 hectares of the site were landscaped and dedicated as nature protection or conservation areas. Stormwater at Rieselfeld is not channelized and driven out of the project into culverts, but retained on-site and managed naturally through a series of interconnected bioswales and wetlands. On-site stormwater management practices are ubiquitous, planned into green rooftops and green parking lots between units. Like Vauban, the houses at Rieselfeld are low-energy and do not exceed 65 kWh/m². District heating, combined heat and power, biofuels (woodchips), and solar

Box 3.1

Freiburg KIOSK

KIOSK is a civic organization in Freiburg that started in 1996, at a construction trailer near a city-owned sludge disposal site. (KIOSK is an acronym for Contact, Information, Organization, Self-Help, Culture.) The purpose was to bring out multiple creative ideas from the citizens and residents about Rieselfeld's conversion from a waste site into a residential and livable area for a broad demographic of the city. The first meetings were held in the "glass house" club at the disposal site.

KIOSK has operated an information center, where it hosts family lunches, prints a community newspaper, and organizes flea markets. It has even assisted in the organization of protests to protect trees near the site. Altogether, KIOSK has elicited help from more than one hundred volunteer residents inside the city. There are monthly meetings to discuss the activities of the organization, along with its strategy and outreach. There are membership fees associated with KIOSK, €15 per person or €20 per family. KIOSK has a board of seven residents, each elected every two years. Their tasks are (1) political representation; (2) cooperation with the city; (3) public relations; and (4) contact with local councils and institutions in the sludge disposal site.

KIOSK has an advisory board, which councils the board and promotes exchange between the various interest groups involved with the project. The reactions of Rieselfeld citizens to KIOSK are overwhelmingly positive, as they see the organization as a neutral arbitrator on difficult or challenging planning issues.

photovoltaics dominate residential and commercial energy sources. Studies have already suggested that housing at Rieselfeld emits 20% less CO_2 than conventional housing in Germany.

The development of Rieselfeld was financed mainly by land sales (approximately €115 million) and development fees (€922.5 million), but also from public and county funds (€7.5 million) in the form of subsidies and prefinancing. The revenues, approximately €145 million, were brought into a trust-company fund. With this capital, the project team had to finance public buildings (€52 million), streets and utilities (€35 million), landscaping (€13 million), planning, managing, and marketing (€19 million), and public relations. These costs amounted to approximately €144 million. To prefinance the public and social infrastructure, the development agency had to take a loan of €40 million from the state bank of Baden-Wuerttemberg. Because Freiburg lacked funds, both Rieselfeld and Vauban were developed without any money from the city's budget. All costs were calculated and then divided into square meters of selling ground. That is, every square meter was assessed for the infrastructure and utility costs, which were then factored into the sale price of the unit.

Conclusion

As cities and urban regions around the world struggle to respond to the forces of globalization, urban planners will be encouraged by the work, vision, and results of cities such as Freiburg. It is uncommon to witness a city so totally and comprehensively planned for sustainability (see figure 3.7). Integrated transportation, land use, and open space planning have all

Figure 3.7 Freiburg's compact urban form provides for large blocks of forests and agricultural lands, in close proximity to the city, and a sharp, clear urban edge. Credit: Wulf Daseking, City of Freiburg.

been thoughtfully merged to enhance energy conservation, air and water quality, economic development, and social prosperity. Urban and environmental planners around the world will appreciate the work that Freiburg has undertaken, as it reflects that sustainable urban environments are not marginal, but mainstream.

Quo vadis, Freiburg? The core of the city's planning for the future will be to continue pursuing the course of sustainable development laid out over the past three decades. The focus of development will be infill within the city's existing built areas, and energy efficiency and climate protection will be environmental priorities. The further expansion of public transit, and the suppression of private cars, will form the core of the city's mobility efforts. In addition, the strengthening of the universities and their integration with all other educational and research institutions will remain part of Freiburg's development strategy, as will social inclusion and integration.

References

Beatley, Timothy. 2000. *Green Urbanism: Learning from European Cities.* Washington, DC: Island Press.

Buehler, R., and J. Pucher. 2011. Sustainable Transport in Freiburg: Lessons from Germany's Environmental Capital. *International Journal of Sustainable Transportation* 5: 43–70.

Keeley, M. 2007. Using Individual Parcel Assessments to Improve Stormwater Management. *Journal of the American Planning Association* 73, no. 2: 149–60.

Sperling, Carsten. 2002. Sustainable Urban District Freiburg-Vauban. Retrieved December 22, 2011. http://www.forum-vauban.de/.

Stadt Freiburg. 2011. Retrieved December 14, 2011. http://www.freiburg.de/.

Wörner, Dieter, 2012. "Personal Communication." Freiburg Department of Environmental Protection.

4

Copenhagen, Denmark: Green City amid the Finger Metropolis

Michaela Brüel

Introduction

Copenhagen has a long tradition of being a "green" city in the sense of practicing sustainable urban planning. This characterization ranges from the green regional planning of the 1930s and the region's pattern structure, laid out in the "Finger Plan" from 1947, to the objectives of the municipal plans that have been updated every four years since 1989 and prioritize public transportation and introduce guidelines for sustainable urban renewal and construction and climate planning.

Regional Planning

Copenhagen is in the favorable position of being located at the southern gateway of the Sound of Øresund between Kattegat and the Baltic Sea. Copenhagen is in the peculiar situation that only half of the city's periphery is landlocked—including the island of Amager. The rest of the city is bordered by water. Counting the whole of Amager as part of Copenhagen, two-thirds of the periphery is waterfront. This gives Copenhagen relatively less through-going traffic, but relatively longer distances in the urban development directions, to the south, the west, and the north, compared with other cities of the same size. The city of Copenhagen, with a population about 528,000 (part of a larger metro region of 1.7 million), occupies a land area of about ninety square kilometers.[1] Until a reform of the municipal and regional structure in 2007, the greater Copenhagen region covered the central municipalities of Copenhagen and Frederiksberg and the three surrounding counties of Copenhagen, Frederiksborg, and Roskilde. In 2004 the new, liberalist Danish government made an agreement with a right-wing political party to introduce a new administrative structure in order to modernize public administration and reduce what they considered unnecessary bureaucracy. One of the specific objectives was to improve service in the health sector and to sustain Danish hospitals with the necessary population to keep up specialist knowledge. Consequently, fourteen counties were abolished and replaced by five regions. There are now four metropolitan administrative units. The county of Roskilde to the south was to join the rest of Zealand in a region of its own. The metropolitan region contains the national center of government, business, and education.[2]

The landscape in the metropolitan area is rather flat and easy to develop, which in the middle of the 20th century created a conflict between building interests and recreational interests. This was true especially in the northern parts, where the urban development up until then had been most intensive, and where the countryside is the most varied and charming with small woods, lakes, hills, and beaches well suited for bathing. Lots of summerhouses and cottages are located in North Zealand, predominantly along the seashore. During the first decades following the Second World War, Danish society was characterized by an unprecedented growth of wealth, which had a vital impact on urban development. The migration from countryside to towns was increasing, and the demand for dwellings was tremendous, especially the demand for individual garden houses. The total number of dwellings built annually in the 1940s amounted to ten thousand, the number rose to twenty thousand in the 1950s, thirty thousand at the beginning of the 1960s, and reaching as many as fifty thousand dwellings in 1970. This increase was driven by strong growth in industrial production, followed by growth of trade and public service, which caused the urban industrial zones to become too small with nowhere to expand. Consequently, the companies had to move to new and more spacious business areas at the periphery of the towns. The tremendous construction activity was difficult to handle with the available legislation and the municipal structure of that time, including more than 1,300 Danish municipalities and 27 counties varying in size. Further, many provincial towns were so small in area that urban development tended to take place in the neighboring municipalities. This scattered, "diverted" urbanization represented a growing problem. Rural municipalities next to larger towns pinched the good taxpayers by offering inexpensive construction sites in natural surroundings, leaving the urban municipalities with worn-down industrial areas and dwelling neighborhoods hosting low-income groups. The need to regenerate new areas in urban growth was greater than ever, as was the need for more robust physical planning.[3]

The limited urban planning taking place in the middle of the 20th century was based on the Urban Planning Act of 1938, which required that municipalities with more than one thousand inhabitants produce an urban plan. This applied to approximately 230 out of Denmark's 1,300 municipalities. The Planning Act was supplemented in 1939 by a government paper inventing the term "master plan," being an overall, noncommitting plan covering the entire municipality.

The need for planning was most urgent around the major cities, so in 1949 the Danish parliament passed the Act of Urban Regulation. This act made it possible to work out "urban regulation plans" across municipal limits, dividing the area into "inner zone," "intermediate zone," and "outer zone." The planning proceeded as a joint municipal exercise in "urban development committees," constituted on the occasion with participation by the municipalities involved, and chaired by a government official.

Parallel to these activities, the Danish Town Planning Institute, a private committee of planners, had appointed a Regional Council in 1929. This was done according to negotiations with the municipalities involved. The objective was to prepare a regional plan, including regulation of land use and traffic. The council started its work with a draft proposal of a "green plan" for the region, including areas for recreational purposes for the benefit of the region's population. The plan for the "Green Areas of the Copenhagen Region" was completed in 1936. In 1938 the Danish parliament supported the initiative by passing an amendment to the Act of Natural Preservation, making it possible to create a complete preservation plan for the region.[4]

The Finger Plan

The green plan was followed in 1947 by the Finger Plan (see figure 4.1), which directs new urban development to be concentrated along suburban train lines radiating from the city of Copenhagen. Within a distance of forty to fifty kilometers there were five provincial towns whose growth had been slowed. Instead of letting the growth of the city take place in concentric layers, urban development would be like fingers to the palm of the existing built-up areas. In between the fingers, the open land is reserved for recreational purposes. At this time, there were only two suburban railways. Consequently, the plan advocated the idea of building, in stages, a number of electric railways into the surrounding country. Around the stations on these lines, local centers with shops and institutions would naturally develop. From each center there would be frequent and convenient connections directly to the center of the city. The transportation time to the city was to be thirty minutes at the most.[5]

Although the original Finger Plan has been adapted to accommodate growth in population, housing, business, and—especially—traffic, the leading elements of the plan have been retained. Regional and local planning still operates according to "urban fingers"—green wedges and a radial, circular traffic structure. The fingers have been extended with electric train lines to the five provincial towns of Køge, Roskilde, Frederikssund, Hillerød, and Elsinore.

The main goals of the Finger Plan are the following:

- To minimize dependence on car use in the urban district through improvement of public transportation. Opportunities for traffic relief in urban centers are created, and consequently the environmental conditions are improved in terms of reduction of noise and pollution and an increase in traffic safety.
- To promote mobility to the large group of citizens without access to a car, by sustaining the highest possible amount of jobs and other activities in the urban center or zones with good access to public transportation.
- To create an integrated, high-density mix of existing urban areas in an environmentally correct manner. This reduces the need for urban development of greenfields, and therefore avoids scattered development, as this is irresponsible in terms of traffic, public service, and preservation of the landscape.

With increased urbanization resulting in more car traffic and air pollution, it is more vital today that we maintain and strive for these aims.

"Finger Plan, 2007," presented by the Ministry of the Environment, constitutes the formal directions of physical development for the thirty-three municipalities in the metropolitan region.[6] The fingers were extended to accommodate an additional one hundred thousand dwellings. The 2007 plan opens four-kilometer-wide growth areas for urban development. Office buildings with more than 1,500 square meters of floor space must be located within 600 meters of a train station. According to the ministry,

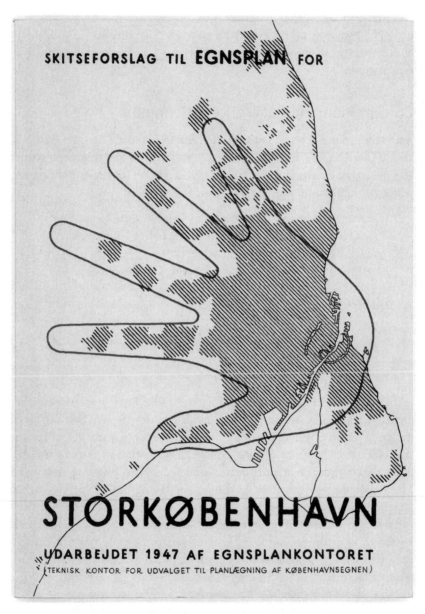

Figure 4.1 The famous 1947 Finger Plan is Copenhagen's regional plan for guiding growth along the major rail corridors in the metropolitan area. Credit: Danish Town Planning Institute (Dansk Byplanlaboratorium).

research documents that good access to train service encourages people to use public transportation. After thirty years, the emission of CO_2 might be reduced by one hundred thousand tons per year by directing growth in this manner.

Current Planning Legislation in Denmark

According to the objects clause in the Danish Planning Act,[7] its goal is to assure that society's interest is reflected in land use and to protect nature and the environment in respect of human conditions of life and the preservation of fauna and flora. The act aims particularly at

1. securing appropriate development in terms of a methodical and socioeconomic general assessment in the country as a whole as well as in each county and municipality;
2. creating and preserving valuable buildings, townscapes, and landscapes;
3. preserving open coastlines as an important natural and landscape resource;
4. preventing noise inconveniences and pollution of air, water, and soil; and
5. involving the public in the planning process as much as possible.

On the national level, the Ministry of the Environment publishes a national planning statement with guidelines on themes that are to be incorporated in physical planning over the following four years. On the regional level, the county councils have an obligation to prepare regional plans, which must be in agreement with the national planning statement. The regional plans map out guidelines for laying out of space of urban zones and summer cottages, the situation of greater public institutions and infrastructure, the position of polluting industries, the regional retail trade structure, agricultural and forest interests, natural protection interests in the open land, the position of potential wetlands, areas for leisure purposes, exploitation of stone, gravel, and other natural resources, and the use of streams and lakes.

Every municipality must prepare a so-called municipal plan, which is passed by the city council and must be revised every fourth year. The city council is to decide whether the plan should be revised as a whole, revised in part, or prolonged for another four years. The municipal plan is the "superior" planning document of the municipality. It lays out an overall structure, maps out land use (housing, industry, public institutions, and leisure purposes), density, and traffic structure, and defines areas of preservation, urban renewal, and urban redevelopment. It is possible to prepare an amendment to the municipal plan changing the land use or density, though the municipal plan must remain in agreement with the regional plan.

The most detailed plans are the so-called local plans prepared by the municipal councils. Any building or construction of a certain size requires the preparation of a local plan. In Copenhagen, a practice in deciding whether a building requires a local plan has developed over the years: a new building with more than forty dwellings or two thousand square meters of office space requires one, since these dimensions are considered to have a substantial impact on the surrounding environment. This is a general rule, but each situation must be evaluated concretely. A local plan must be in agreement with the municipal plan, which defines the land use and density of any registered site. The local plan determines the detailed land use of the new building (e.g., shops on the ground floor and dwellings on the upper stories), the exact density (floor space per ground space), the number of stories, the plan of the building, the building materials, the maintenance of cultural heritage (e.g., buildings, vegetation), the function and design of the open space, the parking, the environmental conditions, and so forth.

Since 2007, when the counties were abolished, no regional plans have been presented. The regional development plans are a collection of policies and principles, but not coherent physical plans.

Copenhagen's Municipal Planning

The first municipal plan of Copenhagen dates from 1989 and has been revised every fourth year. The plan currently in force is "City of Copenhagen Municipal Plan, 2009."[8] The municipal plan includes a so-called main structure with thematic guidelines of urban development, housing, trade and industry, public institutions, green areas, and environmental sustainability.

The following are abstracts of four selected themes (urban development, transportation, Metro in Copenhagen, bicycle policy), with particular interest in Copenhagen as a green city.

Urban Development Strategy

The urban development strategy of the city of Copenhagen supports a traffic structure based fundamentally on public transport services, primarily the railway network, and an overall road network, gathering the traffic on a few regional roads to keep the dense, built-up local areas as uncongested as possible.

One of the overall objectives of the municipal plan is to develop a sustainable transport pattern in which urban development and traffic infrastructure are harmonized. The goal is for the traffic requirement to be met by the lowest possible level of individual car traffic. The city of Copenhagen constitutes the central part—the palm—of the Finger Plan of the greater Copenhagen area. This accessibility gives the municipality special opportunities to utilize and develop the public transport system. Both urban development and urban conversion make it possible to relocate travel destinations and consequently change the traffic pattern. A location close to a station strengthens, other things being equal, the competitiveness of public transport, increases the number of passengers, and makes possible a continued improvement of public transport on market terms.

In accordance with the regional plan, it is an objective in the municipal plan that urban development be localized close to stations so that an environmentally sustainable urban and transport pattern is promoted, and so that urban development is of a high quality in terms of architecture, urban planning, and the environment.

The urban development strategy of Copenhagen prioritizes major construction and development projects in the municipality that are close to a station and have amenity value. The areas around the best-served stations are given the highest priority regarding the location of traffic-generating functions and densely built-up areas.

A distinction is made in urban development between (in order of priority)

- junction stations according to "Finger Plan, 2007," where all regional lines can stop and therefore have the potentially highest accessibility;
- Metro stations that have a high-frequency rail connection to the city and Nørreport Station;
- other stations.

A high level of importance is attached to regional public transport accessibility for the greater Copenhagen area when locating business and industry. Clerical and service enterprises and other employee- and visitor-intensive urban functions, which generate particularly large traffic volumes, are preferably to be located within six hundred meters of well-served traffic junctions.

Traffic and Transport Facilities

Development and economic growth often go hand in hand with growth in car traffic, resulting in a negative impact on human health and the environment. For a number of years, commuting from homes outside the municipality to jobs within the municipality has been a dominant feature. Increasing car ownership and increased commuting by Copenhageners to locations outside the city requires new regulations on car traffic. The objective is not to adjust the existing city to the increasing car traffic, but rather to create, through regulations, sustainable traffic development adjusted to the existing city so that energy consumption, the nuisances of the traffic, and environmental impacts are minimized. Aside from the municipal plans, obligated by the Planning Act, many municipalities have chosen to work out traffic and environmental plans, specifying these two themes—but of course remaining in accordance with the overall municipal plan.

An overall objective is to create a sustainable and coordinated urban development and transport pattern in which the largest possible share of the traffic takes place either by means of public transport, or by bicycle or on foot, and with individual passenger car traffic constituting as small a share as possible.

In accordance with these objectives, a number of initiatives have been taken.

Bridge between Copenhagen and Malmö in 2000

Recognizing that urban development of the island of Amager was no longer prevented by busy boat traffic through the port of Copenhagen, the Danish national parliament passed two important acts in 1991: the Act of a Fixed Link across Øresund and the Act of Ørestad, a new urban development on the island of Amager.

These acts resulted in important investments in infrastructure. First was the opening of the Øresund Bridge in 2000, which carries a highway as well as a train line between Copenhagen and Malmö, Sweden. Since 2000, regional train lines have been running frequently between Copenhagen and not only the five provincial towns of Køge, Roskilde, Frederikssund, Hillerød, and Elsinore, but also Malmö, at intervals of ten to twenty minutes.

The Ring Line, completed in 2006, was made possible by the bridge, as the Danlink ferry connection of goods transportation between Copenhagen and Malmö was closed. The Danlink was connected with tracks running through densely built-up districts of Copenhagen, the closing of which made it possible to integrate the tracks into the metropolitan S-train system, creating a circular connection of the radial train lines.

The most spectacular station on the Ring Line is Flintholm, connecting the Metro with the Ring Line and the S-train. Flintholm is the third most important station in Copenhagen, surpassed only by the Central Station and the city station of Nørreport. Flintholm is especially impressive because the three train lines in two levels, and bus lines in street level linked with stairs, escalators, and elevators, are covered by a huge glass roof (designed by a respected Danish architect firm).

Metro in Copenhagen

A Metro in Copenhagen had been discussed for decades with no results, since no organization or public body was able or willing to cover the huge expenditure. The solution to the problem came with the Act of Ørestad. The construction of the Metro was to be financed by the selling of sites in Ørestad, and the new urbanization of Ørestad was to be sustained by first-class public transportation.

The three first stages of the Metro, the lines between city and the island of Amager to the east and Frederiksberg to the west, opened in 2002, 2003, and 2007. The total cost of these three stages is estimated to be 11 billion Danish kroners or 1.5 billion U.S. dollars.

The total length of the first three stages of the Metro is twenty-one kilometers. Eleven kilometers are aboveground as an elevated railway. Ten kilometers are in a drilled tunnel, running twenty to thirty meters underground from Frederiksberg to Amager.[9] The effect of the fixed link between Sweden and Denmark is a sustained focus on the train service.

The nine tunnel stations have been excavated from above. Each station is created as a twenty-meter-deep, sixty-meter-long, twenty-meter-wide excavation. Before the excavation of the stations, watertight outer walls of concrete piles were constructed in order to prevent a lowering of ground-water level, which would harm the old city buildings. The tunnel stations are designed with open space from the platform to the glass roofs, creating bright and open station areas. Daylight is let in through glass prisms from the pedestrian precinct to the platform, twenty meters below.

The longest stretch of the Metro does not run in tunnels, but above ground, either at ground level or on elevated tracks. In Ørestad the Metro runs as an elevated construction, in some places with traffic passing under it, in other places with tracks laid on a low embankment. Thirteen stations are built at street level or aboveground.

The Metro will be extended with a City Ring to open in 2018. The City Ring will have seventeen stations, all located underground, and a control and maintenance center of its own. The line will connect the radial S-train lines even more efficiently than the Ring Line.

Bicycle Policy

Copenhagen is known far and wide as the "City of Cyclists." This is due to its long-standing and lively cycling tradition—and in recent years, its bike share program.

Cycling is a socially acceptable means of transport; in fact, it is not uncommon to see Danish ministers or mayors cycle to work. Bicycle traffic in Copenhagen has grown in recent years, and as of 2011 one out of three Copenhageners cycle to work.

In Copenhagen, cycle planning is an integral part of mainstream traffic planning. The Copenhagen cycle track network of some three hundred kilometers was built over the course of almost a century. Copenhagen bicycle traffic is thus considered a distinct traffic category with its own separate road area—on a par with motor traffic and pedestrian traffic.

In 2002 the city of Copenhagen for the first time published a bicycle policy.[10] The purpose of the policy is to draw attention to the fact that bicycling is an environmentally desirable and effective means of transport. The bicycle policy objectives are to increase the proportion of the workforce that travels to work by bicycle, to improve safety and a sense of security when cycling, and to increase traveling speed and bicycling comfort.

Green Cycle Routes

Green cycle routes are intended as a new option for cyclists, particularly those who have a long way to go. Cycle routes are laid out at a high standard, and usually include a wide cycle path and separate pedestrian walkway. When possible, cycle routes run in their own discrete area through green surroundings, and are designed to minimize the stops cyclists have to make because of automobile traffic. In addition to serving as routes between home and work, they are also intended to serve a recreational purpose.

The report "Proposal for Green Cycle Routes"[11] describes the twenty-one planned routes, which will cover a total of one hundred kilometers. The length of the routes varies from less than two kilometers to more than eight kilometers. Part of the network already exists, but at a lower standard than intended in the future.

The plan for laying out the first cycle route, the Nørrebro Route, was approved by the City Council in 1997. The Nørrebro Route was built in several stages beginning in 2006 and is not yet completed in the western portion. The Nørrebro Route is divided into several sections, many of which run through the Nørrebro Park, laid out on a former railway site (see figure 4.2).[12] The route crosses Åboulevarden, the busiest street in Copenhagen, by a light bridge opened in 2008.

The city also features squares, open spaces, and streets designed to form beautiful and harmonious settings for human recreation and activities. This objective is detailed in the "Metropolis for People"[13] vision and objectives for urban life in 2015: more urban life for everybody, more people walking, and more people staying longer in the public open spaces.

Recreation and Leisure: A Green Policy

In a densely built-up city, the green and blue (water) recreational areas are valuable—for the urban environment, for the opportunities for active open-air recreation, for the health and well-being of Copenhageners, and for the environmental balance. They are also an important part of the cultural heritage of the city. The importance of these elements has been confirmed by surveys of people's reasons for moving to Copenhagen. The appearance of the neighborhood as well as access to green areas and open spaces are more important to the residents than other features.

Trees, green spaces, the natural environment, and monuments of the past are protected and developed in Copenhagen so that the city's green capital is increased for the benefit of future generations (see figure 4.3). Copenhageners have daily easy access to beautiful parks, green "backyards," and fine playgrounds near their homes. Beautifully landscaped parks,

Figure 4.2 The Green Cycle Routes program is intended to provide opportunities for bicycles to commute into the city alongside or through parks and green areas. Eventually there will be twenty-one routes, covering a distance of one hundred kilometers. Credit: Timothy Beatley.

Figure 4.3 Copenhagen is a city of parks and green areas, and residents are never very far from nature. Pictured here is the Amager Strandpark. Credit: City of Copenhagen.

squares, and other green areas are a natural part of a modern metropolis. Green spaces should be seen as a sort of capital, increasing the city's value and helping to develop it into a modern, competitive metropolis.

The city's 2004 "Parks Policy" emphasizes the improvement of recreational possibilities along harbor and coast and the improvement of water cleanliness. The objective is to make it possible to swim along the whole coastline of the municipality and in the harbor. Copenhagen is now host to three swimming sites in the heart of the city, giving residents ample opportunity to have a splash in the clean harbor water (see figure 4.4). Previously, most people would probably have rejected the idea of taking a dip in the harbor, but thanks to the large underground rainwater reception basins established by Copenhagen Energy, the water is now clean enough to allow a cool swim on a hot summer's day.

Multiyear investment and planning efforts are needed to achieve major environmental improvements. But it is through such efforts that the impossible may turn out to be feasible, as exemplified by the good quality

Figure 4.4 There are now three swimming areas in the city's old harbor, made possible by municipal efforts to clean up these formerly polluted waters. Credit: City of Copenhagen.

bathing water in the harbor. And the efforts will not stop until the water in the entire harbor is clean.

The city also aims to manage the green areas in such a way that Copenhagen becomes more sustainable and the UN Agenda 21 obligation is also met. Cooperation with user groups of the individual squares, open spaces, facilities, and parks is to continue. Environmental considerations are a prerequisite in both the establishment and the running of all public recreational areas.

The characteristic features of Copenhagen's green landscape are to be found in low-lying natural areas, fortifications, royal parks and commons, and, when it comes to water, the coast, harbor, lakes, streams, marshes, and meadows. The historical and scenic features that have left their mark on the city's development are to be preserved and made more prominent.

The city's green structures, areas, parks, natural assets, and trees are to be protected through preservation and the drafting of maintenance and development plans. Most Copenhagen parks are protected by law.

The city's valuable plant and animal life is to be registered, protected, and developed better than it was before, and open green spaces are to provide a wealth of outdoor experience. Close to home, trees help clean the air, and the green wedge along the harbor and the western section of Amager is a vital green lung for all of Copenhagen.

The greatest challenge is to find spaces for the greening of the under-privileged districts of Copenhagen. But there are ample opportunities to be found in disused railway and abandoned industrial areas. The municipal average of open space is approximately 25 m² per inhabitant. The districts with the fewest open spaces are densely built housing areas (Nørrebro, Vesterbro, and Sundbyvester), with an area of approximately 2–3 m² per inhabitant.

The closest green space should be no farther away than the bus stop, two hundred meters. Where green spaces are few and far between, the areas should be utilized more flexibly. For example, sports facilities could be designed so that they can also be used for more general recreational purposes. In other cases, to compensate for a lack of space, focus can be put on enhanced quality, while link-ups for cyclists and pedestrians and green street spaces could encourage citizens to avail themselves of green areas that are somewhat farther away.

Some of the city's disused military, port, industrial, and railway areas, as well as sections of the island of Amager and some of the older, outer urban areas, are rapidly being transformed into attractive, new districts. There is at present a unique opportunity for Copenhagen to meet the recreational needs of all those who already live in the city, and to create attractive green spaces for guests, tourists, and future citizens.[14]

Copenhagen Urban Spaces

The process of creating a policy of city spaces was started in 2004 with a number of workshops including architects, designers, civil servants, and the citizens. The "Policy of City Spaces" was followed in 2006 by the "Action Plan for Urban Spaces."[15] The shopping corridor Strøget was the first pedestrian street in Copenhagen (and all of Denmark, in fact). In November 1962 the narrow, medieval streets of Østergade, Vimmelskaftet, Amagertorv, Nygade, Nytorv, and Fredriksberggade, busy with car and bus traffic, were converted into a calm pedestrian area. The shopkeepers' concern that they would lose customers soon proved unfounded: the customers more easily managed their way to the city shops by foot, bicycle, or public transportation. Within a very short time, Strøget became a success—the "rambla" for Copenhageners to stroll, watch others, and get fresh air.

In 1962 the pedestrian area in Copenhagen amounted to 13,700 square kilometers, comprising Strøget and the King's New Market, the two most important squares in Copenhagen. By 1973 the pedestrian area in the city had been increased to 50,150 square meters, including the transverse streets of Fiolstræde and Købmagergade, other important shopping areas. By 1996 the net of traffic-free or almost-traffic-free zones—including the "Alley" or the "Parallel Strøget," a 15-kmh zone giving priority to pedestrians and bicyclists, had been extended to almost 94,000 square meters.[16]

During recent decades, the pedestrian net has been extended to neighborhoods outside the medieval city, such as Sankt Hans Torv in the district of Inner Nørrebro and Enghave Plads and Halmtorvet in the district of Vesterbro. Squares formerly dominated by asphalt, car traffic, and parking, today are filled with various kinds, sizes, and patterns of granite, trees, and cafés. New open spaces of high-quality architectural design have enriched the lives of Copenhageners with new leisure opportunities.

Copenhagen's long-term process of shifting spaces from cars to pedestrians has been aided immensely through the research and passionate advocacy of the resident pedestrian guru architect Jan Gehl, until recently a professor at the Royal Danish Academy. Gehl has studied the Strøget and the other pedestrian spaces of Copenhagen over decades, extracting lessons and inspiration he applies now to cities all over the world, from London to New York to Melbourne.[17]

Environmental Sustainability

In accordance with the city of Copenhagen's standard of values, the development of Copenhagen as the capital of Denmark, and as the center in the Øresund Region, is to take place on a sustainable basis. As the "Environmental Capital of Europe," the municipal government will work toward the sustainable development of the city.

The fundamental task of the continued greening of Copenhagen is to plan and organize the city's part of the ecological cycle in such a way that the city does not destroy its own environment or the environment in the hinterlands, which supplies its resources or receives its waste substances.

It is an important objective that the planning of the city's supply of electricity, gas, heating, and water, as well as the disposal of waste and sewage, is based on an urban ecology principle. The planning can contribute to a reduction in the consumption of materials, energy, and water, and a reduction in the impact on the environment from, for example, waste and environmentally foreign substances in water, air, and soil.

Another objective is to promote a practice based on urban ecology principles to secure a better urban environment, to achieve significant resource savings in connection with urban renewal and new construction, and to improve the quality and life span of buildings.

An important municipal task is to support the urban ecological development in dialogue with citizens, property owners, and users to encourage a further development of concrete urban ecological initiatives and objectives, and to establish the framework for new initiatives and objectives.

The local government of Copenhagen has passed a set of guidelines of sustainable urban renewal and new construction, laying out requirements and recommendations that should be included in connection with the planning of building and construction works (see below).

Agenda 21

Agenda 21 is the UN action plan for sustainable development in the 21st century. It was adopted in 1992 at the UN summit in Rio. A wide range of environmental problems are rooted in local conditions, and solutions presuppose local action. Local authorities play a pivotal role in this work. Copenhagen is facing the challenge of creating a sustainable city. In 2000, Local Agenda 21 was included in the Danish Planning Act.

Even before it was a formal demand, the city of Copenhagen launched a range of environment activities aimed at making Copenhagen more sustainable and a better place to live.

In 1997, Agenda 21 in Copenhagen was translated into five key points:

1. Active Copenhageners: A central aspect of Agenda 21 is that citizens, companies, and associations act in an environmentally conscious way.
2. Nature's cycle: Since nature absorbs only a fraction of our pollution, environmental impacts should be assessed in relation to the ecological cycle.
3. Long-term perspective: Our actions reach into the future, into the life times of our children, grandchildren, and great-grandchildren. This is why we need to think in long-term perspectives.
4. Globally and locally—Environment problems know no city and country boundaries. But local decisions may have global

implications, as in the case of control of the greenhouse effect and holes in the ozone layer

Context: We need to perceive the environment in the context of our lifestyles. The environment should be considered in an overall framework of social conditions, education, unemployment, and so forth. Cooperation across sectors is imperative.[18]

In 2004, a more formal Agenda 21 plan was passed by the local government. The formal basis of the plan is the Danish Planning Act. Before the expiration of the first half of the election period, all municipal councils must publish a statement of their strategy for the municipality's contribution to a sustainable development in the 21st century. The statement must involve the politically agreed-on objects of the following efforts:

- Reduction of the environmental impact;
- Promotion of sustainable urban development and redevelopment;
- Promotion of biological diversity;
- Public involvement in local Agenda 21 activities;
- Interaction in decisions concerning environmental, transportation, industrial, social, sanitary, educational, cultural, and economic matters.[19]

The city of Copenhagen, however, intends to make a stronger effort. In 2001 Copenhagen joined the Dogme 2000 alliance with four other Danish municipalities, committing themselves to draw up a forward-looking Agenda 21 plan with specific options and actions of the joint environmental effort. The Dogme 2000 members commit themselves to fulfill the agreed-on options, and an external auditor is to control the performance.

The three overarching tenets of Dogme 2000 are the following:

1. Human impacts on the environment must be monitored and measured.
2. An Agenda 21 plan must be drawn up.
3. Environmental work must be anchored locally.[20]

The Agenda 21 plan includes the following themes:

- Sustainable urban development: How to convert the superior visions of the urban development into action concerning sustainability in local planning, construction and urban renewal, transportation, biological diversity, and recreation

- Resources: Dealing with the ecological latitude of the city of Copenhagen and the Copenhageners, the consumption of resources and production of garbage, the consumption of energy and emission of CO_2, and the consumption of water and water quality
- Environment and health: Focusing on environmental factors with an impact—positive or negative—on public health. Negative factors are air pollution, noise, and pollution of soil and subsoil water, aside from chemical substances and products. Positive factors are better and healthier conditions in buildings and open spaces, in addition to improved eating habits and physical exercise, especially in children and young people.
- Anchoring: Highlighting the importance of environmental efforts being anchored in local communities. This is being seen through to campaigns like the Environmental Festival and the Environmental Traffic Week, Agenda 21 centers, and the Copenhagen industrial network. Other important elements are environmental education of children and young people, green guidance, and information.
- "Putting one's own house in order": Dealing with the city of Copenhagen's own initiatives regarding environmental certification, environmental assessment, green budget and accounts, environmental purchasing, transportation, ecological food, sustainable building and construction, consumption of energy and water, and waste disposal.

"Environmental Accounts"

Since 1996 the city of Copenhagen has published Copenhageners' "Green Accounts" every year, and since 1999 annual "Green Accounts" of the city of Copenhagen itself. The green accounts are important in terms of monitoring the human impacts on the environment. The most recent of the three Copenhagen "Environmental Accounts" was completed in 2009.

Copenhagen's "Environmental Accounts" give documentation of Copenhageners' consumption of resources (water, electricity, gas, and heating), their manner of waste handling, and their traffic patterns. The accounts also describe the general "green" state of the art in Copenhagen and supply Copenhageners with green tips and advice. The most important challenge facing Copenhageners is bringing down the increasing traffic and increasing CO_2 emissions. Whereas the total rate of CO_2 emission decreased 15 percent from 1990 to 2002, it increased slightly in 2003. On average, two people in a flat without electric heating consume 2,000–2,500 kWh per year. The objective was to reduce the total CO_2 emissions from energy, transportation, and waste by 35 percent over the period from 1990 to 2010. Concerning water, the consumption rate is 127 liters per Copenhagener per day, and the objective is 110 liters. Copenhageners are getting better at separating waste, and the amount of waste delivered at the four recycling centers is steadily increasing. Around every sixth household in the city of Copenhagen suffers from an unacceptably high noise level.[21]

Environmental Manual

In 1998, the city of Copenhagen passed a set of guidelines for sustainable urban renewal and construction. The guidelines, which were revised in 2001, 2005, and 2009, cover the following themes:

- sustainable planning
- energy and CO_2
- materials and chemicals
- water and drainage
- urban space, life, and nature
- waste disposal
- noise
- indoor climate
- the construction site

The guidelines consist of minimum demands that must be followed, and recommendations to be used for inspiration. All subsidized municipal building and construction, urban renewal, and social housing must follow the guidelines. Private contractors are urged to follow the guidelines as well—and many do so, especially when they benefit from demonstrating a "green profile" (see figure 4.5).[22]

Public Participation

Public participation has been a vital part of the Danish planning legislation since the Planning Act of 1975. It requires physical plans—at any geographical level—to be sent into public hearing for a minimum of eight weeks. The city of Copenhagen has decided that the period of hearing should be at least two months—not counting the month of July (summer holiday), Christmas, and Easter.

Figure 4.5 A city-run ecological kindergarten, designed and constructed under Copenhagen's new green building standards. Credit: Bergit Jorgensen.

The requirement of public participation in the Danish Planning Act is limited to a demand of the public hearing the proposal of the plan. The city of Copenhagen, however, puts great emphasis on public participation. Since 2001 the annual budget has included an entry of almost 1 million Danish kroners to finance the "Citizen Dialogue Project." Proposals of local plans are presented to the citizens at meetings or at neighborhood walks, on the home page of the planning administration, and at exhibitions at the local libraries. At some public meetings, the plan is presented by the civil servants, followed by a discussion with the audience. Other meetings include a panel of politicians. Some meetings are very popular—the most "spectacular" plans have attracted as many as four hundred participants, more than two thousand visits on the home page, and more than three thousand questions.[23]

"Eco-Metropole: Our Vision for Copenhagen, 2015"

Leading up to the COP-15 Climate Summit in December 2009 in Copenhagen, a number of the policies described above were compiled into

"Eco-Metropole: Our Vision for Copenhagen, 2015," a policy passed by the city government in October 2007.

The policy envisions Copenhagen as becoming

1. the world's best city for cycles;
2. a center for world climate policy;
3. a green and blue capital city;
4. a clean and healthy major city.

The goals for 2015 regarding biking include the following:

- At least 50% of people going to their work or educational institution in Copenhagen will travel by bike (in 2010, the rate was 36%).
- The number of seriously injured cyclists will drop by more than half compared to today (in 2010, 118 cyclists).
- At least 80% of Copenhagen cyclists will feel safe and secure in traffic (in 2010, 58%).

The green and blue capital city goals for 2015 include the following:

- Ninety percent of Copenhageners must be able to walk to a park, a beach, or a swimming pool in less than fifteen minutes (in 2010 this percentage was about 60%).
- Copenhageners will visit the city's parks, naturals areas, sea swimming pools, and beaches twice as often as they do today (in 2010 Copenhageners visited recreational sites every other day, for about one hour on average).

The goals for making Copenhagen a clean and healthy major city include the following:

- Copenhageners will be able to sleep in peace, free from health-damaging noise from street traffic. All schools and institutions will be subject to low noise levels from street traffic during the daytime (there are no current measurements on these phenomena).
- Air cleanliness will be so high that Copenhageners' health will not suffer (like most other major cities, Copenhagen finds it difficult to live up to the air quality specifications for nitrous dioxide and large particles).
- There will be at least 20% ecological food in the city's food consumption, with the municipality taking the lead with at least

90% ecological produce in municipal institutions (about 7% nationwide).
- Copenhagen will be Europe's cleanest capital and one of the cleanest capitals in the world. For example, rubbish on public streets will be removed within eight hours (today, thirty-six hours elapse in some streets before trash is cleaned up).[24]

The City of Copenhagen's Climate Plan

Copenhagen's overall ambition is to be the world's environment metropole by 2015. The goals of the city's climate plan, outlined below, will be revisited in 2012:

- Reducing CO_2 levels 20% by 2015, and becoming CO_2-neutral by 2025, by extending the system of district heating, establishing windmills, and encouraging more cyclists;
- Switching production of energy from fossil-fuel sources to unceasing sources;
- Reducing waste of energy in buildings;
- Reducing consumption of energy;
- Introducing initiatives in the fields of traffic and urban planning;
- Including Copenhageners and business in the planning process;
- Launching initiatives to cope with the expectations of 40% more rain during the 21st century;
- Introducing a new infrastructure for cars running on alternative means of power (e.g., electricity and hydrogen).[25]

Conclusion

Copenhagen has been a global leader in sustainability and a pioneering green city in many ways. The city has adopted and is implementing a variety of innovative green practices and initiatives, including the following:

The bicycle policy is developing and refining the cycling tradition of Copenhagen with tracks along all major roads (not highways) and a network of green bicycle routes.

Area planning in municipal and local plans has given priority to public transportation by allowing construction with high density close to train stations.

Urban space planning since the 1960s has developed pedestrian areas of a high standard, promoting urban life and security.

In addition to these important green initiatives, the city has developed exemplary guidelines for sustainable urban renewal and new construction since 1998, promoting environmentally sane construction. The guidelines are mandatory to municipally financed construction, but have been adopted by private contractors as well, since the "green options" are considered to be of high status.

Copenhagen's ambitious green agenda has largely been successful and there are many important lessons from the city's experience. The bicycle policy is a success. One-third of all Copenhageners use the bike when going to work or school. Still more Copenhageners have adopted the ugly bicycle helmet as a clever investment in safety. The bicycle-parking problem has not yet been solved: outside and above train and Metro stations, bicycles are scattered on the pavement instead of being placed in the bicycle parking stands (often farther away).

Despite these bicycle successes, Copenhagen is still dominated by cars. Restrictions to car traffic are not efficient. Copenhagen's efforts to introduce taxes on car driving in the city center have been rejected by the liberalist government since 2001. More will need to be done in the future, but it is likely that Copenhagen will maintain its reputation and status as a green urban pioneer.

Notes

1. "Planning in Greater Copenhagen," Kai Lemberg, director of general planning, City of Copenhagen, 1970.

2. "Regional Planning in the Greater Copenhagen Region, 1945–1978," Hovedstadsrådet (Metropolitan Council), May 1978.

3. "Bidrag til regionplanlægningens historie" (Contributions to the History of Regional Planning), preliminary report, Ministry of the Environment, March 2004.

4. "Københavnsegnens grønne områder" (Green Areas of the Copenhagen Region), Egnsplanudvalget, 1936.

5. "Skitseforslag til egnsplan for Storkøbenhavn" (Finger Plan), Egnsplankontoret, 1947; "Copenhagen Regional Plan," a summary of the preliminary proposal, 1948–49.

6. "Finger Plan, 2007," national instruction of the physical planning in the metropolitan area, July 2007.

7. "Bekendtgørelse af lov om planlægning, lovbekendtgørelse nr. 93 af 24. september 2009" (Danish Planning Act), 2009.

8. "Københavns Kommuneplan, 2009" (City of Copenhagen Municipal Plan, 2009), Finance Administration, 2009, http://www.kk.dk/kommuneplan.

9. "Metro," Ørestadsselskabet (Ørestad Development Corporation), 2002.

10. "Cykelpolitik, 2002–2012" (Bicycle Policy), July 2002.

11. "Grønne cykelruter" (Green Bicycle Routes), City of Copenhagen, 2001.

12. "Byrumshandlingplan" (Action Plan for Urban Spaces), City of Copenhagen, 2006.

13. "Metropol for mennesker" (Metropolis for People), City of Copenhagen, 2009.

14. "Parks Policy," City of Copenhagen, 2004.

15. "Byrumshandlingsplan" (Action Plan for Urban Spaces), City of Copenhagen, 2006.

16. "Byrum i København" (Copenhagen City Spaces), City Architect's Department, 1996.

17. See Jan Gehl, *Cities for People*, Washington, DC: Island Press, 2010.

18. "Local Agenda 21," City of Copenhagen, 1997.

19. "Københavns Agenda 21," 2004–2007.

20. "Dogme 2000: Environmental Management toward a Sustainable City," Copenhagen Environmental Protection Agency, 2001.

21. "Københavns miljøregnskab, 2009" (Environmental Accounts of Copenhagen, 2009), 2009.

22. "Miljø i byggeri og anlæg" (Environment in Construction), City of Copenhagen, 2009.

23. "Borgerdialogstrategi" (Political Decision on Citizen Dialogue), City of Copenhagen, 2001.

24. "Miljømetropolen" (Eco-Metropole: Our Vision for Copenhagen, 2015), City of Copenhagen, 2007.

25. "Københavns Klimaplan" (Copenhagen's Climate Plan: CO_2-Neutral in 2025), City of Copenhagen, 2009.

5

Helsinki, Finland: Greenness and Urban Form

Maria Jaakkola

Helsinki is an essentially green maritime city with a particularly rich shoreline. The location of the city core far north on a peninsula penetrating the Finnish Gulf defines its character and provides a starting point for its radial city structure. The greater landscape formed by geomorphology—granite cliffs and river valleys between them—forms the framework for the urban structure.

The ice-worn bedrock creating steep hills and an array of isles and peninsulas; the coniferous woods; the modernist architecture—all contribute to the Helsinki cityscape. The landscape structure is still visible in the city structure, the highest peaks accented by public buildings or parks providing views. The dense urban structure meets the water's edge, and natural shores of granite and sand can still be found in the city center. The city has over a hundred miles of shoreline on the mainland, and a vast majority of it, including most of the 315 islands, is in public use.

Two-thirds of Helsinki is in fact sea. The total area of Helsinki has expanded in the recent years from 686 to 716 square kilometers, due to a substantial land acquisition of the Östersundom area from Helsinki's eastern neighbor Sipoo in 2009.

The city of Helsinki was first established in 1550 by Gustav Vasa, the Swedish king, on the mouth of Vantaa River. From that location, some two miles northeast, the city center was relocated to its present site in 1640.[1] Few structures remain from the 1700s apart from the UNESCO-listed Suomenlinna island fortress. The existing check (grid) pattern in the central urban structure, including the city's oldest park, is heir to the first city plan, commissioned in the 1810s by the Russian tsar Alexander I and authored by Johan Albrect Ehrenström.

Helsinki is a young city among the European capitals. It was declared the capital of Finland only in 1812, after which it started to take on its contemporary appearance. After the construction of its first railway in 1862, the city started to grow more rapidly. A major part of the existing city structure was constructed in the 20th century.

The city is compact but green. Green areas cover around 46% of the land area of Helsinki (if green is defined broadly, to include, for example, nonusable green areas such as agricultural fields or roadsides; see figure 5.1).

The population of Helsinki was 583,350 at the beginning of 2010, which makes it the largest city in Finland, accommodating 11% of the country's population. Population density in Helsinki is thus about three thousand inhabitants per square kilometer. It is also characteristic of

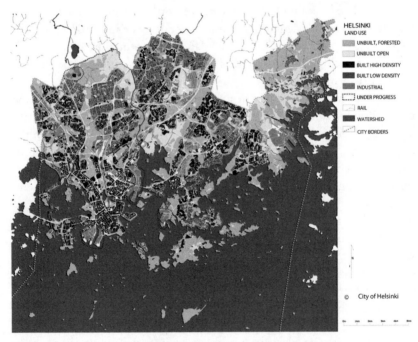

Figure 5.1 Land use in Helsinki in 2010. Note the new redevelopment areas indicated with a dotted line. Helsinki's geographical location stimulates the interests in redeveloping the waterfront. The ongoing developments will create new homes for an estimated 120,000 people over the next thirty years. © City of Helsinki, Törrönen 2010.

Helsinki to live in crowded spaces; the average floor area per person is thirty-three square meters.[2] A vast majority of the inhabitants of Helsinki live in apartment blocks.

The Helsinki region[3] attracts immigration nationwide, especially that of young people preferring the urban way of life. Helsinki has also had very high ranking in some international comparisons of urban livability.[4] The region offers metropolitan amenities, and yet the countryside is not far away. Obviously there are economic reasons, too, with there being more jobs than workers in Helsinki.

Residents and tourists value the greenness of Helsinki and its proximity to the sea. The statistics tell us that two of the top three tourist attractions in Helsinki are situated in green areas: the Suomenlinna historic island fortress and the Korkeasaari Zoo.[5]

Helsinki is facing its biggest land use change in a hundred years with the 2008 relocation of the commercial harbor and the development of the former harbor sites into an integral part of the inner city. The old industrial areas, warehouse areas, harbor areas, and railway yards are being replaced by shops, offices, hotels, dwellings, parks, seaside promenades, and other modern city functions. This transition is facilitated by the fact that the majority of land use changes involve city-owned land, which makes up 68% of the city.

Planning for Sustainability and Equity

Helsinki's greenness is a result of the strategies on a municipal level that guide all planning activity, as well as the characteristics of the urban planning and design. These strategies are based on European- or global-level decisions that are interpreted regionally and locally.

Agenda 21, a UN plan[6] of action for addressing human impacts on the environment, along with the European-level Aalborg Charter,[7] are the basis for sustainable development planning in Helsinki. In 2002, the Helsinki City Council approved Helsinki's Action Plan for Sustainability, a long-term strategic program prepared in accordance with the principles of the Aalborg Charter. The action plan included the strategic outlines for advancing ecological, economic, social, and cultural sustainability in city development during the 2002–2010 period. Helsinki has a separate Strategy Program for 2009–2012, which is described later in the chapter.

In 2003 Helsinki was presented with a Certificate of Distinction of the European Sustainable City Award competition. The City's Sustainability

Action Plan was one of the specific achievements of Helsinki emphasized by the competition jury. The other achievements cited were the development of a participatory planning process, the district heating system and cogeneration of heat and electricity, the development of the public transport system (local train, metro, tramways, and bus services), the enhancement of biodiversity, the creation of the urban green area network, the actions taken for the prevention of social seclusion and segregation in housing policies, urban planning, and social work, and the support for citizen-initiated, small-scale sustainability projects.

After the Sustainability Action Plan, Helsinki has laid out sectored strategies to guide sustainable development, but all-encompassing environmental programs have not been established. The work has become more fragmented, but it includes a wide range of authorities and expertise.[8] On the one hand, there is the global- and national-level discussion about challenges of long-term climate change mitigation and adaptation; on the other hand, concrete measures must be taken to respond to acute local problems, like sea-level fluctuation or air- and water-quality issues.

The Helsinki Metropolitan Area Climate Strategy 2030 seeks to reduce greenhouse gas emissions to one-third of the 2004 level by 2030, achieving a level of 4.3 tCO2e per resident. The greenhouse gas emissions of the Helsinki Metropolitan Area in 2004 were about six tons of carbon dioxide equivalent (tCO2e) per resident, and the total emissions of the region's population accounted for about 8% of emissions for the whole of Finland. Reckoned by consumption, the largest causes of greenhouse gas emissions and energy consumption in the Helsinki Metropolitan Area are the heating of buildings (43%), electric power consumption (28%), and transportation (23%). Electricity consumption and transport are the fastest growing of these causes.

Energy production generates a substantial amount of carbon dioxide emissions. This can be explained partly by the heating required during the long winter.[9] Although the district heating is a sustainable method of distribution, most of the energy is produced from fossil fuels. There is, however, a significant change in the horizon, since the main producer of this energy has recently drawn up a long-term development program based on 80% decrease of emissions by 2050. This will require a significant amount of investment in new technology.[10]

The consumption of fuel by private cars is also considerable. The Finnish way of life, with faraway second homes,[11] is partly responsible for this.

Of all domestic trips, 6% are for driving to the summer cottage and back, and about a half are connected with leisure activities in general.[12]

However, Finland's role in global emissions is extremely small and Helsinki's is virtually nonexistent,[13] and since Helsinki is a seaside town in a vulnerable location, focus is needed on climate-change adaptation strategies.[14] Providing basic ecosystem services such as clean water and unpolluted air and soil remain of utter importance and should not be overwhelmed by the energy discussion.

Adjusting stormwater management and flood-prevention practices to increase absorption and infiltration is one of the key strategies in terms of the climate-change adaptation processes. The Helsinki stormwater strategy was ratified by the City Council in 2007. Extreme weather conditions occur especially in the winter in the form of sea-level fluctuation and increased precipitation.[15] Apart from a few examples,[16] approaches involving stormwater management are yet to become more than a marginal phenomenon in city planning. In climate-change mitigation strategies, emphasis is placed on energy-efficient and compact urban structure, energy-efficient housing, and public transport. A key challenge is to increase eco-efficiency.[17]

The Nordic welfare state has kept Helsinki's income differences to a minimum, and city planning has managed to prevent housing shortages as well as social segregation. According to a Dutch study,[18] the past development of the Helsinki region is somewhat exceptional in international terms in its leveling out of spatial socioeconomic differences. A major trend in city planning in Helsinki has been a close connection between housing policy and social policy. There are indicators now that socioeconomic differences are on the rise in the city, but they are still on a very modest scale compared with the global situation.[19]

The Finnish Planning System

The basis for all planning in Finland, including Helsinki, is the Three-Stage Planning System. The Finnish land use planning system operates on regional and municipal levels. The regional land use plan is applied to large areas covering multiple governmental units (towns or municipalities). Particular attention is given to ensuring an appropriate regional and community structure, preserving landscape values and ecological sustainability, and providing proper conditions for business and industry. The master plan covers a town or municipality or a certain part thereof, and can be either a more strategic or visionary strategy to coordinate the spatial needs of different sectors, or a more specific plan to guide building activity directly. The detailed plan regulates the location of functions, the size and type of buildings, as well as the formation of the townscape and all its elements, including infrastructure and green areas. The plans are submitted to the municipal or city council for approval, and can vary from a broad zoning document to outlined planning permission. Only the detailed plan has the legal sanction to establish development on a site.[20]

The Finnish Constitution states that responsibility for nature and its biodiversity, for the environment, and for the nation's cultural heritage is shared by all. Public authorities must strive to ensure for everyone the right to a healthy and safe living environment, as well as the opportunity to influence decision making concerning it.[21] The Land Use and Building Act, the most recent version of which took effect in 2000, aims to promote sustainable development and participation. The main objectives are to assure that land use and construction result in high-quality residential environments, to promote ecologically, economically, socially, and culturally sustainable development, to ensure that everyone has the chance to participate in open planning processes, and to guarantee the quality of planning decisions and solutions.[22] According to this law, town plans may not decrease the quality of the environment. Every plan needs to have a participation and evaluation element, which defines and involves all individuals and institutions whose living and working conditions will be affected by the plan. All stages of the planning process must include citizen engagement. Further, an environmental impact assessment must be conducted at the start of every local and regional plan.

The most important planning tool to bring forth sustainability aims is the master plan. From the 1960s onward, Helsinki has produced a strategic, structural land use plan approximately every ten years. In Helsinki, important lines of action were defined in the master plan of 1992 in terms of sustainable development and environmental values. The main issue in this plan was to gain the inner-city shoreline for housing and recreation and to move the big harbors farther east. The latest master plan of 2002 strengthens the structural thinking of green areas and emphasizes their qualitative viewpoints, cultural meaning, and identity. At present, Helsinki and its neighboring municipalities Vantaa and Espoo are negotiating stronger cooperation on the master planning level for the next plan, which will have to take into account the regional aspects in increasing depth and define the boundaries of city growth.

The Green Areas Network as Part of a Sustainable City

Green cities facilitate and encourage more sustainable, healthy lifestyles.[23] Green areas have an important role in providing services such as sustainable potential for recreation, commuting routes in an attractive environment, and recovery from mental fatigue. In a green city, green areas are diverse and functional, from an ecological as well as an experiential point of view. The (bio)diversity concept should be expanded in an urban setting to signify and include an array of recreational possibilities for its residents and the potential to experience different landscapes. This requires that the green areas be located in the right places according to local cultural and ecological values, sufficient in size, access, and frequency. They also need to possess characteristics of a healthy ecosystem such as a well-functioning hydrologic circle.

Green areas promote sustainability and respond to climate-change issues in various other ways, too. They provide cooling of the local climate, cleaning and filtering of water and air, habitats for biodiversity, and biomass for carbon sinks. They also make buffer zones for detention and flood control by providing large areas of unpaved, absorbing, and filtering surface in the urban setting. And these are only a few examples. Indicators like biodiversity can also be strongly affected by the location and character of green areas in the city. The accessibility of those areas by sustainable traffic forms is part of a sustainable transportation policy. The high quality of the green areas system is a key factor in keeping Helsinki attractive, and city culture, including a functional public transit system, is possible only when enough people choose to live in the compact city.

Cultural sustainability includes aspects of sustaining and managing the values of shared cultural heritage. Often these aspects manifest themselves within the green areas system. The Helsinki city core peninsula accommodates most of the historic parks and squares. Islands and seashore are dotted with historic manor houses and villas with gardens, especially in the eastern part of the city. The historic parks, gardens, and cultural landscape were classified and preserved by a special concept of "landscape culture" defined in the latest master plan. The criteria used to define the landscape culture areas include the historicity as well as the aesthetic, garden architectural, and cultural values of the place. Nonetheless, many historic parks in the city center lack the legislative status of preservation or a detailed plan with conservation aims. Thus they may be subject to traffic or other solutions (tunnel entrances, service buildings, etc.) that diminish their cultural, historical, and landscape values.

The total area of green space per capita[24] in Helsinki is as much as 110 square meters, but 95 square meters of this are forest, pastures, roadsides, and agricultural fields. In contrast, there are only about 15 square meters of designed and constructed parkland per capita.[25] The green areas are somewhat thoroughly interconnected but quite modest in scale.

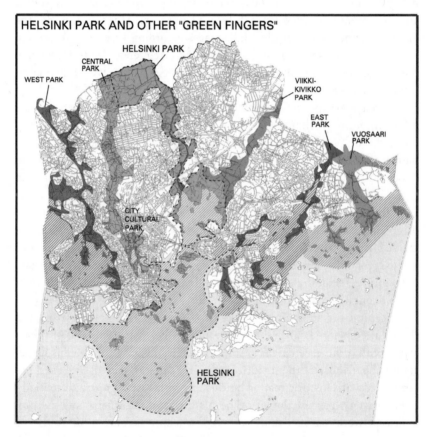

Figure 5.2 The green fingers as defined in the master plan of 2002. © City of Helsinki.

The radial green wedges, or "green fingers," form the backbone of the green areas system in Helsinki (see figure 5.2). They extend from the seashore to the city limits and beyond in a radial manner, and have been a structuring element in the city planning since the master plan of 1970. They follow either a natural feature, such as a river corridor, or a symbolic entity, such as the Keskuspuisto Central Park. The sea area and archipelago make up another wide entity connecting the green fingers to one another.

Green fingers promote diversity by each having a distinct character according to their situation in the landscape and the urban structure. They are interconnected by a network of square parks, boulevards, pedestrian walkways, seaside promenades, narrow strips of nature, greenbelts, and green corridors, and serve recreation and outdoor activities as well as everyday life connections to schools, shopping areas, and workplaces. The larger ones also act as ecological corridors.

When green areas are continuous and interconnected, like the green fingers of Helsinki, they form greenways, which are defined as linear open spaces "established along either a natural corridor, such as a riverfront, stream valley or a ridgeline."[26] Greenways are also characteristically integrated functional networks linking urban and rural.[27] In Helsinki they also link seaside with forest. Ecological, cultural, and recreational values coalesce in greenways.

Unfortunately the continuity of the green fingers has not been resolved in every aspect, and the ring roads traversing them diminish their integrity and attractiveness. These roads, however, are the most essential connections between different parts of the city, and their effectiveness as traffic corridors for public transit enforces the sustainability strategies in other ways. Reconciliation and compromise are needed to give way to both functions in the city, green and recreational versus mobility. Continuous pedestrian/bike traffic is possible, however, thanks to the extensive ski trails and connecting bridges.

Harbors and swimming beaches are an important part of outdoor life in a seaside town. There are a dozen supervised beaches in Helsinki and an uncountable number of unsupervised ones. The increasing popularity of winter swimming ("hole in the ice") has transformed the use of many of them to be intensive year-round.

Numerous cemeteries, allotment gardens, and housing areas with a gardenlike character complement the green areas. The city encourages household gardening by providing either allotment gardens (with a cottage) or cultivation lots, which are rented out to the citizens. Currently

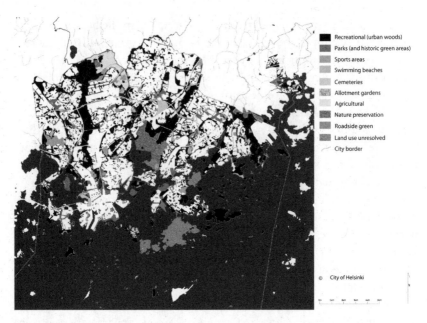

Recreational (urban woods)
Parks (and historic green areas)
Sports areas
Swimming beaches
Cemeteries
Allotment gardens
Agricultural
Nature preservation
Roadside green
Land use unresolved
City border

© City of Helsinki

Figure 5.3 Green areas in Helsinki are moderately small in scale but evenly spread and diverse. Every city district has its own district park, toward which limited upkeep resources are targeted. The amount of historic parks intensifies on the core peninsula.

there are about fifty of those areas, providing numerous plots inside the city limits.[28]

There are also a total of forty nature preserves (covering 460 hectares) in the city area, three of them with EU-level protection (see figure 5.3).[29] Most of the biotopes within nature-protection programs in the Helsinki area are seashore pastures or luxuriant (deciduous) biotopes, rare on the national level. Birdlife also plays a key role in the protection scheme. Many of the islands have restricted access in order to protect the wildlife, and a number of islands are in military possession.

Waterscape is given specific attention in Helsinki's green areas planning (see figure 5.4). Not only does it provide multisensory experiences, but it also serves as a diverse habitat for wildlife and has potential for stormwater runoff treatment and detention. Natural shore is also important for sustainable landscape—when shoreline is left to natural processes, it stabilizes in time (as opposed to high-cost, high-maintenance concrete walls that crumble from the increasing wave or ice burden). Helsinki must

Figure 5.4 Urban core meeting seafront. (Central railway station to the right.) © City Survey Division, City of Helsinki.

increasingly promote watersheds, especially river valleys, by reserving green areas around them to form greenways, instead of hiding them under the technical infrastructure of a city.

Infill and Green City Strategies

As part of Helsinki's Strategy Program for 2009–2012, there are objectives concerning urban structure and housing. The strategy aims at safeguarding the quantity and quality of housing and the diversity of the urban environment and harmonizing (densifying) the urban structure in response to climate change. It strives at promoting infill development (especially along railroads) and sustainable traffic forms. This includes developing railway systems and other public transit services, as well as enhancing bicycle and pedestrian infrastructure. The Helsinki City Strategy Program also contains a principle that unified green areas and green connections be preserved.

These goals can conflict. If the existing structure of green fingers is compromised with infill development aims, the flexibility for promoting sustainability with the help of green areas, for instance by providing comprehensive ecosystem services or by implementing climate change buffers, can be dramatically decreased. At the same time, residents also value their small neighborhood parks, so should infill developments be done at their expense? According to city strategies, the goal of planning for five thousand new dwellings every year requires considerable densification in the suburbs, potentially threatening the congruity and integrity of the green areas network.

Fortunately, though, 75% of these new dwellings are to be produced on former brownfield areas in the following ten years, so the problem is not at the doorstep yet. Helsinki needs to define in the following decades, however, the essence of its attraction, and join the international discourse on landscape-sensitive urbanism.[30]

Regional democracy means accessibility to green areas for all citizens. Urban planning has so far brought diverse open space, from forests to playgrounds, into the very heart of the city. The aesthetic and functional quality draws people into using a park and thus makes it a desirable option for leisure activities. Increased and diversified use of parks by bigger and more diverse crowds, even new ways of using them like skate-boarding or BMX biking, sets new kinds of preconditions for their planning and design. A denser city structure requires higher maintenance levels, not least to evoke and restore the feeling of safety and social control.

To define the future of the green fingers and other green areas in city planning, a project to make an Open Space Strategy for Helsinki has been initiated in the Environmental Office of the Helsinki City Planning Department.[31] The work, which will also look at climate change strategies for the first time from the green areas point of view, has started with a landscape analysis for Helsinki.[32]

Transportation and Mobility

Sustainable transportation has been emphasized in the city planning strategy as well. The network of pedestrian and bicycle path connections is quite extensive, as is the coverage of public transit. Public transport represents a substantial share of the daily traffic of Helsinki, and works better the closer one is to the city center. There are more than a hundred active bus lines in the city. The share of public transport in passenger traffic was 64% in the Helsinki central area (the peninsula) in 2009. Public transportation systems include tram, bus, metro, and train. During the morning peak time (6–9), the share of public transport of all vehicle traffic toward the city center was as high as 72%. Of all trips made in Helsinki, 34%

were made by walking, 7% by bicycle, 16% by bus, 7% by train, and 3% by metro. That means 67% of all transport was by some method sustainable traffic (cycling, walking, public transit).[33] The goal is to still increase this share by three percentage points by 2012. Even in the larger and more scattered metropolitan area, the share of public transport is as high as 27%. In the Helsinki region of fourteen neighboring municipalities, however, this share is only 10%.

The BEST survey for 2010 placed Helsinki, together with Geneva, at the top of the charts for the smooth running of its public transport and the standard of its service.[34] (The other cities in the survey were Stockholm, Oslo, Copenhagen, and Vienna.) Overall satisfaction with the Helsinki service is extremely high, and the city came top of the league for the reliability of its public transport.

The bicycle and pedestrian network serves recreational as well as commuting purposes. The network consists of national-, metropolitan-, and district-level routes. Six radial routes on the national level start from the center of Helsinki. The whole bicycle route network is represented in the regional outdoor recreation map, which is handed out in city offices free of charge.

There are about 2,100 kilometers of paths reserved for cyclists and pedestrians in the city of Helsinki. About 75% of the paths are set within a recreational environment, which comprises not only green areas but also places like the seaside streets. Four kilometers of new paths are completed annually. The network includes more than two hundred underpasses and bridges. The standard width of the usually gravel paved pathways is three meters. The majority of these routes are also lit, which is essential in the dark seasons.

The path network is intended for the pedestrians and cyclists as well as cross-country skiers in the wintertime. The ski track network as planned is about 240 kilometers, whereof forty kilometers are located on ice outside Helsinki coastline. The city is responsible for their management. All the routes connecting to a street, and a remarkable share of the ones on the green areas, are ploughed free of snow in the wintertime.

The new cycling strategy of Helsinki in 2010 aims at making cycling a real alternative for commuting, thus shifting the emphasis from the former recreational network to more effective systems. There is a strong need for this in order to meet the ambitious goals set by the Strategy Program, since for the past fifteen years, the share of cycle traffic has not increased significantly, despite the efforts made in this area.

Conclusion: Helsinki as a Green City

It seems obvious that a prerequisite for sustainable urban development is a strong planning tool that enables actors with environmental expertise to participate in the planning process. In Helsinki, the regulatory planning system and economic factors such as land ownership make it possible to act on the city areas. The master plan is an effective tool to manage the increasing growth of population, boasting a 95% rate of implementation.[35] The successful implementation of sustainability aims also requires governmental policy in terms of carbon and fuel taxes, subsidies, and so forth. Helsinki has good potential in terms of knowledge, innovations, and research.

To tackle housing and traffic issues in a wider sense, even better regional integration of planning within the whole Helsinki region will be necessary. Instead of competing with one another for the best taxpayers, neighboring cities will have to cooperate. There is political will on the national level to run this kind of metropolitan policy.

Helsinki is an example of the coexistence of greenness—in all its forms and interpretations—and urban form. The dense city structure has made it possible to preserve green areas in the outskirts and in entities between the town districts. Current redevelopments in the Helsinki area are closely linked to sustainability aims; by reusing brownfield areas efficiently, the city becomes even more compact and precious greenfield areas can be saved. Moreover, these brownfield areas are often accessible by public transport, and new dwellings can be easily linked to existing infrastructure and services.

Helsinki is also a global green city measured by the amount of green areas per capita. These areas are also quite interconnected and forested by nature. Numerous natural areas are preserved, even near the city center. Probably the most distinguishing feature among other capitals is the amount of natural shoreline that has been preserved for public use with a conscious policy. Green areas and the ecosystem services they provide rank high in terms of quality of life. Helsinki has great potential in being able to provide pleasurable and healthy green living environments.

While the next Master Plan for the Metropolitan Area is still missing, however, it might happen that Helsinki alone faces the pressures of infill development in the suburbs. This development needs to be controlled and guided so that the cultural and ecological values of the green areas system can be sustained for future generations. The finger structure is the essence of Helsinki green areas system, and the changes it tolerates need to be defined soon. Future research is also needed to provide facts about the sustainability of urban solutions at the master planning level. The popular densification trend in Finnish urban planning is based on the philosophy that the denser an urban form is, the more sustainable it will be. The denser the urban structure, the more public transit and other services one can provide. This trend emerged in the last decade or two as an antidote for the sprawling of "forest neighborhoods" of the 1960s and 1970s. To a certain extent this is certainly true. It is, however, essential to acknowledge the limits of this development, and the appropriate scale of the urban clusters, so that reasonable accessibility to services provided by green areas for every resident can be kept. Will there still be possibilities in Helsinki to experience the forest feel that is so essential for the Finnish way of life? The farther away one needs to travel in search of "nature," the more unsustainable the lifestyle.

Pasi Mäenpää, with his concept of wide or open (minded) urbanism,[36] suggests that the particular Finnish way of building cities, manifested in Helsinki suburbia's open landscape spaces and quarter structures, which is often considered "urban sprawl," is in fact responsive to the site and sensitive to the particular local urbanism.

Threats placed on the green areas system include monoculture of the cultural heritage—if only the most valuable bits can be preserved, the continuity is compromised and diversity lost. Although the inhabitants appreciate the landscape, cultural heritage often loses the battle of values.

In order to meet the requirements of new city dwellers, special emphasis should also be placed on the high-quality design of green areas. To fund their implementation, innovations need to be sought. Besides forest green, the growing city also needs more intensively built and managed neighborhood parks. Green areas increase the economic value of nearby housing, and a question should be raised of whether and how this extra value could be guided toward their better design and management.

As for sustainable traffic, public transit and cycling must be made more desirable options everywhere in the city, and at the same time car traffic should be made more undesirable. These two have to happen at the same time in order to have a real effect on people's choices. It can be said that the recreational bicycle and pedestrian network, resting on the green areas network of Helsinki, hardly has an equal, but there are still challenges to promoting utility cycling (errand-running and commuting), in terms of mobility management and enhancing accessibility. The dominant role of cars, especially on the regional scale, appears to be a difficult issue for decision makers. The metro line will at long last be extended westward to the neighboring town of Espoo, but measures to decrease individual car traffic[37] have not yet been implemented.

The local residents possess a significant amount of "quiet knowledge"[38] about what it's like to live in an area, and this experience is increasingly included in the planning processes. Square footage, however, is a lot easier to assess statistically than the quality of a living environment.

The experience of a place is the key to assessing its quality. For instance, a well-planned, well-designed, and well-kept recreational system (see figure 5.5), possessing the particular feel of being inside and outside the city at the same time, is understood at an intuitional level, and experienced as meaningful or beautiful (or both).

Reliable tools to evaluate how planning efforts have actually succeeded need to be developed in order to access this realm of information. The urban green is used and "signified" by the inhabitants,[39] attaching meanings and values that cannot be reduced to and revealed by natural scientific evaluations or planning related surveys.

The significance of contact with "living things" in a particularly "Helsinki" way must be cherished in the future. Whether it be an old tree to observe the passing of seasons, or a forest view seen from the bedroom

Figure 5.5 Helsinki seen from the southeast. Note the recreational isles with restaurants in the foreground. © City Survey Division, City of Helsinki.

window, or a gentle granite cliff to stretch one's legs on a sunny day, there need to be such places and things left untouched. They will still possess their healing capacity after any technical innovation has been outdated.

References

Ahern, Jack 2003. Greenways in the USA. In Tapiola 50: Roots and Seeds of the Garden City, Tapiola Case. September 4.

Beatley, Timothy 2000. Green Urbanism: Learning from European Cities. Washington, DC: Island Press.

City of Helsinki, Green Areas Program 1999. Helsingin viheralueohjelma 1999–2008: Helsingin kaupungin rakennusviraston julkaisuja. Helsinki City Public Works Department.

City of Helsinki 2006. Helsingin kestävän kehityksen toimintaohjelman seurantaraportti (monitoring report of the Sustainability Action Plan) 2002–2005, Helsingin kaupungin hallintokeskuksen julkaisuja.

City of Helsinki 2009. City of Helsinki Strategy Program.

City of Helsinki 2009. Statistical Yearbook of the City of Helsinki.

City of Helsinki 2010. Annual Report 2009.

City of Helsinki 2010. Environmental Sustainability Issues and Challenges in Helsinki, 2010. City of Helsinki Environment Centre.

City of Helsinki, Environment Centre 2009. Helsingin ympäristön tila: teemakatsaus 1/2009.

Finnish Transport Agency 2004–2005. National Travel Survey, 2004–2005. Liikennevirasto, WSP Finland Oy.

Hellman, Tuija and Lilleberg, Irene 2010. Liikenteen kehitys Helsingissä vuonna, 2009. Helsinki suunnittelee: 4, Edita Prima Oy, Helsinki.

Helsinki Action Plan for Sustainability 2002. Approved by the City Council June 12. Agenda 21, Helsinki, Helsingfors.

Helsinki Master Plan 2002. Helsingin Yleiskaava, 2002, ehdotus, selostus: Helsingin kaupunkisuunnitteluviraston julkaisuja. City Planning Department.

Helsinki Metropolitan Area Council 2007. Metropolitan Area Climate Strategy, 2030. YTV Helsinki Metropolitan Area Council.

Jaakkola, Maria 2010 (unpublished). Viheraluestrategia: Vihreä ja merellinen Helsinki mutta millainen ja miten? Draft for the Open Space Strategy for the Helsinki City Planning Department.

Jaakkola-Kivinen, Maria 2002. Phenomenology as a Means of Understanding Landscape: Towards a Phenomenology of Landscape Architecture. Working Papers, University of Art and Design in Helsinki, UIAH, Kokeiluja—Experiments 3, Future Home Graduate School.

Lapintie, Kimmo, Maijala, Olli and Rajanti, Taina 2002. GREENSCOM: Communicating Urban Growth and Green Work. Package 6, Finland, Case Studies Helsinki and Tampere. Helsinki University of Technology.

Mäenpää, Pasi 2008. Avara urbanismi, yritys ymmärtää suomalainen kaupunki toisin in Lehtonen Hilkka, 2008. Asuttaisiinko toisin? Kaupunkiasumisen uusia konsepteja kartoittamassa. Helsinki University of Technology, Yhdyskuntasuunnittelun tutkimus- ja koulutuskeskuksen julkaisuja B95, Yliopistopaino Oy, Espoo.

Pol, Peter and Speller, Carolien 2004 (unpublished). City Port Redevelopment, Helsinki Case. EURICUR, Rotterdam, The Netherlands.

Santasalo, Tuomas 2004. Matkailukohteiden kävijämäärät, 2003. Matkailun edistämiskeskus MEK E:48.

Staffans, Aija 2004. Vaikuttavat asukkaat: Vuorovaikutus ja paikallinen tieto kaupunkisuunnittelun haateina. Helsinki University of Technology, PhD thesis. Yhdyskuntasuunnittelun tutkimus ja koulutuskeskuksen julkaisuja A 29, Espoo 2004. Yliopistopaino Oy, Helsinki 2004.

TOPOS: International Review of Landscape Architecture and Urban Design Vol. 71/2010. Landscape Urbanism.

Törrönen, Sirpa 2010. Landscape Analysis: Helsinki. Aalto University of Technology, master's thesis.

YTV Helsinki Metropolitan Area Council 2007. Pääkaupunkiseudun ilmastostrategia, 2030. Climate Strategy for the Helsinki Metropolitan Area to 2030.

Primary Sources: Discussions and Conversations

Helsinki City Planning Department
  Town Planning Division: Olavi Veltheim, Matti Eronen, Jyri Hirsimäki,
    Maria Karisto, Liisa Kuokkanen-Suomi, Matti Kaijansinkko
  Traffic Division: Marek Salermo, Antero Naskila, Kaisa Lahti, Irene Lilleberg,
    Tuija Hellman
  Master Planning Division: Douglas Gordon, Markku Lahti, Maija Immonen,
    Aimo Huhdanmäki, Rikhard Manninen
Helsinki Environment Centre: Kari Silfverberg, Kaarina Heikkonen
Uusimaa Regional Council: Seija Elo
Ministry of Environment: Anne Koskela
Helsinki Information Centre: Erkki Korhonen, Ilkka Niemi
Helsinki Region Transport: Johanna Vilkuna, Marja Salo

Notes

1. Finland belonged to Sweden until 1809, when it became the Grand Duchy of Finland under Russian rule. Finland declared its independence in 1917.

2. Statistical Yearbook 2009, City of Helsinki, 84.

3. The Helsinki region includes neighboring cities Espoo, Kauniainen, and Vantaa (the Helsinki metropolitan area, with a population of close to a million people), which cooperate on many regional issues, and fourteen other municipalities.

4. Helsinki scored fourth in Mercer's Quality of Life Survey, fourth in the Personal Safety Rankings, 2010, and fifth in the *Economist*'s recent Most Livable Cities index.

5. Measured by the number of visitors, the Linnanmäki amusement park in

Helsinki is the number one draw in the country as well as in the city, with about one million visitors every year. See Statistical Yearbook of Helsinki 2009.

6. Conference on Environment and Development in Brazil 1992.

7. European Conference on Sustainable Cities and Towns in Denmark 1994.

8. Discussion with Kari Silfverberg of the Helsinki Environment Centre.

9. The average annual temperature for Helsinki is 5°C, and there are seven months where the temperature is usually below that.

10. Helsinki Metropolitan Area Climate Strategy 2030.

11. One million Finnish households own a summer cottage in the countryside.

12. National Travel Survey 2004–2005.

13. Finland's contribution to global emissions was 74.6 million tons (CO2-ekv) in 2010, and Helsinki's about 6 tons. The total of global greenhouse gas emissions was 44,000 tons (CO2-ekv) in 2005 (www.ilmasto-opas.fi, www.stat.fi, EU Life Program, Finnish Environmental Institute, Aalto University, Finnish Meteorological Institute). Furthermore, approximately 75% of land area in Finland is covered by forest, which acts as a carbon sink for 35 million tons of CO2-ekv annually.

14. Helsinki Region Environmental Services Authority is currently drawing the Adaptation Strategy for the Helsinki Metropolitan Area, due in March 2012. http://www.hsy.fi/climatechange.

15. In Helsinki, at 60 degrees latitude, rainfall is often snow.

16. See the Kuninkaantammi and Honkasuo city planning projects.

17. Environmental Sustainability Issues and Challenges in Helsinki 2010, City of Helsinki.

18. Poll and Speller 2004 (unpublished).

19. Discussion with Rikhard Manninen of the Helsinki City Planning Department, referring to Urban Audit, Eurostat European Statistics.

20. Helsinki City Planning Department. Detailed plans are updated according to land use needs; and about fifty to eighty are drawn up in the Helsinki City Planning Department every year. Their validity is checked every thirteen years.

21. Ministry of Environment.

22. It is important to note that planning is in Finland an activity dominated by architects, in best cases leading a multidisciplinary planning group involving traffic engineers, geographers, landscape architects, and researchers. In smaller cities, however, many of these other experts may be lacking.

23. Beatley 2000, 7.

24. In "the old Helsinki," excluding Östersundom, which is dominantly agricultural.

25. Green areas statistics, Helsinki City Public Works Department.

26. Little, quoted in Ahern 2003.

27. Ahern 2003.

28. There are 9 community gardens (with individual huts) and 39 areas with rentable cultivation lots in Helsinki. (Helsinki City Public Works Department data on green areas).

29. Under the Natura 2000 program; information from Helsinki City Environment Centre.

30. TOPOS 71/2010.

31. Jaakkola 2010 (unpublished).

32. Törrönen 2010.

33. Hellman and Lilleberg 2010.

34. For more on Helsinki public transit, see http://www.hsl.fi/; for info on the BEST survey, see http://best2005.net/.

35. As of 2004; interview with Douglas Gordon.

36. Mäenpää 2008, 183, comprehends the city as consisting of diversified milieus and ways of life without domination of a certain type of urbanity.

37. For instance, the issue of a toll at the inner-city borders has been raised in discussion.

38. Staffans 2005.

39. Lapintie et al. 2002.

6

Venice, Italy: Balancing Antiquity and Sustainability

Marta Moretti

Despite being a city held in the collective imaginary—indeed one based on a wealth of images, words, sounds, and colors gathered over centuries of culture—Venice needs to be understood as a modern city in which a person still wants to live and work.

Situated in the heart of its lagoon along the Adriatic Sea in the north-eastern part of Italy, the city of Venice is generally known worldwide as the "city on water," given the extreme nature of its relationship and involvement with the natural element. It comprises 117 small islands. Dwelling, trading, moving: all activities have to do with water, taking advantage of it or protecting against it. In short, Venice is a de facto, ongoing laboratory constantly attempting to adapt to human and natural transformations (figure 6.1).

In terms of territory, the city of Venice covers a surface of 413 square kilometers, of which 253 square kilometers are covered by water, with a total population of 270,772 residents.[1] Venice relies heavily on the tourist economy, but for more than a century political leaders have been express-ing the need to transform it into a modern industrial city. The borders of Venice have spread to the nearest mainland, developing at the same time as a huge industrial area along the water, and turning Venice into one of the main chemical and oil centers of Europe.

Further, Venice has an important port, which is one of the largest in Italy and employs, with all the activities linked to it, eighteen thousand workers.[2] Located at the top end of the Adriatic Sea, as well as at the inter-section of the main European transport corridors and of the Motorways of the Seas, the Port of Venice is in a position to act as the European gateway for trade flows to and from Asia.

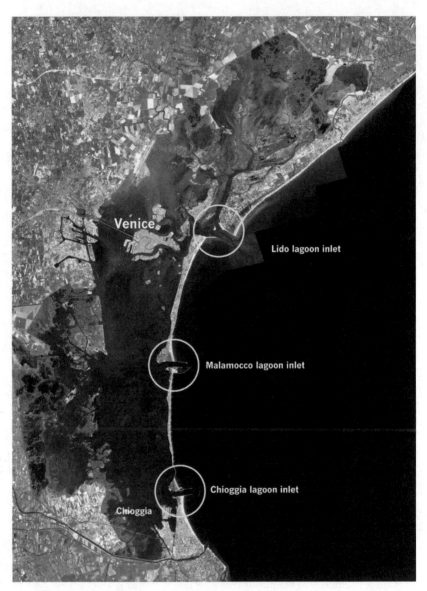

Figure 6.1 Venice, the "city on the water," comprises 117 small islands inside the lagoon. The locations of the inlets are shown here. Credit: Ministry of Infrastructure and Transport—Magistrato alle Acque (Venice Water Authority), concessionary Consorzio Venezia Nuova image archive.

So, to talk about modern-day Venice one must consider four different facets: the historical city, which has a fishlike shape (*forma urbis*) when viewed from above; the modern city (Mestre); the industrial city (Porto Marghera); and the archipelago of islands of the estuary. Taken together, they represent a more complex kind of urban settlement. Water acts as the connecting element, the common denominator that links all these separate parts together. This concept was particularly strong in the past, when Venetian waters—lagoon, canals, basins, but also rivers and the Adriatic Sea—were greatly taken into consideration and defended, through specific laws and physical interventions. There was the awareness and conscious-ness of the fundamental role played by these waters in the construction of the power, greatness, and wealth of the Serenissima.

Water was also instrumental in terms of fishing and trading: it is through water that ships built in the Arsenale were "catching the wind." Only three inlets today separate the Venetian Lagoon from the Adriatic Sea—Bocca di Lido (800 meters wide), Malamocco (400 meters wide), and Chioggia (380 meters wide)—and guarantee the natural tide flow. Twice a day, the tide flows in, bringing the clean water into the lagoon from the Adriatic Sea. Even the natural environment of the lagoon is the result of a set of constant interventions by the Venetians over centuries to harmonize these two main bodies of waters: the waters of the Adriatic Sea, and those, semi-salted and semi-fresh, of the Venetian Lagoon (figure 6.2). The natu-ral environment is, in reality, an artificial structure that requires a great deal of work, technology, and knowledge to maintain.

What we see today is the end product of a number of important op-erations devoted to its preservation. First, in order to avoid flooding, the main rivers flowing into the lagoon—Brenta, Bacchiglione, Piave, and Sile—were diverted directly to the open sea, between the second half of the 18th century and the first half of the 19th century. Also, using differ-ent technologies and materials, barriers have been set on the seashore as defense from the waves—at the beginning made with wood piles and then, since the 18th century, with big stones called *murazzi*.

Water-related issues were such a concern for the Serenissima that spe-cific institutions were created to control and manage them. Water defense is still a critical issue today. If high tides and flooding always belonged to the story of Venice—the first traces appear in documents dating to the 6th century[3]—in recent decades Venice and other built-up areas in the la-goon have been flooded more frequently and with greater intensity. Due to global change, Venice as well as other coastal cities and regions will likely

Figure 6.2 The Chioggia, one of the three inlets that connect the Venetian Lagoon and the Adriatic Sea. In the foreground, the temporary gate housing caisson prefabrication site and the double lock for fishing boats and emergency vessels. In the background, Chioggia. Credit: Ministry of Infrastructure and Transport— Magistrato alle Acque (Venice Water Authority), concessionary Consorzio Venezia Nuova image archive.

be exposed with particular strength to the risk of flooding. This increase in the frequency and amplitude of flooding is due to the relative drop in the height of the land with respect to the sea—more than twenty-three centimeters from the beginning of the 20th century[4]—as a result of the rise in sea level (eustasy) and the drop in land level (subsidence).

Yet, since the 19th century, the city has shown signs of being less interested in the sea, and, conversely, has begun to look toward the neighboring territories of land. Arguably this began centuries before, when the Stato da Mar (the Empire on the Sea) of the Serenissima was facing its decline and the Republic of Venice began to look to the mainland. The dimension of insularity, at times total and exclusive, started to be counterbalanced by a stronger connection with the mainland—first through the construction of a railway bridge in the mid-19th century, followed by a road bridge, Ponte Littorio, then Ponte della Libertà, in 1934.

Even if water is still the most important means of transportation within the historical city—accommodating port activities, leisure time, and tourism—the increased access to Venice by road and rail brought with it a cluster of problems. With fewer than sixty thousand permanent residents on the historical island,[5] according to the available data, Venice is visited every year by more than twenty million tourists. There is an increase each year in tourism (with the exception of 2008 due to the global economic crisis) and a decrease of population, due to high costs of living and to a general low birth rate in Italy. The tourist "season" is getting longer and longer, even though there are peaks throughout the year and on weekends. There is a heavy impact on the city in terms of services (transport but also public toilets and garbage, just to mention a few), and the physical structure of the city itself is not prepared to meet the needs so many visitors. Despite the attempts by local authorities to combat this trend, tourism is almost the monocultural economic activity of the city, accounting for 20% of its income. The risk is that Venice loses its own characteristics as a real "city," and turns into a site used only by visitors. The constantly increasing number of shops selling goods of "first need" that switch into stores for tourists is impressive and makes us wonder what type of city Venice is going to be in the future. More than the danger of environmental impacts for the city—which mostly involves wave movement for traffic, great amounts of garbage, and a general overuse and waste of the city's resources and infrastructures—the quality of life and services for both residents and visitors is suffering.

If the physical maintenance of Venice, Chioggia, and other urban areas is taken care of by the state, through specific bodies, the Veneto region (the local administrative body of the region around Venice) is responsible for pollution abatement while local authorities are responsible for the maintenance and restoration of the architectural and built fabric.

Yet the structural side is not enough to keep a city alive and affordable for residents and visitors, since to safeguard a city in all its meanings is to guarantee as many functions and services as possible. The socioeconomic development of the city, which is the charge of the Municipality of Venice, is equally important in order to consider Venice a "normal city," complex and diverse, rich with different activities and social classes, with local needs and metropolitan responses.

For that reason, sustainability has become a great concern for the city of Venice—as evidenced by the city's enrollment in the Aalborg Charter,[6] and its commitment to address the main issues of the Venice Local Agenda 21,[7] mainly regarding the following critical points: sustainable tourism, urban quality and environment, and production.

A Strategic Plan for the City, 2004–2014

According to EU indications, to be a livable city, quality of life has to be achieved through a good balance between environmental, social, economic, and special aspects.

In this regard, the city has defined its development strategies to promote structural and functional transformations of the urban system. Through its Strategic Plan—the document that defines the objectives, actions, and projects of the city, approved in January 2006—the city of Venice identifies a number of policy lines, then resulting in feasible actions, and main areas of development recognized as being important for the future of the city.

The identified structural conditions of the plan have been summarized in three main lines of action:

1. *The city of inhabitants*: plural, inclusive, sustainable, a city where the residential aspect will be preserved while remaining welcoming for immigrants and sustainable for all.
2. *Physical and functional structure of the contemporary city*: a city restored and preserved in its physical historical layout but also including functions and services according to contemporary needs.
3. *Metropolitan city*: a city capable of "thinking" globally at the metropolitan scale, looking at a wider territory in terms of services and infrastructures.

The strategic lines of the plan are organized around seven main statements related to the different characters of the city's future development: International City, City of Culture, City of Waters, City of Tourism, City of Higher Education, Research, and Innovation, City Top-Level Logistic Node,[8] and City of Material Production and Services.

So, even if composed by two different urban "souls," a number of measures of a different nature have been adopted with the purpose of both limiting the consumption of natural resources and at the same time protecting the historical and natural environments.

Urban Regeneration, Industrial Reconversion, and Environmental Requalification

Today, the historical "city on water" (including the island of the Giudecca) counts approximately 59,080 inhabitants. The modern "city on land"—Mestre, Marghera, and its surroundings—boasts a total of 181,950 residents, while the estuary (including Lido, Murano, Burano, and the rest of the islands) has 29,742 inhabitants: a total of 270,772 (as of October 2011).[9]

This breakdown gives us an idea of the weight of each single component of this complex system. Despite its unity in terms of territory and management, for many years this system was partly managed and developed in a disharmonic and inorganic way, as if any single part was autonomous and not connected to the others. This fact caused a strong push toward the political and administrative separation between the "city on water" and the new "city on land," to which citizens have been called to express themselves four times through referendums over the past thirty years (1979–2003), without success. In the mid-1990s, the city administration drew up a new plan that considered the city as a whole and attempted to reconnect the constituencies.

The 1996 Master Plan of Venice—still a reference with all its variations—gave a global vision of the city as a whole, looking at the "city on water" and the "city on land" as two elements of the same urban body, each one with its functions and objectives. It put forward the idea of a "possible Venice," a concept combining history and innovation, the conservation of its cultural and artistic values alongside the development of the available resources. This was instrumental in finally highlighting the historical identity and individuality of Venice, using the safeguarding of the environment as an impetus and giving consideration and attention to long-neglected areas—the entire island of Giudecca, part of the glassmaking island of Murano, and the abandoned islands in the lagoon, some of them former asylums, others former military parade grounds. These various elements were imagined as part of the urban fabric, selected according to several criteria: accessibility, internal mobility within the daily urban system, functionality, suitability for reconversion, capability to attract investors, and so forth. For example, in the old town, former port or industrial buildings on the waterfront were selected to host university services or housing in order to both revitalize marginalized areas and reuse valuable structures. On the mainland, too, underused areas with a great deal of possibility in terms of conjunction and connections were devoted to public services or organized as public areas.

TRANSFORMATIONS OF GIUDECCA AND OTHER SITES IN THE CITY CENTER

Due to its physical restrictions and limitations in terms of both space and conservation of its heritage, the historical center has recovered and transformed as no other city in Europe, bringing all available buildings and areas back to urban uses.

Several areas on the island of the Giudecca, the seat of the first industrialized era of Venice in the 19th century until the development of Porto Marghera, have been restored to create new residential areas. This redevelopment helps to meet the demand for new and more functional houses for both residents and the second-home market. Also in Giudecca, the former shipyard CNOMV[10] and the huge former flour mill, a neo-Gothic complex once occupied by Molino Stucky, both of which closed in the 1950s, have been transformed. They have been redeveloped into a complex area of different services: small craft and productive activities, mostly connected with boat building and restoration, housing, public offices, a retail center, and a brand-new Hilton hotel and conference center. Further, the former slaughterhouse in the *sestiere* of Cannaregio has been transformed into university facilities. On the island of Murano, in the seat of the famous glass bead factory Conterie, an articulated set of urban uses will be implemented.

Even most of the abandoned or derelict islands in the lagoon have been regenerated over the last decades. San Servolo, owned by the Province of Venice, is now the seat of Venice International University,[11] a higher education and research center, founded in 1995 as a joint venture between eleven renowned international universities and important Italian institutions. On the other side, the island of San Clemente has been sold to private investors and is now a five-star resort and hotel. On the island of La Certosa,[12] a former military shooting range, the Vento di Venezia Yachting Center in 2004 succeeded in creating a multifunctional complex: more than five thousand square meters with a range of services from mooring, maintenance, and refitting to the construction of new boats in wood and courses in navigation and marine culture.

The city of Venice combines conservation and respect of its original structures and features, and requires that developers look to reuse existing spaces and buildings for new purposes. Therefore Venice really is an extraordinary laboratory of urban regeneration.

Porto Marghera and the VEGA Park

The functional and physical transformation of the city not only involves the old city but engages the industrial area as well. Porto Marghera, one of the largest industrial areas in Europe (2,200 hectares), has lost a number of companies due to the decline of chemical activities that began in the early 1970s. This resulted in a large number of empty spaces for new construction, but also opportunities to transform, reuse, and "green" the existing industrial infrastructure.

The main project for this area, highly developed over the past ten years, is called VEGA, or the Venice Gateway for Science and Technology.[13] VEGA is a science and technology park—a network of universities, research centers, and the manufacturing businesses—aimed at promoting and developing scientific research initiatives to help the transfer of knowledge, and to stimulate technological development and the competitive spirit of companies. It focuses on the cutting-edge sectors of technological innovation: nanotechnologies, information and communications technologies, and the green economy. VEGA ranks among the most important science and technology parks in Italy, a model of environmental redevelopment acknowledged through the international certifications granted for the quality of its environment management system (ISO 14001). Further development plans involve in particular those areas facing the Venetian Lagoon or served by a navigable canal, where the presence of water represents added value in terms of real estate and quality: the "Venice waterfront." The park project was planned at the beginning of the 1990s, with the primary mission of redeveloping one portion of the first industrial area of Porto Marghera by applying an environmentally sustainable development model. The European Union classified this area as a "depressed industrial area," allocating public funds (the FESR European structural funds, managed by the Veneto region) to support a total investment of roughly €70 million. The growth and development of VEGA was articulated in four basic stages between 1993 and 2004, organized into four adjacent areas covering a total area of thirty-five hectares.

Yet the problem of Porto Marghera is not just a matter of spaces. As stated above, the idea of building an industrial area on the lagoon's edge started at the beginning of the 20th century when there was less awareness of environmental issues. For many decades, these industries were dumping toxic substances in the lagoon's waters (figure 6.3). The presence of heavy metal in the lagoon on one side, and the drain of nutrients used by agriculture on the other side, severely affected the lagoon's fauna and caused for some years an extraordinary production of seaweed and phytoplankton in the shallow waters, with consequent decomposition.

The program for the recovery and the regeneration of the entire area of Porto Marghera—recognized as a site of national interest—aims first to decontaminate the soil (a total of around 5,200 hectares, made of water, canals, and emerged land, of which 1,900 hectares are industrial spaces, which makes it the largest polluted area in Italy), then to convert dangerous activities to sustainable, clean, hi-tech ones, trying to find new investors at the international level. Several entities at different institutional levels

Figure 6.3 In Porto Marghera, a large former industrial site, there are many opportunities to transform, reuse, and green these areas. Credit: Marta Moretti, Cities on Water archive.

are involved in this operation, but the Veneto region has been delegated the lead role in the remediation operation. Since the area of Porto Marghera is partially public and partially private, the intervention procedures seem to be quite complex and slow (and extremely expensive). A specific master plan for the reclamation works of the area was drawn up and approved in April 2004[14] by the Veneto region and the city of Venice, under the umbrella of the Ministry for the Environment, outlining guidelines, strategies, costs, and timing: ten years for the environmental reclamation and for securing only the priority areas (the 60% occupied by industrial infrastructure), and a provision of €1.5 million for the cost of the depollution process. There are many public bodies and entities involved with the drainages, embankment of industrial channels and basins, and public land reclamation (e.g., the Magistrato alle Acque and Port Authority), as well as the private companies entitled for plant management and soil contamination treatment.

San Giuliano Park

The most advanced transformation process involves a waterfront-facing polluted rubbish dump between Venice and Mestre in a huge public green area, the San Giuliano Park.[15] For Venice it is surely one of the most significant urban revitalization projects, given its complexity and heterogeneity, as well as the serious environmental decay of the site. The proposal for the environmental reclamation and the marine ecology remediation—which today is a complex, critical, and rapidly progressing sector—represents the starting point of a conservation and protection policy of the lagoon habitat. The Plan Guide of San Giuliano Park, prepared by the architect Antonio Di Mambro, winner of the appropriate international competition and approved by the Local Council in January 1996, affects an area of 700 hectares, of which 475 are land and 225 are canals, salt marshes, and lagoon. The plan comprises the following elements:

- Creation of a wide range of recreational activities and diversified structures for cultural and economic activities
- Interconnection of those activities and structures with an appropriate network of pedestrian paths within the green areas, limiting car traffic to parking lots
- Removal of physical, visual, and psychological obstacles placed between the centers of Venice and Mestre

Thanks to the park foundation, the area of Punta San Giuliano, used for many years as an industrial and urban waste dump, now acts as connecting hinge between the "city on land" and the "city on water."

When finished, it will cover around seven hundred hectares, becoming the largest urban park in Europe. The first portion of it, opened to the public in May 2004, has an area of 74 hectares and is divided into "Lotto A2" (12.4 hectares) and "Lotto B1" (61.6 hectares) (excluding the future nautical pole). These areas comprise environmental protected spaces (30 hectares), parking lots (10,800 square meters), foot and cycle paths (approx. 14 kilometers), water stretches (17,400 square meters), buildings (a total of 1,550 square meters, including the north gate, a skating rink building and a skating center dressing room, football ground dressing room, entrance bar, fifty bathrooms, and two shaded areas), squares and resting places (9,691 square meters), of which 515 square meters are allocated for the entrance bar square and 475 square meters for the gazebo area. The green area covering more than sixty-eight hectares consists of recreational grazing lands (187,671 square meters), environmental grasslands (490,273 square meters), meadows of humid sites (1,800 square meters), flower meadows (1,197 square meters), alveolar turf surfaces (16,123 square meters), sports grounds (5,500 square meters), and sown grounds for phytoreclamation purposes (5,602 square meters).

To meet the needs of the public while the project is being completed, three temporary structures have been placed within the San Giuliano Park: a 400-square-meter tent in the Punta San Giuliano area, a 1,300-square-meter tent, and a 1,500-square-meter structure that will serve as a restaurant.

Mobility to and within Venice

The needs and problems of the traffic flows of tourists and businesses and locals, with different frequencies, intensities, and timing, must be addressed. The combination of water traffic in the historical city—public means, *vaporetti*, water taxis, work boats for the delivery of goods of any kind, private boats for tourism and for leisure, cruise ships—with the traffic to reach it from the mainland (road, train, buses) makes mobility a crucial issue for Venice.

The solution proposed in the 1996 Master Plan to diversify the flows by using different arrivals was never really accomplished. The main terminal of Piazzale Roma at the end of the bridge crossing the lagoon is supposed to be used exclusively by residents and commuters, while the heavy traffic of tourism buses is supposed to be diverted toward several areas along the lagoon coast. There are three terminals involved in the plan to improve the flow of incoming traffic: Fusina, Tessera, and Punta Sabbioni. Fusina, located on the southern coast, allows access to Venice by water transport along the Zattere. But the land acquisition and approval procedures are slower and more complex than expected, and this terminal functions today only in a reduced form.

Punta Sabbioni is a terminal serving bathing tourism coming from camping and beaches located on the eastern coast. Such category of tourist usually comes to Venice just for a one-day trip. This terminal is functioning and was reorganized and rationalized in 2003.

Finally, for Tessera, an increase in the water connections—a semipublic service—between Marco Polo Airport, the third busiest in Italy, and the northern side of the city has been realized, with a wider range of routes. The Venice Gateway project, designed by the architect Frank Gehry, envisions a "water terminal" to the city, car parks, and a hotel and conference center for three thousand people; it has been planned since 2001 but only recently gained final approval (January 2012). Another planned project for the airport is a stop of the Metropolitan Rail System (SMFR). The SFMR is an undergoing project, financed by the Veneto region, providing a regional and suburban rail service at high and regular frequency (every fifteen to thirty minutes) along some existing railways in Veneto, developing new stations and a wider network integrated with the road system. A project for a fast sub-lagoon connection between the airport and the north side of the city has also been under discussion, but in addition to questions about how it will be financed, this proposal poses many question marks for its impact on the lagoon. On the other hand, there is no doubt that faster connections to and within the city is an indispensable precondition for the future of Venice itself.

Even the pedestrian paths in the old city—still the main network of getting around—have been reorganized with new connections close to the "exit" of the city. The exit is a new bridge—the fourth over the Grand Canal—designed by Santiago Calatrava and called Ponte della Costituzione (figure 6.4). Completed in the spring of 2008, the bridge directly connects the railway station to the car terminal of Piazzale Roma. From here, a suspended light transport system, the People Mover, opened to the public in April 2010 to connect the terminal of Piazzale Roma with the car park on the island of Tronchetto and the Maritime Passenger Terminal in the port, for cruise and ferry users (figure 6.5).

Figure 6.4 The new Calatrava-designed bridge over the Grand Canal, called the Ponte della Costituzione. Credit: Marta Moretti, Cities on Water archive.

Figure 6.5 Completed in 2008, this People Mover connects the city's railway station to the car terminal of Piazzale Roma. Credit: Marta Moretti, Cities on Water archive.

The construction of the first two sections of a "green" electric tramcar connection within the first urban belt on the mainland has been completed, and the hope is that it will help manage traffic and reduce air pollution. The main aims of this connection are accessibility, punctuality, comfort, and environmental friendliness. The first proposal for the electric tramcar was presented in 1992, but lately the road system was chosen instead of the rail for a cost, time, and impact evaluation. The final plan, supported in part by the state, included variations on the tracks (two main lines being Favaro Veneto-Mestre-Venezia and Mestre-Marghera) and work started in 2004, with several stops and starts—partially due to the lack of financing, partially due to the need to remove services from the ground (gas, electricity, sewage, etc.). Part of the track was completed at the beginning of 2010, with great appreciation from its users, while the connection with the Venice historical center will be included in a second phase of the project (to be finished between 2015 and 2018), when all the indispensable infrastructures will be built along the Liberty Bridge.

The goal is to achieve a balanced budget within fifteen years. When completed, this new connection will represent a consistent contribution to traffic decongestion around Mestre and to the reduction of air emissions.

It is worth mentioning an interesting system adopted by the city in 2009 to better organize tourist arrivals and service provision. A website, VeniceConnected.com, manages the online sale of public transport and recreational services (e.g., museums, foundations, general attractions, public parking, toilets, Wi-Fi Internet accesses) to any user who desires to make use of them within the territory of the Municipality of Venice, subject to registration and payment of the fees indicated.

Maintenance of the City and Water Protection

In addition to the issue of congestion compromising mobility, overuse of the waterways is contributing to problems with water quality and quantity as well as damage from the waves caused by motor craft. Too many motor vessels cruise the urban waters for the distribution of goods and urban transport, making reduction of traffic very complicated. Many restrictions have been put in place in terms of speed control and of the boat typologies allowed to enter St. Mark's Basin; in addition, new technologies for low-wash crafts are currently under study. But the problem of wave-induced impact in the city is still very severe in terms of damage to old buildings, the *fondamenta*, and the city's edges, and the destruction of the lagoon bed and its environment.

Since wave motion is also causing the deposit of debris, particularly in the inner canals, the municipality should be doing constant dredging, which is essential for ensuring the navigability of inner waterways even in low-tide conditions. This duty was once the Republic of Venice's priority but was then forgotten by local administrations. In the mid-1990s this was started again on a continuous basis through a semipublic company called Insula Spa, responsible for urban maintenance such as dredging canals, renovating bridges, and systematizing underground infrastructures.

Venice, due to its peculiar structure, does not have a real sewage system, so urban waste has always used the canals, taking advantage of the natural exchange of waters. It is hard to believe, but this mechanism functioned pretty well until the mid-20th century. Even as late as the 1950s, people would swim in certain inner canals.

As mentioned at the beginning of the chapter, Venice has always faced the challenge of serious floods, which have become stronger and more frequent in recent years (figure 6.6). The terrible flood of November 4, 1966, submerged a large part of the city for several hours. It appeared that the city was under a serious risk of destruction because of the power of the waters. From that moment forward, safeguarding Venice and its lagoon has been considered a problem of "primary national interest," to be faced also by the international community. The first practical action to address this issue was the promotion of a Special Law for Venice. This act was promulgated in 1973 (law no. 171/73) by the Italian government and then regularly revised, bringing to the city special funding for its protection, and also defining (in particular with law no. 798/84) the entities entrusted with the safeguarding. At the same time, a number of international private committees started to organize themselves and to raise money on focused projects, mainly for the restoration of the city's historical heritage.

The MOSE Project

A special concessionary body, Consorzio Venezia Nuova (CVN), was set up in 1984 with the aim of safeguarding the physical infrastructure of the city, on behalf of the Italian Ministry of Infrastructure and Transport–Venice Water Authority (Magistrato alle Acque).[16] The aim of CVN was to realize

Figure 6.6 Venice has a major flooding problem during its frequent periods of *acqua alta*, or high water, but has developed a number of strategies for adapting to these conditions. Credit: Marta Moretti, Cities on Water archive.

a very important project, MOSE (Modulo Sperimentale Elettromeccanico, or Experimental Electromechanical Module). The project defends Venice from high tide (defined as higher than 110 centimeters above sea level). This includes, together with reinforcement and the raising of quaysides and paving in the lowest lying urban areas, the construction of mobile barriers to be raised as needed at the three inlets of the lagoon, which are the openings along the coastline where lagoon water is in continual contact with seawater (see figure 6.7).

When not in operation, such buoyancy flap gates are full of water and rest in caissons on the waterbed, allowing the regular traffic of commercial and cruise ships that reach the Port of Venice through the lagoon inlets. If a high tide is forecast, compressed air is introduced into the gates, expelling the water. As the water is expelled from the gates, they rotate around a hinge axis until they emerge and block the tidal flow from entering the lagoon. In this way, the amount of water accessing the lagoon would be less consistent and forceful. The mobile barriers remain in position for the duration of the high-water period.

Figure 6.7 Venice is building a series of floodgates, a system called MOSE, which can be deployed in periods of expected high water. Credit: Ministry of Infrastructure and Transport—Magistrato alle Acque (Venice Water Authority), concessionary Consorzio Venezia Nuova image archive.

The total cost of the MOSE System is extremely high—the sum of €5.493 billion has been recently revised (July 2011)[17] and does not include the necessary maintenance. The debate around this project lasted more than twenty years, with many different decision levels involved. But finally, in May 2003, after many international evaluations, the formal go-ahead was given by the president of the Council of Ministers, along with a number of top-level representatives of the institutions taking part in the Committee for Policy, Coordination, and Control: the Ministry for Infrastructure and Transport, the Ministry for Environment, the president of the Veneto region, and the mayor of Venice.

Work has been proceeding in parallel at the three inlets, from north to south, of Lido, Malamocco, and Chioggia, and now is 65% complete (as of December 2011).[18] Four mobile barriers are under construction at the lagoon inlets (two at the Lido inlet, one at Malamocco, and one at Chioggia), for a total of seventy-eight gates (from the 18.5 x 20 x 3.6 meters of the smallest gate in Lido and Treporti, to the 29.6 x 20 x 4.5 meters of the largest gate, in Malamocco).

In the future, the phenomenon of high waters could be further aggravated by the predicted rise in sea level produced by global climate change. Regarding this problem, MOSE (together with the reinforcement of forty-six kilometers of coastal strip) has been designed based on a precautionary criterion to cope with an increase of up to sixty centimeters in one hundred years.[19] Management of MOSE is flexible enough to cope with an increase in high waters in various ways. Depending on the situation, the defense strategies can involve simultaneous closure of all three inlets, closure of one inlet at a time, or partial closure of each inlet, as the gates are all independent.

To allow port activities to continue when the gates are in operation, one lock for large shipping is necessary at the Malamocco inlet, while three small locks (two at Chioggia and one at Lido-Treporti) will allow for the transit of fishing boats and other smaller vessels.

Approximately three thousand people are currently employed (directly or indirectly) in the construction works. To avoid interfering with the fragile coastal areas, the work sites are organized to receive almost all material by sea. In addition, the work is always concentrated in half of each inlet to avoid interrupting transit of the channels and to reduce any possible negative effect on economic, maritime, and port activities.

The realization of the MOSE system foresees three phases, for a term of eight years. The first phase is completed, and involves construction of the complementary structures (the external breakwaters at the Malamocco and Chioggia inlets) and a series of other activities prior to installation of the mobile barriers (e.g., trial areas for experiments on bed consolidation, underwater surveys to identify possible archaeological remains, securing of military devices left from the war, design of mechanical components).

The second phase is also largely completed, and involves realization of the carrying structure of the system: consolidation of the seabed, abutments, barrier support structures, and associated civil engineering works (at the Lido and Chioggia inlets, refuge havens and navigation locks for fishing and pleasure boats and emergency vessels; at the Malamocco inlet, the navigation lock for large ships).

The third phase is also under way, which involves the construction of the concrete caissons and the hinges. Still to come is the fabrication of the gates, and their assembly.

Four rows of gates will be realized: one at Malamocco inlet (with nineteen gates), one at Chioggia inlet (with eighteen gates), and two at Lido inlet (on the Treporti Canal with twenty-one gates and on the San Nicolò Canal with twenty gates). An artificial island, housing the control buildings and the gate operation system, connects the two rows at the Lido inlet. Completion of the construction work is scheduled for 2014.

Contemporaneously, morphological restoration work is under way in the most deteriorated areas, using the material obtained from dredging at the three inlets, when compatible with the lagoon environment. More and more, the lagoon is giving way to the sea. Since the beginning of this century, salt marsh expansions have been reduced by one-half, and if erosion rate continues, by the year 2050 mudflats and salt marshes could totally disappear. This transformation has serious consequences for the survival of the lagoon ecosystem and for the structures created by humans. The principal elements at risk, besides the lagoon morphology itself, is the lagoon's biodiversity, due to the disappearance of animal and plant species and the destruction of urban centers and the structures protecting them, due to the increase in wave motion. In order to combat erosion, widespread and systematic maintenance measures are currently carried out; in recent years, about four hundred thousand cubic meters of sediment a year, deriving from the dredging of lagoon channels, were kept within the lagoon when found compatible for the reconstruction of mudflats and salt marshes.

Other Works

During the twenty years of debate over the MOSE project, Consorzio Venezia Nuova was able to undertake many other works, based on a General Plan of Interventions. The safeguarding activities delegated to the state and carried out by the Ministry of Infrastructure and Transport–Magistrata alle Acque (Venice Water Authority) via the CVN, are divided into distinct but interrelated lines of action: defense from high waters (local defenses of urban centers, MOSE system), defense from sea storms (beach and dunes reconstruction), environmental defense (securing the banks of polluted canals, improvement of water and sediment quality, protection and reconstruction of mudflats and salt marshes habitat and structure), and control and management (studies, surveys, monitoring, data banks).

During recent decades, as a result of the effects of eustasy and subsidence, high water in Piazza San Marco has become an almost daily occurrence. Located in the lowest part of the city, the piazza is subject to the most frequent floods (lately, more than 250 times per year, enough for tide to reach a height of sixty centimeters), with obvious consequences to Venice's most precious and representative buildings. The high waters result in the damage and degradation of architectural structures and paving, deterioration of the stone blocks, surface damage, and the collapse of underground rainwater drainage conduits.

The aim of the measures is to protect the area from the most frequent flooding, restore paving, and improve the subsoil, while maintaining the architectural relationships between the various elements in the piazza and the static equilibrium of the buildings. The Superintendence of Cultural Heritage–Archaeology project involves the consolidation, restoration, and elevation of at least 100 centimeters of 150 meters of lagoon bank along the basin. In addition, to avoid flooding caused both by flow-back though the drains and by seepage through the subsoil, the old system of underground conduits will be isolated from water coming from the small canals surrounding the area. The deteriorated conduits will be restored and, at the same time, a new rainwater collection and conveyance system will be constructed, to enable the water to flush out to the lagoon during high tides. Further, to counteract flooding caused by seepage though the subsoil, a bentonite (special clay) membrane will be laid forty centimeters below the level of the paving, not altering the hydrogeological equilibrium of the subsoil.

Besides this, work to reinforce the bell tower has recently begun. It is one of the city's most recognizable and best-known monuments, affectionately called by the Venetians "el paròn de casa" (the master of the house). Collapsed at the beginning of the 20th century, reconstructed during the 1910s, and afflicted by insidious damage for some time, the monument is undergoing meticulous and sophisticated reinforcement work as part of the activities to protect Piazza San Marco from high waters.

Since early 2000, the Magistrata alle Acque (Venice Water Authority) either directly or through the CVN has been implementing a program of work to secure and restore the historic buildings in the northern part of the Venice Arsenale, where the maintenance and management of MOSE will be located, committing considerable financial and operational resources. The work was made necessary by the widespread and serious degradation affecting the architectural structures, leading to deterioration of masonry, widespread instability, and in some cases collapse of structural parts, with the loss of elements of great historical value.

This marked the start of a more general program to reclaim the area, made possible thanks to synergy between the institutions and authorities concerned, already anticipated by the company Thetis, which transferred its head office to the Arsenale more than ten years ago. So, locating the "brain of MOSE" in the Arsenale was also a tool to transform the safeguarding of Venice and its lagoon into a major opportunity for compatible development and high-quality employment.

Consorzio Venezia Nuova is also active on the mainland side, along the polluted borders of Porto Marghera. The reduction of pollution in the lagoon is approached in various ways—through the interception and purification of pollution inflows from the drainage basin and residential and industrial settlements along the edges or within the lagoon area itself; through the blocking of pollutant seepage from abandoned dumps; and through reclamation of the lagoon bed in polluted areas. In particular, this means isolating the pollutants present in dumps formerly used to dispose of waste of various origins (including industrial), and eliminating the industrial residues accumulated over time in canals in Porto Marghera (beds and banks).

Widespread action must also be taken in other areas of the lagoon to block the release of pollutants accumulated over the years in the sediments, to construct phytopurification systems to reduce the pollutant load deriving from the drainage basin, and to perform periodic harvesting campaigns to prevent the risk of environmental crisis due to seaweed proliferation.

Port Activities, Cruise Traffic, and Green Policy

The Venice Port Authority was opposed to the gate project, in defense of the commercial and tourism traffic, which are so essential for a city that has very few economic drivers. The risk of having a negative effect on port activities seems to be reduced, since the gates would be closed only a few times per year (three to five times per year with the current sea level) and since a lock to allow the transit of large ships is included in the system, in order to guarantee port operations even when the gates are opened. Venice became in recent years the leading homeport for cruise ships in the Mediterranean Sea (two million passengers in 2010, the majority of which were cruisers),[20] and the combination of "fly and cruise" seems to be a very popular tourist option. The entrance and exit of these "floating cities," right in front of St. Mark's Basilica, is a great boost for tourists. In order to facilitate services for passengers, a new and more functional Maritime Terminal was realized in 2002 on the eastern border of the city. But the passage of these "giants of the sea" is out of scale for the dense and urbanized city, and is posing many questions in terms of safety, induced wave motion, and general sustainability. To reduce the impact of the port on city life, the Venice Port Authority has recently developed a plan of action articulated in three parts: open port, safe port, and green port. Established more than ten years ago, all the activities aim at strengthening the relations between the port and the city of Venice. Regarding safety, the port is launching a training, information, prevention, and control initiative while providing constant monitoring of the port's sensitive areas, the main internal navigation channels, and the road and railway access points that lead to Venice tourist and commercial infrastructure. Finally, the Port Authority has signed an agreement to reduce smog and powder emissions, and control noise pollution and wave movement. In addition to air quality monitoring and assessment, the port has started a number of projects aimed at cutting dangerous emissions and promoting the use of alternative energy. Quaysides have been designed to avoid any contamination, and the Marittima rainwater is collected and filtered before flowing into the main pipes.

The port has recently been reorganized on the mainland, at the border of Porto Marghera, to allow for more functional connections and transport, which will facilitate commercial activity. This development was made possible thanks to an understanding between the Port Authority and the city of Venice. According to a national legal provision (law no. 84/94), the development plans of cities and ports have to find shared and integrated solutions regarding spaces, areas, services, and uses. Accordingly, due to soil remediation ongoing in this area, the industrial land of Porto Marghera under the Venice Port Authority will be reclassified as port land.

Fishing is also an important resource for the lagoon, in particular for the island of Pellestrina and the city of Chioggia. For centuries, traditional fishing in the lagoon was considered a difficult profession requiring a great deal of knowledge and skill. It was an activity compatible with and respectful of the cycles of nature. But in more recent years, the cultivation of a kind of Philippines clam changed this approach severely because it does not require any specific training for workers but pays very well. Sometimes the clams were cultivated with no control, beyond the legal regulations. Recent rules to this area were able to integrate the two different activities and maintain respect for the environment.

Conclusion

As described above, Venice appears as a city of great contradictions. In its permanent search for a balance between innovation and conservation, the Venice historic core is probably the city in Europe that has undergone the fewest changes over the centuries in terms of space, layout, and general way of life. In my opinion, Venice can still be considered among those cities with higher quality of life. So the city of the past—with little capacity of accepting and containing modernity in itself, with reduced adaptation to modern life needs—ends up becoming "modern." I am referring to its pedestrian dimension, which is now seen as a model for sustainability. In most cities, we assist in a transformation of the historical centers to accommodate pedestrians, in order to be more sustainable and improve the quality of urban lives. It is amazing that the "pedestrian city" is still a model to be looked at and studied; in fact, every year a very consistent stream of foreign universities organizes field trips or courses in Venice just to study its model.

Looking at the numbers of the entire population of the municipality, Venice can be included with medium to small cities, but in terms of services, infrastructures, and connections—as well as its place in the collective imagination—Venice can be ranked with larger cities. In fact, Venice must also be seen as the main pole of attraction of the Veneto region, as well as one of the most important catalysts of northeastern Italy. Just to give an example, for the forthcoming candidacy of Venice as European Capital of Culture 2019, Venice is the focus of a wider territorial system involving the Veneto region, the Friuli Venezia Giulia region, and the Provinces of Venice, Trento, and Bolzano.

With a population in constant decline since 1968, reinforced in 1999 by the detachment, through referendum, of the area of Cavallino-Treporti, Venice is a city with a growing phenomena of second homes (an increase of 100% from 1994 to 2004), becoming many people's dream for its very special position in the global tourist market as a cultural destination of excellence.

Another contradiction is that Venice is an excellent city for kids—safe, with social control, a sense of community, no car dangers, plenty of open spaces despite a lack of green areas—but it is inhabited mostly by aged people, toward whom it can be unfriendly (no elevators, bridges, and mandatory walks, etc.).

In fact, due to longer life expectancies and declining birthrates, the population of Venice is continually aging, with severe consequences in terms of generation turnover, a balanced demographic evolution, and a change in family composition. Due to the cost of living, young people move out from the historical center to find work and affordable housing on the mainland. Besides the permanent residents, there is an important segment of the population—very difficult to calculate—gravitating around Venice and its perimeter for functional reasons: commuters, students, services users, and others.

But if we want to look at Venice from the sustainability point of view, we can say that the municipality has invested over the decades a great amount of money in social issues, becoming one of the most involved administrations in Italy for issues concerning foreigners, disadvantaged population, and so forth. On the other hand, looking at the state of the art of the green economy in Italy, according to a list of indicators defined by the Index of Green Economy (energy coming from renewable sources, biologic agriculture, separate waste collection, energy efficiency, etc.), conducted in 2010 by Fondazione Impresa,[21] the Veneto region is sixth at the national level, thanks to separate waste collection and waste disposal. In fact, the waste collection has been applied on the mainland, through road collectors, for dry waste, while in the historical center a differentiated collection of humid recyclable waste, paper, and glass/metal/plastic—door-to-door—has been in place for several years, with good results. For the remaining indicators, energy efficiency and the production of energy from water sources are fairly good, while agriculture and energy production from other renewable sources are less advanced.

Venice has undergone an extensive process of transformation over a long period. In this context, Venice can be considered an international city, with relevant resources in terms of safety and quality of life, and it is playing once more the "water card" that makes Venice unique.

During its long history, Venice experimented with a very tight cohabitation with water and, at the same time, has accumulated a huge concentration of knowledge in dealing with and managing the problems connected to it. This capacity of adapting to the natural conditions and finding solutions compatible with the environment is an important factor of sustainability. Water nowadays is a big issue all over the world, and this knowledge is valuable to share and exchange.

The story of Venice shows all the potential of water: too often considered an enemy to fight with, dangerous and violent; if studied, observed, respected, and known, water could fully regain its positive aspects and act more as a sort of *fil rouge* that keeps different urban realities together, in a complex variety of aspects, instead of being an element of separation. To this extent, Venice can be considered a sort of ongoing workroom for studies regarding water and, in particular, its relationship with the city.

Water can still be Venice's "blue-green" element of sustainability for several aspects—work, transportation, mobility, and leisure—in view of a better quality of life.

Notes

The collection of data has been realized with the collaboration of Antongiulio Zanrosso.

1. http://www.comune.venezia.it/.

2. http://www.port.venice.it/.

3. Paul the Deacon (ca. 720–799), also known as Paulus Diaconus, in his *Historia Langobardorum*, III, 23.

4. http://www.salve.it/.

5. http://www.comune.venezia.it/.

6. Charter of European Cities and Towns Toward Sustainability, approved by the participants at the European Conference on Sustainable Cities and Towns in Aalborg, Denmark, on May 27, 1994. See http://ec.europa.eu/environment/urban/pdf/aalborg _charter.pdf.

7. The Venice Local Agenda 21 is the UN action plan for sustainable development, applied at the local level as a partnership process among local bodies.

8. "City Top-Level Logistic Node" is one of the development lines identified by the Strategic Plan. Venice, for its strategic geographical position and for the availability of spaces along the waterfront, can play the role of a logistical pole for services, distribution, and stock of high-level goods.

9. http://www.comune.venezia.it/.

10. http://www.venicecube.it/.

11. http://www.univiu.org/.

12. http://www.ventodivenezia.it/.

13. http://www.vegapark.ve.it/.

14. http://www.regione.veneto.it/.

15. http://www.parchidimestre.it/.
16. http://www.consorziovenezianuova.com/; http://www.salve.it/.
17. http://www.cipecomitato.it/.
18. http://www.salve.it/.
19. Ibid.
20. http://www.port.venice.it/.
21. http://www.fondazioneimpresa.it/.

7

Vitoria-Gasteiz, Spain: From Urban Greenbelt to Regional Green Infrastructure

Luis Andrés Orive and

Rebeca Dios Lema

Located in the north of Spain, Vitoria-Gasteiz is the capital of the Autonomous Community of the Basque Country (figure 7.1). It represents one of the three main Basque cities, together with San Sebastian and Bilbao. Although it is a very small Autonomous Community of over two million people and a land area of almost eight thousand square kilometers, it has a great cultural and identity strength, as well as an important economic and political weight.

The great investment of the Basque government in technological innovation and its strong support to face environmental challenges has been widely recognized. The most recent award has come from the European Commission, appointing Vitoria-Gasteiz as the European Green Capital for 2012.

Vitoria-Gasteiz is well-known for its environmental strategies, its highly controlled and well-planned growth, and its high quality of life and urban fabric. The city has one of the highest incomes per capita in Spain, and its rate of unemployment is much lower than the national average. It has the largest industrial area in the north of Spain, where factories like Michelin and Mercedes-Benz, now developing the first electric car in Europe, are the most recognized at the international level.

Figure 7.1 Vitoria-Gasteiz was among the first European cities to sign the Aalborg Charter. Credit: CEA (Environmental Studies Center).

During the last thirty years, social, ecological, and environmental issues have been key factors in guiding the city to what it is today. In the late 1980s Mayor José Ángel Cuerda, with the support of all the political parties, created the CEA (Environmental Studies Center), a public municipal organization in charge of research and education on environmental issues. This showed extraordinary enthusiasm for the emergent ideas and strategies that were then being carried out in the sustainability field. With an interdisciplinary technical team of more than twenty specialists, the CEA became a pioneer municipal structure, designing the basis for a more sustainable future in Vitoria-Gasteiz, just as was happening with Curitiba, Brazil, at that time.

The UN Conference on Environment and Development held in Rio de Janeiro in 1992 and the Aalborg Charter of 1995 meant strategic and integral support, in a global context, to the environmental initiatives in Vitoria. Vitoria-Gasteiz was the first Spanish city to sign the Aalborg Charter and also the first to design a local Agenda 21. Issues including hydrology, pollution, noise, and energy were being taken into account in an integral manner. This process has enjoyed a great deal of support ever since. It has become a leading development in the city and has been reinforced by the pride of its citizens, helping to ensure its success.

Of these strategies, the greenbelt has been the most successful in terms of social acceptance and international recognition (see figure 7.2, page 161). The restored areas in the peri-urban fringe of the city that make up the greenbelt are highly regarded by citizens as they enjoy these spaces in their daily walks (the most popular pastime in Vitoria). It is due to the traditional management of the relationship between the city and the countryside that Vitoria-Gasteiz has been able to maintain a sustainable balance over the years. Most of the agricultural and forestry landscapes of the region are owned by rural communities distributed all over the territory, and historically have been managed by the Provincial Council. The woods, prairies, and wetlands that sustain and make up the greenbelt are publicly owned.

The management of public land has had an enormous influence on ecological policies today. Our ancestors showed us what sustainability was about by preserving the natural resources that we enjoy today, despite the poverty and devastating famines suffered by Spain historically.

First Steps toward Ecological Planning: The Urban Fringe

With a population of almost 240,000 people, the Municipality of Vitoria-Gasteiz covers an area of almost twenty-eight thousand hectares and is the largest in the Basque Country. It is located in a wide valley of fertile land watered by the River Zadorra and edged by extensive forested mountains. This environment provides the backdrop for the medieval quarter of the city, originally situated on a hill of marl soil, called La Llanada (or plains of Alava), on which the capital is situated. The valley boasts an enormous hydrological network of rivers and streams that fill two reservoirs (a water supply for 1.8 million people) and a large, deep aquifer. It has the highest biodiversity index of the region. The reasons for this are twofold, namely, its transitional geographical position between the Mediterranean and Eurosiberian biogeographies, and the large proportion of publicly managed land.

In the late 1980s, the CEA highlighted the characteristics of this landscape that should be focused on for environmental planning purposes: a compact city, peri-urban areas, the agricultural matrix, and the natural mountain systems.

A COMPACT CITY

The slow, controlled growth of the population and the special care taken in planning issues had given shape to a well-defined, compact city until the 1950s. During the 1960s and 1970s agricultural and farming traditions changed as a result of heavy industrialization and an extraordinary increase in population levels. In less than twenty years, the city doubled in size (in both population and land mass) and new industrial areas were created on its outskirts, attracted by lower land prices and the proximity to communications infrastructures and the river.

During the economic crisis of the 1980s, special efforts were made to restore urban cohesion, and restrictions were placed on any further expansion. Bold efforts were also made to improve social services: the first and exemplary network of civic centers was established in order to provide a full range of services in every neighborhood (sports, schools, health care centers, etc.), and green areas and plazas were planned and designed to play a fundamental role in social integration. As a result, Vitoria-Gasteiz is known for its high environmental quality and its clear separation between the urban fabric and the countryside, including a large expanse of parks and tree-lined avenues that make it one of the greenest cities in Spain, and also structure it with great connections to the surrounding areas.

Peri-urban Areas

Despite the success in creating a compact city, the process of heavy industrialization had a great impact on the peri-urban areas of the city, reducing their ecological value and increasing the size of marginal spaces due to the expected changes in land uses from agricultural to urban or industrial uses. This led to critical social and economic changes, as the countryside was highly devalued.

In the late 1980s there was still a series of seminatural, mostly abandoned and highly degraded areas on the urban fringe. Despite being subjected to great urban and human pressures, they still maintained valuable spaces with great potential for "framing" the urban core, acting as an ecotone between the city and the surrounding countryside. This is what has come to be known as the greenbelt.

The Agricultural Matrix

Almost 40% of the municipality is made up of farmland (almost 108 km²), complemented by a series of sixty-three small villages that represent 2% of the population (almost five thousand inhabitants). Most of these villages are very well integrated into the rural landscape with carefully designed *caserios* (Basque rural houses) and traditional churches.

The position of the municipality on an extensive aquifer provides this area with a large network of rivers and streams. All of them drain into the main river, the Zadorra, connecting the Alava plains with the Mediterranean valley of the River Ebro. This ecological corridor defines and feeds the entire agricultural plain. Unfortunately, both urban development and agriculture have reduced the riversides, and some tributaries have become much degraded or even absorbed by the sewage systems.

In addition to the agricultural land, there are a number of important island woods, small, natural relicts spread throughout the municipality that preserve the historical and natural memory of the region. Although they have been reduced, many of them remain as a reminder of the plains of Alava that were once covered with oak forests. These are areas of great biodiversity within the agricultural matrix.

THE NATURAL MOUNTAIN SYSTEMS

On the outer limits of the municipality, another 40% of the land is made up of a series of mountain ranges with forests and grazing meadows of great ecological and landscape value. Both the mountain ranges of Badaya and Arrato (west) and Vitoria (south) are publicly owned and full of native, leafy species of trees. The latter constitutes the main natural system of the municipality with high importance for conservation, given its great botanical and faunal value and its source of the main rivers that run through the city toward the River Zadorra.

Solutions within the Framework of Landscape Ecological Planning on the Urban Fringe

Following this preliminary analysis made by the CEA, it was understood that the areas on the edge of the city were subject to heavy pressure from urban developers and also contained the highest proportion of degraded areas. As in so many other Spanish cities at that time, the city/country-side interface was not well resolved and the symptoms of environmental degradation were clear: shantytowns, illegal vegetable gardens on the riverbanks, garbage dumps, abandoned gravel pits, quarries, burnt shrubs and forest areas, and all kinds of illegal hunting, fishing, tree felling, cattle breeding, and so forth. All these uncontrolled landfills were coexisting with new infrastructures and industry areas, surrounded by brownfield sites, vacant and residual spaces, near high-quality landscapes, villages, historical icons, and churches, connected by badly damaged tracks.

The CEA study came to three main conclusions:

1. Vitoria-Gasteiz had an extensive territory of good ecological quality, with large amounts of publicly owned land and a great

deal of potential to conserve and enhance the landscape and biodiversity. First proposals included one thousand hectares of land to be protected as a greenbelt.

2. Vitoria-Gasteiz concentrated its efforts on developing the city center, at the expense of the outlying areas of the city. This was especially clear on the edges of the city where the levels of degradation and environmental hazards were very high, especially in areas near the lakes and rivers.

3. Once they had been restored, all these landscapes on the urban fringe would be capable of playing an extraordinary role in improving the functional ecological networks at a regional scale. They could also be used to define the urban model and therefore have a positive impact on the quality of life of all city dwellers.

Initial restoration works focused on those areas that suffered high levels of degradation, or that boasted exemplary natural values. Other factors included availability, budgets, social and institutional support, and the educational and illustrative value of the land and its aptness for public use.

The first restoration projects began with a very modest budget of approximately €100,000, and with the help of students and workers participating in a public employment plan developed during the economic crisis of the late 1980s. New peri-urban parks were implemented in the 1990s, combining ecological, landscape, environmental, economic, and social factors. The gravel pits were restored, the public tracks were improved, the plowed areas were sowed and planted, and a number of adaptations were made for public use in more highly frequented areas—almost always at points of contact with the city.

The Greenbelt Strategy: Toward a Greener City

It was in the early 1990s when the CEA launched the plan to create an entire green peri-urban system. Although it was seen as an overall solution to the problem of the degraded areas between the city and the countryside, it was soon realized that the benefits of this restoration went far beyond ecological and social improvement. It was a multifunctional strategy with the aim of introducing landscape ecology concepts into planning decisions.

The networks of ecological connectivity that were created with the greenbelt formed the core of this ecological planning strategy. It was necessary at that time to "attack" the causes of territorial fragmentation by enhancing biological connectivity.

The first proposal for the greenbelt in 1995 was defined by the main natural systems: a river that marks the boundary of the city to the north (Zadorra), a mountain system to the south, and a drainage system with small rivers and streams to the east and west of the city. Moreover, there were a number of small "island woods" (Armentia and Zabalgana) and a consolidated peri-urban park with its traditional procession and popular festivities (Olarizu). A few decades ago, a number of drained wetlands (Salburua), before being occupied by farming land, had provided habitats for communities of plants and animals, and played a regulatory role by helping to control flooding, so there was considerable support for their recovery. Despite the fact that many of these spaces were degraded, there was huge potential for their recovery.

Implementing the Greenbelt Strategy: Main Projects and Functions

In addition to restoration actions, key planning tasks were introduced in order to assess alternatives and projects in the spaces that were experiencing the greatest development pressure. A broad range of functions were gradually added to the strategy as the greenbelt started to become reality.

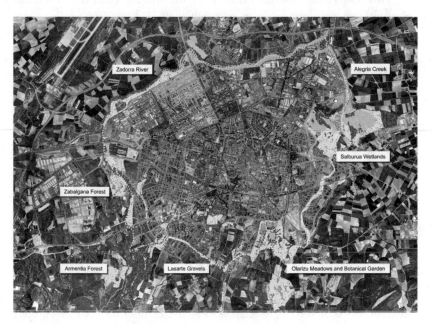

Figure 7.2 Greenbelt of Vitoria-Gasteiz. Credit: CEA.

Regulating the Hydrological System

As in so many other cities, successive expansions had been made at the expense of the water meadows, in this case of the River Zadorra and its small tributaries that run down the forested mountains of Vitoria. Five of these streams had been embedded into the sewage system as they entered the city. Two critical aspects came together:

- The introduction of the clean waters of the creeks into the urban drainage system meant an excessive volume of water for treatment.
- The saturation of the sewage system in rainy periods created flooding hazards in the urban area, and even led to the dumping of dirty water in the main river at critical points.

In addition, two of the main industrial areas were laid out on the Zadorra floodplains during the 1970s, and they suffered greatly from regular flooding episodes. There was a great deal of controversy at the beginning of the 1990s when, in order to avoid the frequent economic consequences of the river overflowing, the Basque government and the Provincial Council of Alava proposed to transform the river into a large concrete channel.

This project was rejected outright by the citizens because of the critical environmental and social impact, which forced the authorities to try other, more imaginative ways of resolving the conflicting degradation and hazards. Detailed hydraulic and ecological restoration studies led to much "greener" functional solutions. But the most important achievement was the decision not to develop the floodable areas on the right bank of the river (figure 7.3). This would allow the establishment of a boundary for urban growth and the preservation of agricultural areas, which would also serve as natural separation pools when needed.

An integrated plan was launched in 2001 with the aim of preventing the river from bursting its banks, recovering the fluvial ecosystem, and ensuring the continuity of the northern sections of the greenbelt. The project affects a surface area of 251 hectares over a distance of thirteen kilometers and comprises five phases and a large number of actions. Some of these have been already undertaken, mainly relating to the environmental restoration of the riverbank and to the implementation of pathways. In 2005 the first stage of the hydraulic equipment installation was launched, affecting 1,300 meters of the canal. As of 2011, eighty-two hectares have been successfully recovered, conciliating the different aims of hydraulic

Figure 7.3 Multiple projects for ecological regeneration and hydraulic adaptation have been implemented over the last few years. The city of Vitoria-Gasteiz is situated over a huge underground aquifer, and the adequate management of the water has been of great importance for recognizing the "tangible" values of the greenbelt. Credit: CEA.

corrections, ecological restoration, and social involvement. The natural conditions of the River Zadorra have been restored and preserved, in part due to its inclusion as a vital corridor in the European Ecological Network Natura 2000 as a Site of Community Importance.

Back in 1989 there were very ambitious proposals for other floodable area in the eastern part of the city, known as Salburua. These proposals included theme parks or golf courses. Fortunately, these were never realized. Instead, research on the history, evolution, and identity of Salburua helped to support the more ecological and economic alternative of restoration to its original conditions.

Before these wetlands had been drained to support farming in the 1850s, they provided habitats for communities of plants and animals and helped to control flooding. Once the agricultural drainage system was cut off, the wetlands were naturally reborn. The high quality of the park and its high level of biodiversity led to its inclusion in the Ramsar Convention on wetlands in 2002, and it is one of the most important wetlands in the Basque Country, only three kilometers from the city center and with the highest rates of visitors, especially bird-watchers (figure 7.4).

Most of the investments made to create this park came from European Union funds, since the complex served a great natural hydraulic role. The wetlands take the overflow from two of the streams coming from the south and both purify the aquifer and reduce the high economic impact, especially on the nearby industrial areas. The two streams were redirected to the River Zadorra so they no longer ran through the sewage system.

CREATING CONNECTIONS, IMPROVING ACCESSIBILITY, AND INTEGRATING PUBLIC USE IN NATURAL SURROUNDINGS

One of the initial goals of the greenbelt was to seek a harmonious compromise between ecological tasks and social use. A network of pathways and walks was implemented within each new park of the greenbelt, allowing people to enjoy, recognize the value of, and protect these newly restored areas.

The long-held tradition among the inhabitants of Vitoria-Gasteiz of going for walks plays a very important role in the success of the greenbelt. Walkers made use of the newly created or restored routes immediately, and multiple educational and sporting activities helped to reinforce the citizens' identification with the greenbelt.

It has been demonstrated that people can collaborate actively in the work of conservation, acting as de facto watchdogs of the spaces crossed by tracks, substituting for or complementing formal monitoring services. This also obliges us to be more careful with the maintenance of these spaces and to be especially vigilant.

PROMOTING PEDESTRIAN AND BICYCLE MOBILITY

The implementation of the different parks and walks along the greenbelt increased demand for better accessibility from the city. In 2003 work began on the Urban Pathways Plan to guarantee an adequate connection of the city center and suburbs to the greenbelt parks. An entire network was designed by means of quality radial urban axes for pedestrian or cyclist mobility. All the planned paths are now available for use, but many await specific improvements. Each urban pathway also connects main urban areas such as plazas, parks, civic centers, sports facilities, and schools. These pathways lead to information points about the other sporting, leisure,

Figure 7.4 Only a twenty-minute walk from the city center, the Salburua wetlands have become a hotspot on bird migration routes, as several species choose this area to stop for shelter or even for breeding. Credit: Quintas.

environmental, and educational activities that can be pursued along the greenbelt.

These pathways complement a free bicycle-lending service, managed by the city council. The inauguration ceremony for this service in 2004 was attended by a large number of institutional representatives (e.g., the Minister for the Environment, the President of the Senate, the Mayor, the Delegate of the Basque government, the President of the Environmental Studies Center, the President of the Caja Vital Savings Bank), since it was the first system of its kind in Spain. This scheme has been very successful, with more than 50,000 users and around 155,000 uses in 2009 (425 uses per day). Users only have to show their ID card the first time at one of the seventeen lending points (civic centers, tourist offices, etc.) and enjoy for a few hours one of the three hundred bicycles available.

The great increase in bicycle users over recent years, together with the city–countryside connections demanded by the greenbelt users, have given impetus to the promotion of alternative forms of mobility (figure 7.5). As a result, a new Plan for Sustainable Mobility and Public Space was launched in 2006 in order to promote public transportation, to improve

Figure 7.5 The success of the Paseo de la Senda in connecting the city center with the countryside—today's greenbelt—has been a great reference for the new Plan for Sustainable Mobility. Credit: Quintas.

pedestrian accessibility and quality of urban spaces by reducing car use and presence on the streets, and to implement an ambitious network of bikeways and walkways of around 150 kilometers (91 kilometers are already in use today).

REASSESSING AGRICULTURAL ACTIVITIES AND PRESERVING RURAL LANDSCAPES

It was in 1997 when the Olarizu meadows and prairies were added to the greenbelt. The headquarters of CEA were placed in the rehabilitated "house of the meadows," which has become a focal point for educational activities on environmental and ecological issues, as well as an urban planning watchdog for the introduction of sustainable issues on decision making.

Another great project implemented in this area is the Environmental Park, known today as the Market Gardens (figure 7.6). The central activity of this park is ecological horticulture, with the intention of creating a place for people over fifty-five years old who are interested in growing healthy foods in a pleasant, social atmosphere.

More than one hundred vegetable gardens are in use in the Market Gardens, including a community garden in which users can develop their practical skills. The initiative became so popular that fifteen hectares of ecological horticulture facilities were added at the north of the city in the Zadorra River Park. Work began in 2006 designing a system with a capacity for 250 gardens to promote ecological agriculture to farmers of all ages. This project was 100% financed by the Izartu Program of the Basque government, with urban rehabilitation objectives and funds. The project has played an important role in connecting socially neighboring districts.

Another space of about fifteen hectares is being designed to promote ecological agriculture among young farmers on the adjoining land, property of the town hall. A more ambitious strategy will be designed to include quality agricultural spaces (agronomic or landscape) closer to the city, in order to make it possible to bring fresh food to urban consumers and familiarize city dwellers with the principles of ecological production.

INCREASING BIODIVERSITY AND BIOCAPACITY

The restoration of degraded areas has brought about a significant increase in biodiversity. In fact, this is one of the main reasons why most of these initially threatened areas are now protected. The aim of the INBIOS project (a Spanish program to improve local biodiversity) currently under way in the greenbelt is to increase the numbers of species in danger of

Figure 7.6 The Market Gardens of Vitoria-Gasteiz provide horticultural education and facilities, integrating agricultural activities right next to the city. Credit: CEA.

extinction and improve their habitats, such as through the reintroduction of the European mink.

A new project is also being implemented, designed as a showcase of European ecosystems. This includes a seedbed for the preservation of continental native species under the threat of extinction. The Olarizu Botanical Garden of European Threatened Woods is the only one of its kind in Spain and covers fifty hectares of land. Besides the conservation aims, these ecosystems will be used for education and for scientific research.

One of the goals of the restoration projects in the greenbelt is to encourage the participation of city dwellers in reforestation activities. The campaign "Adopt a Tree and Grow with It" began in 1996, and more than twelve thousand schoolchildren and hundreds of adults have planted more than forty thousand trees and bushes. The increase in the plant canopy favors biodiversity and mixed landscapes, but also works on climate and environmental regulation by increasing biocapacity rates.

CONDITIONING URBAN PLANNING AND DESIGN

Back in 1998, when the municipal government began to outline the criteria for revising the General Urban Development Plan, the greenbelt had just come into existence. The undoubted soundness of this project had provoked a great deal of debate about matters of significance for cities, such as compact development versus urban sprawl, building density and sustainability, alternatives for mobility, water management, and the city/country binomial.

The physical consolidation of the strategy was helped greatly by a photomontage of the proposed greenbelt that was posted everywhere, together with the external recognition and the social acceptance of the spaces that were under restoration. The greenbelt project began before the areas planned for new urban expansion were finally approved in 2003. Consequently, the spaces reserved as parks and corridors for ecological connectivity were incorporated as structural elements and key aspects of the new urban development. This has been possible thanks to the fact that a high percentage of the population has become familiar with the importance of urban ecology and ecological connectivity.

Providing Economic Benefits

Initially, this green icon generated some fear in the real estate sector, where it was seen as a corset around the city, a restriction on future urban growth. The economic benefits relating to ecological planning are widely recognized. The greenbelt has helped the image of the areas nearby, and it is clear that real estate promoters have improved their sales by taking advantage of the proximity of their new buildings to these natural spaces. In fact, the main urban developments to the west and east of the city bear the names of the parks of the greenbelt that preceded them: Zabalgana and Salburua, respectively. Other sectors, like the tourist industry, look on the greenbelt as a feature that attracts new visitors to the city.

But support from private investments has not yet become part of the strategy. Designing new methods of including them in stewardship initiatives or promoting private funds would be another way to achieve the goals of the greenbelt.

The Main Threats and the Issues on Hold

Most of the intense work was carried out during the first fifteen years of the greenbelt (1990–2005). During that time, several well-funded pressures threatened the greenbelt. These included shopping centers, theme parks, golf courses, luxury low-density residential areas, and gray infrastructure, all of them planned for development without considering ecological principles or sustainability.

But the most aggressive problems have cropped up during the last ten years. The rapid urbanization process has caused the city to double in size in just a few years. The last urban industrial expansion approved in 2003 involved a considerable increase in the amount of developed land (almost ten million square meters—increasing from 1,800 hectares in 1998 to 3,300 in 2009) and in the number of new houses (more than forty thousand), all in a compact city model that still resists the temptation to sprawl over its extensive neighboring agricultural lands. The need for these expansions has been questioned as the population grew only 8% during this period. It is a very critical situation now that we are in a housing recession.

Even with an Urban Plan that broadly accepts ecological viewpoints, it must be understood that the urban development processes are in themselves very traumatic in terms of ecological impact. Those parts of the greenbelt in direct contact with the new expansions that were not yet implemented, suffered from the conflict between different departments, especially Housing and Environment, and from a lack of understanding of the meaning of integrating ecological criteria in urbanization projects (figure 7.7).

Recent Urban Expansion and Ecological Connectivity in Practice

Studies of the most sensitive contact areas, mainly the fluvial connectors on the east and west sides of the city, identified the representative species and their primary characteristics. It is clear that however conscientious we may be in the development of the Urban Partial Plans, any longitudinal connecting spaces that we design may be very complicated for species as sensitive as the European mink.

The landscape studies performed on sensitive areas of contact attempted to emphasize the need for urban development projects to respect the philosophy of ecological connectivity and of public use. Unfortunately, experience tells us that the implementation of road infrastructure has much more political weight in urban design than do green ecological corridors.

Another example of phenomenon is the proposal for "extra-urban" growth in the south. The southern areas of the city of Vitoria-Gasteiz have always been coveted by urban development promoters because of their excellent strategic conditions: the quality of the existing urban development south of the railway line, in an environment with large sports facilities and the university buildings of the Alava campus of the University of the Basque Country on the one hand, and the nearness of the mountains of Vitoria on the other.

Figure 7.7 Fierce battles have been fought against urbanization processes during the most speculative decade in Spain's history. The greenbelt has been subjected to multiple pressures along its thirty-five-kilometer perimeter. Credit: CEA.

A few months following the approval of the Urban Plan, new private residential sectors were proposed, including a new bypass. Almost immediately, a new proposal came out to build 6,200 more homes in the same area, between the new road that had been designed outside the plan and the consolidated city. This area was classified as agricultural land and had a high risk of flooding.

It was then that it became necessary to work on new defensive strategies against threats to the ecological and functional connectivity between the greenbelt and the mountains of Vitoria. Emphasis was placed on the need to avoid flooding as well as on the ecological qualities of the space. After a great deal of debate during 2007, Mayor Alfonso Alonso made public the decision of the town hall: "The southern part of the city should be a large natural park." This political commitment has halted the urban stakeholders' expectations in sensitive areas. Today, this area of more than fifteen thousand hectares is in the process of being declared an official natural park by the Basque government.

After twenty years of working on the greenbelt strategy, we have come to call it a "history of pulses." Under this denomination, we underline two different viewpoints: a constantly growing pulse of life, as the different areas were being restored, connected with one another, and growing as a living system, on the one hand; and a constant battle between two opposing forces, the natural forces (always present, especially through the water system) and the forces of urbanization and transformation (always in search of new areas for expansion in natural and rural surroundings).

The greenbelt of Vitoria-Gasteiz, with its approximately thirty-five-kilometer perimeter, was and still is a source of permanent conflict between opposing interests. Although it may seem obvious, it is important to highlight this question. Conventional urban development and ecological connectivity are matters that, a priori, do not go well together in Spain. It is true that several exemplary actions have been developed in these areas at the edge of the city, but there is still a long way to go.

Among the one thousand hectares planned in the greenbelt project, almost 80% are already in use in 2011. The 20% that remain will need to allow real connections at those points where the parks are crossed by infrastructures. There are also still a number of streams and lakes to be included in the hydrological regulation plan for the city. The greenbelt is a living part of the city, evolving and changing, and the very next step will be for the implementation of a specific legal planning policy as a tool to preserve and guarantee its maintenance in the future as a green infrastructure.

The Greenbelt: From an Urban to a Regional Scale

The Potential for an Urban Green Infrastructure System

The greenbelt finds its full meaning when providing multifunctional solutions for the city, and it is time to expand its philosophy inward, toward the urban core. In agreement with the European Commission, urban green infrastructures will play a significant role in the coming decades to make cities more livable, more sustainable, and more resilient despite the global challenges we are facing.

The first steps have been taken in Vitoria-Gasteiz by extending the marketplaces of the greenbelt to community gardens in different neighborhoods, and by promoting nonmotorized mobility with the urban

pathways and the bike-lending system. Public participation in the reforestation of outlying parks could be extended to urban streets, avenues, and
plazas. Furthermore, research and proposals for an inner greenbelt are currently under way, directly promoted by the present mayor, Javier Maroto.
We believe citizens are ready for a new initiative, and the planning and
design of an urban green infrastructural system could kick off a new way
of looking for potential within the city.

Vacant spaces, brownfield sites, gray infrastructures, rooftops, "patios"
within blocks, new expansions on hold, and several more areas are waiting
for creative solutions that could introduce biodiversity and enrich urban
life with more complex and attractive urban spaces (figure 7.8). The combination of ecologically based planning, design, and management could
definitely bring about a change of scenario in the urban core and adapt the
real demand to a time of crisis.

Toward a Bioregional Green Infrastructure: The Ecological Network in Alava Province

The municipality of Vitoria-Gasteiz represents almost 10% of the land of
the province of Alava, and as the largest urban center (with 75% of the
population living here) it exerts a vital influence throughout the region.
The great success of the greenbelt strategy has been possible due to the
collaboration and coordination of major regional strategies that go hand in
hand with the conservation of the whole territory.

The greenbelt is part of a wider region, a living system that finds its
sources of sustenance in the greater natural and ecological systems. In order to keep a healthy greenbelt, connections with the main supplying areas
and natural corridors must be preserved. This is proving to be possible
thanks to several initiatives and strategies being implemented at a regional
level by the Provincial Council of Alava. The sharing of common conservation criteria and aims has helped to highlight and protect the value of
these landscapes.

REGIONAL THREATS: FRAGMENTATION AND DEVELOPMENT PROPOSALS

Intense debates have arisen over the last twenty years throughout the region about a large number of regional plans for the Basque Country and
the Alava province itself. Most of them include the capital and its municipality for their central and strategic position on the Paris-Madrid-
Lisbon communications corridor. Away from its natural inherited resources,

Figure 7.8 The greenbelt starts to enter the consolidated city in order to impregnate it with its values. There is great potential to increase urban biodiversity and biocapacity rates. Credit: Quintas.

many entrepreneurs see this territory as the "flat and vacant lands" of the Basque Country. They do not see the value of the land. Farmlands, which are currently without economic prospects for the future, are considered "utterly useless" in these policies. The review and critical analysis of many of these plans has helped us to propose more ecological planning schemes that go beyond the boundaries of the municipality.

THE CONSERVATION STRATEGY IN ALAVA: TOWARD A REAL ECOLOGICAL NETWORK

It is within this context that the Ecological Network thrives. It was considered at that time to be of vital interest to make a decided push toward more sustainable territorial planning, coherent with the propositions of the European Regional Strategy or with the initiatives promoted by the Council of Europe relating to the Pan-European Ecological Network and the European Landscape Convention. Thus a number of strategies were promoted by the Environment Department of the Provincial Council of Alava and by the Environmental Studies Center of Vitoria-Gasteiz for each of the targets. The goal was to include a detailed characterization of essential ecological elements, functions, and processes in the current plans and especially in any new developments, as well as to guarantee the conservation and restoration of key ecological systems, and curb in this way the loss of biodiversity and the progressive degradation of the landscape. Several protection levels have been implemented for this purpose (see table 7.1).

All of them target clear, long-lasting changes that allow a positive evaluation of their contribution to the general sustainability conditions, these being understood to represent an appreciable improvement in the living conditions of the population in their day-to-day life. Within this contribution, special attention should be given to the new legal frameworks developed that guarantee the network's applicability, validity, and stability in time.

Parallel to this and in the light of the excellent results obtained, new, complementary programs, plans, and projects have been added. All of these come within the same line of "regional valuation" in an area with extraordinary resources and potential, in order to aspire seriously to planning its future in terms of greater sustainability.

The Greenways Plan should be highlighted for its importance within this conservation strategy. This plan involves an extensive network of walkways and paths that crisscross the territory. Its aim is to cater to the

Table 7.1   Conservation strategy in Alava province

	1998	2011
Network of protected natural spaces	18,824 hectares	31,201 hectares
Natural parks	2	5
Protected biotopes	0	2
Singular trees	0	11
Ramsar wetlands	0	4
European Ecological Network Natura 2000	0 hectares	79,936 hectares
Special protected areas for birds	0	4
Sites of community importance	0	25
Catalogue of singular and outstanding landscapes	0 hectares	173,584 hectares
Singular landscapes	0	6
Outstanding landscapes	0	56
Ecological Corridors Network	0 hectares	88,000 hectares
Territorial protection areas in the regional plan	0 hectares	136,280 hectares
Green routes	36 km	1,100 km

walking or cycling activities so popular in our territory. The network has also been designed to connect and extend the urban pathways in Vitoria-Gasteiz and the walks along the greenbelt with the main rural settlements and the largest natural areas.

The paths that follow old railway tracks, traditional cattle migration trails, historical pilgrim routes like Saint James's Way, and several other ancient routes associated with cultural activities are being restored to complete and connect the historical heritage and inherited cultural values. New routes have also been added to the network, such as the one that runs around the reservoir, as they are given preferential treatment not only for the benefits to our health, but also for the contribution that these activities make to the conservation of our landscapes.

Today, there are numerous projects to enhance public accessibility to natural and cultural locations of interest, involving private entrepreneurs and community organizations. This network and a plan for its "defense" are in the pipeline. Specific protection and planning policies are being carried out for over 1,100 kilometers of nonmotorized routes.

Among all the aims included in this plan, we can find the contribution to satisfying the growing demand for places for expansion and leisure in contact with nature, on the one hand, and the reinforcement of the functional and identity links of the population with their region, especially of city dwellers. There is an underlying will to encourage our citizens to get involved in decision-making processes that affect the landscape through the promotion of information, education, and participative processes (figure 7.9).

Special importance is being placed on the largest green route included in the plan, as this connects the most beautiful landscapes that can be seen from the top of the mountains that surround the plains of Alava. The Shepherds' Route is an easy mountain itinerary of more than four hundred kilometers (66% of it goes through protected natural areas). As an interregional project, it is now being coordinated by the different Provincial Councils and with the economic support of the Spanish Ministry for the Environment for its implementation.

The International Union for Conservation of Nature has placed great importance on this conservation strategy, as it is understood that this is a "hinge area" for the ecological connectivity of two large mountain systems: the Cantabrian Mountains and the Pyrenees, which are included in their Mountain Corridor Initiative to connect these areas with the Massif Central and Western Alps. The province of Alava joined this initiative in 2005, understanding the importance of social and ecological connectivity.

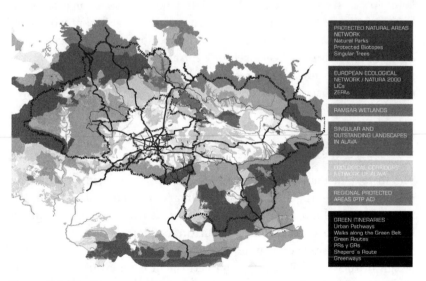

Figure 7.9 The Greenways Network constitutes an essential tool in the conservation strategy toward territorial defense and social valorization. Credit: CEA.

The Upland Ring: A Great New Icon for the Bioregional Conservation Strategy

Under the title "Upland Ring and Functional Ecological Network," the work done in the bioregion of Central Alava was selected as a Good Sustainability Practice and awarded with the highest score to represent Spain at the international competition held by UN-HABITAT in 2010. This assessment as best Spanish practice in "sustainable management of natural resources, the relationship between the city and the natural environment, and sustainable regional development" is a fitting tribute to the important and commendable work of the Provincial Council over the last fifteen years.

Natural and cultural heritage, intangible and identity values, come together and intermingle in the Upland Ring. Each one of the parts of this harmonious ensemble is of great intrinsic value, but it is the overall, global vision that allows us to see its true worth: cultural and historical landscapes, splendid nature, ethnography, ancient traditions, and customs come together in a combination that might well become a UNESCO Biosphere Reserve one day.

As a territorial matrix that guarantees the survival and health of biological processes and cycles, the Upland Ring may be used as an example to help us imagine a functional region in which sustainability proposals are ambitious and carried out in a serious and credible manner. The ecological planning strategies developed in Central Alava may therefore represent the first step toward a bioregion model for innovation and good urban and territorial sustainability practices. The territorial planning of the area around Vitoria-Gasteiz cannot but recognize such a palpable reality.

Conclusion: Toward a Desirable Future

The history of the greenbelt is a story not only of diligent, painstaking care but also of struggle. In almost a military sense, it could be said that it has been developed with a strategic need to keep on moving forward, in both time and space, to stay ahead of urban transformations.

Taking landscape ecology principles into account in the planning and design of the greenbelt has given a permanent counterthrust to regular urban planning. The greenbelt is indeed a physical reality today, but it is also "a way of doing things." This fragile peri-urban system and the city are still two different realities that do indeed coexist and should be directly integrated. We believe that this should be a desirable and feasible step toward making real progress. It would be perfectly possible for the greenbelt to be consolidated as an integrated system in the ecological network of its bioregion, from where it is "sustained."

On the other hand, a healthy greenbelt, as a regulator of the essential processes for the life of sensible species in harmony with responsible public use, is already an enormous heritage, enriching urban resilience and improving the quality of life of city dwellers. This vital system should move into the urban core, enriching it with the most valuable function: life in its diversity. This means going back to its own essence, to the principles that inspired the strategy of the greenbelt: landscape ecology, social integration, balanced land use distribution, and, above all, full awareness and respect for our region, the rural landscape where we all come from and which we all need, today perhaps more than ever.

References

Andrés Orive, Luis. 2003. "City-nature relationships: Towards more sustainable territorial planning models in Vitoria-Gasteiz," at the *Kennedy Lectures: Planning and Design for Sustainable Urbanism*. SUNY-ESF, Syracuse.

———. 2007. "Relaciones ciudad-naturaleza: Hacia modelos de planificación territorial más sostenibles en Vitoria-Gasteiz." In Agustín Hernández Aja, ed., *Arquitectura del siglo XXI: Más allá de Kioto: Jornadas IAU+S 2006*. Ediciones Mairea, Madrid.

CEA. 2001–2010. *Vitoria-Gasteiz Agenda 21*. Available at http://www.vitoria-gasteiz.org/ceac/.

———. 2003. *Anillo Verde Vitoria-Gasteiz Eraztun Berdea Vida Bizitza*. City Council of Vitoria-Gasteiz.

———. 2004. *Salburua, agua y vida*. City Council of Vitoria-Gasteiz.

———. 2009. *2nd Urban Landscape Forum: Green Cities*. City Council of Vitoria-Gasteiz. Available at http://www.vitoria-gasteiz.org/ceac/.

City Council of Vitoria-Gasteiz. 2010. *European Green Capital Award 2012–2013: Vitoria-Gasteiz*. Candidature application for the European Commission Contest. Available at http://ec.europa.eu/.

City Council of Vitoria-Gasteiz and Agencia de Ecologia Urbana de Barcelona. 2007. *Avance del Plan de Movilidad Sostenible y Espacio Público en Vitoria-Gasteiz*.

Dios Lema, Rebeca. 2006. *Greenways Network in Vitoria-Gasteiz and Alava*. CEA, presented at the World Urban Forum III, Vancouver.

———. 2008. *Propuesta de implantación de una red primaria de vías verdes en Vitoria-Gasteiz: Una estrategia territorial*. CEA, Vitoria-Gasteiz. Available at http://www.vitoria-gasteiz.org/ceac/.

Environment Department of the Provincial Council of Alava. 2010. *Upland Ring and*

Ecological Functional Network in Central Alava. Alava candidature for the UN-HABITAT 8th Dubai International Contest for Good Practices.

GEA21. 2010. *GEO Vitoria-Gasteiz: Informe-diagnóstico ambiental y de sostenibilidad del municipio de Vitoria-Gasteiz.* City Council of Vitoria-Gasteiz. Available at http://www.vitoria-gasteiz.org/ceac/.

López de Lucio, Ramón. 2004. *Condicionantes, bases y directrices para la ordenación urbanística y la puesta en valor de los recursos naturales en la zona sur de la ciudad de Vitoria-Gasteiz.* CEA, Vitoria-Gasteiz. Available at http://www.vitoria-gasteiz.org/ceac/.

Mallarach, J. M., et al. 2004. *Análisis y diagnóstico de la conectividad ecológica y paisajística del sector sur del Anillo Verde de Vitoria-Gasteiz.* CEA, City Council of Vitoria-Gasteiz. Available at http://www.vitoria-gasteiz.org/ceac/.

———. 2005. *Catálogo de Paisajes Singulares y Sobresalientes del Territorio Histórico de Álava.* Provincial Council of Alava, Vitoria-Gasteiz.

8

London, England: A Global and Sustainable Capital City

Camilla Ween

City Background and Context

A History of Immigration and Change

London is an ancient and complex city with layers of history. The Romans founded the city shortly after the invasion of England in A.D. 43. They built a bridge over the River Thames and created Londinium on the northern banks of the river. This was a small fortified city of some 350 acres, and remains of the Roman walls are still standing.

The city has seen immigration from Europe probably continuously since the Romans, including the Saxons, the French (the Norman Conquest in 1066), waves of Huguenots, then Jews, and in the 20th century Afro-Caribbean and Asian populations, followed more recently by eastern Europeans after the expansion of the European Union. This has led to London becoming one of the most diverse and multicultural capital cities in the world with over 250 languages spoken.

The physical fabric of the city evolved often in response to dramatic events. The Great Fire of London in 1666 destroyed some thirteen thousand houses and eighty-seven churches, leaving ninety thousand people homeless. The houses were built of timber and were tightly configured within the medieval street pattern, hence the fire spread with devastating effect. The subsequent fear of fire led to expansion outside the walled city, and timber buildings gave way to brick and stone. Widespread destruction occurred again as a result of the bombing during World War II; this memory is now subtly evoked where the rhythm of London's long streets of identical houses is interrupted by postwar infill. It is a dynamic and ever changing city.

The steady expansion beyond the boundaries of the original walled city continued until the 1930s, extending London over an area of 610 square miles. The 1938 Green Belt Act was established to protect the countryside at the edges of the city and put a stop to further suburban sprawl by creating a green cordon around London. Development within the greenbelt is very restrictive, and any proposals must demonstrate a real benefit that outweighs the loss of greenbelt land. As a result, much of Outer London remains a patchwork of countryside and small villages.

Already in Victorian times it was recognized that London needed coordination of strategic functions, and an ambitious municipal authority was established in 1889, the London County Council (LCC). It was an elected body with wide-ranging powers for education, housing, transport, fire, and flood, to name but a few. The LCC built social housing that survives today. It was replaced in 1965 by the Greater London Council (GLC), which was given a larger geographical authority. This body was also elected, and its most famous leader was Ken Livingstone. In the 1980s, however, the Labour-controlled GLC, headed by Livingstone, was so at odds with the Conservative government of Margaret Thatcher that she resolved to deal with the opposition by simply abolishing London's right to local decision making. From 1986 to 2000, London was without any strategic government. This meant that there was no effective coordination of development, with each of the thirty-three London boroughs making planning decisions without a view to London's growth as a whole. There was ineffective transport planning, and public transport investment was severely cut. There was no consistency in transport and local highway projects across borough boundaries, and pedestrian improvements and cycle lane projects regularly ended in the middle of a street, if this happened to be a borough boundary. Any strategic decisions were taken by the central government.

In 1999 the Greater London Authority Act devolved powers to run London from the central government to an elected mayor and the Greater London Assembly. This led to the establishment of the Greater London Authority (GLA). In 2000 Ken Livingstone was elected back to run London, this time as its first mayor (he served two terms), and was succeeded by Boris Johnson in 2008.

Physical Characteristics

London is bisected by the River Thames and is distributed more or less equally north and south of it. The Thames is a powerful body of water and is tidal within most of the London area, with the spring tides rising on average twenty-two feet at London Bridge. Tidal surges, which used to cause periodic and severe flooding, are now controlled by the Thames Barrier (opened in 1984), which can be raised to cut off the advance of the North Sea tide. The river creates a dynamic and ever changing landscape that is the focus for much of the city. Some thirty road, rail, and footbridges cross the Thames within London, reflecting evolving architectural styles and contributing to local character.

One of London's distinctive qualities is that it has evolved from hundreds of small villages and town centers, which still form the focus for community and local economies. It has an exceptionally high proportion of open space (46%),[1] ranging from vast former Royal Parks and hunting grounds, "commons" that are historically owned by "the people," and town squares that were part of the rich legacy of urban development in the 18th and 19th centuries (see figure 8.1).

Transport has, through the ages, also stamped its mark on London, leaving a unique heritage. Many Roman roads remain and are recognizable today, as they are generally very long and straight. The Industrial Revolution produced a network of canals. The Victorian era saw the construction of a vast network of railways radiating out of London from numerous terminal stations. The 1944 Abercrombie plan for London started a strategic highway network, which was implemented in small sections and has left a legacy of odd, disconnected flyovers and underpasses.

The weather is temperate, and though London has a reputation for being rainy, its annual rainfall is only twenty-three inches (Rome's is thirty-three inches). Rain tends to be light drizzle, which means that travel is not particularly affected by weather and it is possible to cycle and walk year-round.

London represents 19% of the UK's GDP and 15% of total UK employment, though it only has 12% of the UK population.[2] Its involvement in the world capital markets is matched only by New York and Tokyo, but the vast majority of businesses are small- to medium-sized, and over 70% of London's employment is private sector–based, with only 17% in the public sector. Manufacturing jobs have dramatically declined since the

Figure 8.1 It is not difficult to find tranquil open space in central London, such as this popular spot in Holland Park. Despite the fact that London has abundant open space, the London Plan seeks to add to this by ensuring new development proposals include open space within their plans to meet the needs of a growing population. Credit: Camilla Ween.

1970s. Tourism and cultural heritage are an important part of London's economy; the city attracts more than twenty-five million tourists a year who spent £16.6 billion in 2009 alone.[3] It is expected that there will be 750,000 more jobs created over the next twenty years. Despite London's economic strength, the city has pockets of deprivation and some of the most disadvantaged communities in the entire UK.

London interestingly saw its population fall because of postwar decentralization, and in 1988 it dropped to a low of 6.7 million. Since then it has steadily grown, standing at 7.8 million in 2009,[4] and it is expected to rise to about 8.9 million by 2031, with the population becoming increasingly younger, but also with the proportion of older people increasing.

Density varies from high in the central area to predominantly low in Outer London. The city is primarily low-rise, with high-rise buildings concentrated mainly in the City of London and Canary Wharf financial districts. Interestingly, however, the Royal Borough of Kensington and Chelsea in central London, which has few buildings higher than eight stories, has a density of 131 people per hectare,[5] higher than the average density of New York City at 102 people per hectare.[6]

Travel

Catering to the city's travel demands is one of London's greatest challenges. In 2007 the total number of journeys on an average day in, to, and from London was almost twenty-four million;[7] this is expected to rise to thirty-one million journeys per day by 2025. About one million people enter London every day. The rail network expects 20%–30% growth by 2030. The London Underground carries 3.5 million passenger journeys per day, which equates to 1 billion per annum. Every weekday about 5.4 million journeys are made on London's buses.

To cater the growing demand, transport capacity will need to be enhanced wherever possible, but a strong emphasis for the future will be on travel demand management, promoting smart travel, walking, and cycling, and reducing personal travel by car.

Traffic congestion was so severe in 2000 that the first London mayor, Ken Livingstone, immediately embarked on the design and implementation of the London congestion charging scheme, aimed at reducing highway congestion. This initiative is described in more detail below.

Key Elements of London's Green City Practice

Ecological Footprint

How cities sustain themselves as access to resources beyond their own boundaries diminishes is one of the greatest challenges for the future. In the mid-1990s Herbert Girardet estimated that London's ecological footprint (the area of land required to sustain all its activities) was 125 times the size of the city itself. A study titled City Limits[8] estimated that in the year 2000 Londoners consumed forty-nine million tons of materials (6.1 tons each) and 154,407 MWh of energy, and produced forty-one million tons of CO_2. Less than 1% of London's energy came from renewable sources. Londoners consumed 6.9 million tons of food, 81% of which came from outside the UK, and 866 billion liters of water, of which 28% was leakage. London produced over twenty-six million tons of waste, of which 71% went to landfill and only 9% was recycled. Sixty-nine percent of passenger miles were by car.

This translates to an ecological footprint for London 42 times its biocapacity and 293 times its geographical area (roughly twice the size of the UK). London's spatial development strategy, the London Plan (detailed below), aims to change the city's dependence on distant resources and establish London as a sustainable city. It is a broad development strategy and spatial development plan, which outlines ways to accommodate London's growth sustainably within its boundaries.

Planning Policy: The London Plan

In the United Kingdom there is a clear and consistent hierarchy of legislation. Overarching policy direction is set by the European Union. National planning policy is high level and must be in conformity with the EU, and regional policy (such as the London Plan) must be in conformity with national policy. At the most local level within London, each of the thirty-three boroughs must have local development plans (called Local Development Frameworks) that must be "in general conformity" with the London Plan.

Creating a strong policy context for growth is central to London's sustainability approach. The Greater London Authority Act (1999) requires the GLA to produce, and keep under review, a spatial development strategy for London, known as the London Plan. It should be an overall strategic plan, setting out an integrated economic, environmental, transport, and social framework for the development of London over the next twenty-five years. The act of Parliament requires that the London Plan take account of three cross-cutting themes; economic development and wealth creation, social development (including crime prevention), and improvement of the environment. The preparation of the plan requires an Integrated Impact Assessment, which includes the legal requirements to carry out a Sustainability Appraisal (this includes a Strategic Environmental Assessment and a Habitats Regulation Assessment), and to ensure that health, equality, and community safety are properly handled. Prior to a plan being adopted, it is subjected to an examination in public, led by an independent panel, which scrutinizes the document and reviews comments from interested citizens. This process is intended to enable public participation in the plan's preparation, and reflects the principles in the EU Aarhus Convention on access to information, public participation, and access to justice in environmental matters. The panel recommends changes that the mayor can consider when finalizing the plan, which is then submitted to the Government Office for London, where ministers decide whether to instruct any further changes prior to the plan being formally adopted.

The first London Plan was published in 2004 and revised in 2008. The current London Plan, which sets out the policy to 2031, was adopted in 2011. It is a comprehensive suite of interrelated policies to support Mayor Boris Johnson's vision for London: "London should: Excel among global cities—expanding opportunities for all its people and enterprises, achieving the highest environmental standards and quality of life and leading the world in its approach to tackling the urban challenges of the 21st century, particularly that of climate change."

The plan sets out to ensure that development is sustainable and that climate change is tackled. It seeks to protect London's natural resources, environmental and cultural assets, the health of its people, and to adapt to and mitigate the effect of climate change. These are covered in six key objectives, ensuring that London is

- a city that meets the challenges of economic and population growth in ways that ensure a sustainable and improving quality of life for all Londoners, and helps tackle the huge issue of inequality among Londoners, including inequality in health;
- an internationally competitive and successful city, with a strong and diverse economy and an entrepreneurial spirit that benefits all Londoners and all parts of London; a city that is at the leading edge of innovation and research; and that is comfortable with—and makes the most of—its rich heritage and cultural resources;
- a city of diverse, strong, secure, and accessible neighborhoods to which Londoners feel attached, which provides all its residents, workers, visitors, and students—whatever their origin, background, age, or status—with opportunities to realize and express their potential, and a high-quality environment for individuals to enjoy, to live in together, and to thrive in;
- a city that delights the senses and takes care of its buildings and streets, having the best of modern architecture while also making the most of London's built heritage, and which makes the most of and extends its wealth of open and green spaces and waterways, realizing its potential for improving Londoners' health, welfare, and development.
- a city that becomes a world leader in improving the environment locally and globally, taking the lead in tackling climate change, reducing pollution, developing a low-carbon economy, and consuming fewer resources and using them more effectively;

- a city where it is easy, safe, and convenient for everyone to access jobs, opportunities, and facilities with an efficient and effective transport system that actively encourages more walking and cycling, makes better use of the Thames, and supports delivery of all the objectives of this plan.

London's Places

Mayor Boris Johnson's vision and objectives will help to create a city that comprises strong neighborhoods and delightful spaces (figure 8.2). The planning system will ensure that new development is designed to be integrated, to ensure community diversity and cohesion, to meet the needs of people at all stages of life, and to provide a sense of place and security. New development should build on existing character or bring new identity where it is lacking. There is an emphasis on high-quality architecture that supports an attractive and legible public realm, streetscape, and wider cityscape. There is guidance on the location and design of tall buildings and the preservation of heritage assets and archaeology. The mayor has designated a list of strategic views in the London View Management Framework, which identifies particular views to be protected.

New development must be and feel safe and secure. This means that new development must be resilient against emergencies, including fire, flood, weather, and terrorism, and local authorities are expected to provide for the spatial aspects of London's emergency plans. All policies of the plan will be implemented in order to reduce noise and support the objectives of the Mayor's Ambient Noise Strategy.

The greenbelt, the "no-development zone" that encircles London, is given the strongest protection, and inappropriate development will be refused. Designated open space within the city, known as Metropolitan Open Land (MOL), is given the same level of protection as greenbelt land, and development that encroaches on the land will not be permitted. Also, the extension of MOL in appropriate circumstances will be supported. Local authorities are encouraged to establish clear strategies for the protection, promotion, and management of biodiversity, geodiversity, and access to nature. Trees and woodland will be protected and enhanced, following the guidance in the London Tree and Woodland Framework, and local authorities will be required to develop local Tree Strategies, linked to their local Open Space Strategies. Food production within the city is encouraged, particularly in the greenbelt, but also close to urban centers. Local authorities

Figure 8.2 This lush canopy over a strategic artery in West London is not atypical, but despite this the mayor has committed to an extensive tree-planting campaign. Credit: Camilla Ween.

should protect existing facilities, such as allotments (leased land for growing vegetables), and identify spaces for the development of community gardens and the productive use of green roof space.

Rivers, canals, ponds, and water reservoirs are being strategically linked through the Blue Ribbon Network. Uses of the water space and land alongside it will be prioritized for water-related purposes, particularly passenger and freight transport and recreation. There is an emphasis on restoring unused and silted-up culverts and increasing habitat value. The River Thames is an iconic feature of London that is protected, and development alongside it requires a Thames Policy Area appraisal.

Supporting the London Plan is a suite of Supplementary Planning Guidance and Best Practice Guides, which provide specific guidance for development proposals. These cover a range of topics, including play space for young people; accessibility; industrial capacity; housing; sustainable design and construction; view management; land for transport functions; equity and diversity; health issues; management of the nighttime economy; biodiversity; use of open space; and better use of supermarket sites.

A recently published supplementary document is Mayor Johnson's Air Quality Strategy. This sets out innovative measures to reduce emissions from road transport (more on that below), and in a radical step toward

making the built environment more sustainable, there are new requirements to ensure there are no negative impacts on air quality from future
developments, requiring them to be air quality–neutral or better. Meeting
these requirements is likely to prove challenging but is seen as important
to realizing sustainable growth and economic development.

The 2011 plan puts greater emphasis on collaborative work with local
authorities that neighbor London as well as those in the London boroughs,
particularly to integrate London into the wider region of southeastern
England. To support London's position as a world city and the economic
engine of the UK, the mayor is committing to collaborate with neighboring authorities to develop wider policies that will support the whole region, particularly in areas of commuting, air travel, skills and education,
managing resources, and handling waste. The mayor will work with neighbors beyond London to develop nationally recognized growth corridors
(where they include part of London), and develop complementary strategies that tackle population and economic growth, infrastructure, and climate change.

The 2012 Olympic Park area of East London is singled out as the most
important regeneration project in the city for the next twenty-five years.
The promised "Olympic Legacy" is to revitalize this low-income area to
provide a new, vibrant, mixed-use district of London with affordable housing, a new media and creative industry cluster, excellent social, leisure,
and open space infrastructure, and exemplary transport links. An Olympic
Park Legacy Company has been established to ensure that this promise is
delivered. Completion of the project will arguably establish the London
Olympics as the most sustainable Olympic games and a model regeneration project.

Within the London Plan, the city is divided into five subregions, which
reflect patterns of working and a subregional character. Further, there is
a concentric subdivision into Outer London, Inner London, and the Central Activities Zone, each of which have strategic priorities. These subdivi-
sions will assist in prioritizing infrastructure development and transport
projects.

The mayor is producing Opportunity Area Planning Frameworks,
which set out high-level planning guidance and development principles
for areas identified in the plan as Opportunity Areas and Areas for Intensification. At the smaller scale, he is encouraging boroughs to identify
Regeneration Areas, where they will promote local quality, economic activity, and social cohesion. London has many town centers, which have

concentrations of commercial activity and are the main focus for commerce outside the Central Activities Zone. In the town centers, the London Plan seeks to strengthen diversity and choice of goods and to facilitate local travel, particularly through good public transport and walking and cycling infrastructure, and to maintain distinctive character and sense of place.

London is well endowed with open space, but it is recognized that with a growing population this needs enhancement. A Strategic Network of Open Spaces is encouraged both to add where there is deficiency and to improve access, linkages, and quality; developers are encouraged to contribute to this through the planning process. The Key Diagram summarizes how all these strategies link together (figure 8.3).

London's People

This chapter of the plan addresses personal well-being, housing, health, and quality of life. Housing is covered in depth to ensure that supply keeps up with demand, that there is sufficient affordable housing, that a wide

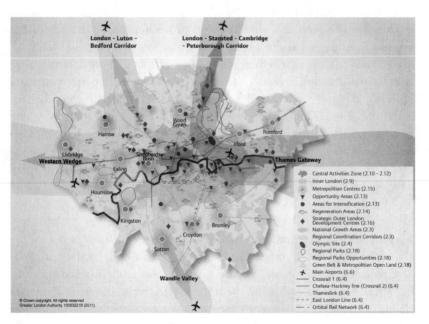

Figure 8.3 The London Plan Key Diagram identifies the main priority areas for growth as well as predicted growth corridors that extend outside of London. © Crown, 2011. All rights reserved. Greater London Authority.

mix of housing types are provided to meet the needs of diverse communities, and that architectural quality is high. The provision of student accommodation, children's play space, and the needs of gypsies and travelers are also specifically addressed. Social infrastructure to support the growing population, such as health care, schools, and sports facilities, is highlighted, and new development proposals will need to include social infrastructure sufficient to support the enlarged community.

London's Economy

The goal is to promote an increasingly diverse economy, to drive the transition to a low-carbon economy, to promote Outer London as a location for business, to support the distinctive central London specialist clusters, to tackle central London deprivation, to encourage enterprise and innovation, and to promote London as a location for European and international agencies and businesses.

For retail, commercial, and leisure development in town centers, the mayor supports an approach of assessing need and location in terms of how they relate to the size, role, and function of a town center and its catchment. The emphasis should be on providing these facilities within the town center, and at the edges of centers only if they can be well integrated with the existing center and public transport. There is strong support for maintaining diversity of choice, convenience shopping, provision of local goods and services, and farmer's markets, which will strengthen local neighborhoods and character and minimize travel miles for goods and consumers. The key objective is to reduce car dependency and improve public transport, cycling, and walking access. There is support for the provision of small affordable shop units to be delivered alongside large retail development.

London's Response to Climate Change

Mayor Johnson is committed to making London a world leader in tackling climate change and in improving the environment both locally and globally, reducing pollution, developing a low-carbon economy, and consuming fewer resources and using them more effectively. In terms of climate change mitigation, the mayor's target is an overall reduction of 60% of London's CO_2 emissions by 2025 (below 1990 levels). The planning process will be used to ensure that new development will minimize CO_2 emissions by using less energy, supplying energy efficiently, and through the use of renewable energy. In line with national legislation, the target for all new development is to achieve zero-carbon residential buildings by 2016 and zero-carbon nonresidential buildings by 2019. Major development proposals will need to include a detailed energy assessment to demonstrate how the targets for CO_2 emissions reduction are to be met.

The mayor will seek to achieve the highest standards of sustainable design and construction to improve the environmental performance of new development. His supplementary planning guidance standards, Sustainable Design and Construction, set out the need to minimize CO_2 and include measures to achieve key sustainability principles, such as avoiding the urban heat island effect; efficient use of natural resources; avoiding noise, air, and urban runoff pollution; minimizing waste; maximizing reuse and recycling; preventing the impact of flood; avoiding the creation of adverse local climatic conditions; sustainable procurement of materials and use of local supplies where feasible; and promoting and protecting biodiversity and green infrastructure. In their design and access statements, development proposals will need to demonstrate how they meet these standards.

The mayor has set a target of 25% of heat and power used in London to be generated using local decentralized energy systems by 2025. This will be achieved through prioritizing the development of decentralized heating and cooling networks and large-scale heat transmission networks. A London Heat Map tool has been created to assist developers in identifying energy opportunities in particular areas, such as major energy consumers, fuel consumption and CO_2 emissions, energy supply plants, community heating networks, and heat density. The intention is to encourage collaboration between development and industry to explore energy-efficient solutions. Local authorities are encouraged to develop energy master plans; for example, if there is waste heat from industry or waste processing, then this can be captured to supply hot water for heating buildings. Development proposals are expected to evaluate the feasibility of inclusion of combined heat and power (CHP) systems and, where appropriate, consider extending these to adjacent sites.

The mayor is also seeking to increase the proportion of energy generated from renewable sources, and has set targets for this increase over the life of the London Plan. Furthermore he is considering the more widespread use of innovative energy technologies to reduce use of fossil fuels and CO_2 emissions, and will seek to promote the uptake of electric and hydrogen fuel cell vehicles, plan hydrogen supply and distribution infrastructure, and maximize the uptake of advanced conversion technologies such as anaerobic digestion, gasification, and pyrolysis for the treatment of waste.

Adaptation to climate change is covered in detail in the plan. A key goal is to reduce the impact of the urban heat island effect, and to ensure that the design of new development avoids overheating and excessive heat generation through measures such as energy efficiency, reducing heat gain and absorption, passive ventilation, and active cooling systems. Demonstration of how this is achieved will be required as part of the planning process.

The mayor will promote and support urban greening, such as new planting in the public realm and green infrastructure. In the Central Activities Zone, the target is to increase the amount of surface area greened by at least 5% by 2030 and a further 5% by 2050. Development proposals will be expected to include measures such as green roofs and walls, tree planting, and soft landscaping.

The mayor will work to protect and improve water quality and ensure that London has adequate sewage infrastructure. Consideration of flooding, buildings within flood zones, and the impact of flood on drainage systems are covered in some detail. Rainwater runoff will have to be managed, and all new development will be required to control surface runoff and will not be allowed to negatively affect London's rivers and waterways. Improvements to London's sewage treatment capacity will be encouraged, using the best technologies. The mayor is supporting minimizing the use of water, promoting the provision of additional sustainable water resources, and promoting rainwater harvesting.

Improved waste management is encouraged, including dealing with hazardous waste, with a target of zero waste to landfill by 2031. This will be achieved by minimizing waste, encouraging reuse, and increasing recycling levels to 60% by 2031. The city's processing and waste capacity will have to be increased, including providing construction, excavation, and demolition waste-management facilities. The plan includes a policy to ensure sufficient aggregates for the construction industry and encouragement for contaminated land to be brought to beneficial use.

London's Transport

An important early policy document was the Mayor's Transport Strategy, published by Mayor Livingstone in 2001, which set an agenda for transport priorities and improvements. Shifting more journeys away from cars and toward public transport, walking, and cycling was the main aim. Tackling congestion in central London was a key aspiration, which led to the congestion charge scheme and the policy of restricting car parking in new development. Bus travel was given high priority; bus services were enhanced and miles of bus lanes were created to improve journey time and predictability. Cycling was encouraged, and as a result all new development must now provide sufficient cycle parking. Walking was promoted through a range of initiatives to improve the public realm, sidewalks, and small urban spaces, and by identifying barriers to walking when new development was being proposed. Mayor Johnson produced a new Mayor's Transport Strategy in 2010, which has a travel horizon of 2031.

It is recognized that transport is central to the achievement of all the London Plan's objectives, but the transport section is intended specifically to meet the mayor's objective to create "a city where it is easy, safe and convenient for everyone to access jobs, opportunities and facilities with an efficient and effective transport system which actively encourages more walking and cycling and makes better use of the Thames, and supports delivery of all the objectives of this Plan," and to ensure that transport and development are properly integrated.

The Mayor's Transport Strategy supports the London Plan and sets out six thematic goals:

- supporting economic development and population growth;
- enhancing the quality of life of all Londoners;
- improving the safety and security of Londoners;
- improving transport opportunities for all Londoners;
- improving the resilience of transport and reducing its contribution to climate change;
- supporting delivery of the London 2012 Olympic and Paralympic Games and its legacy.

The strategic approach is to encourage patterns of development that reduce the need to travel, especially by car, through restrictive car parking provisions; to improve both the capacity and accessibility of public transport, walking, and cycling (by ensuring sufficient cycle parking facilities); to promote development that generates high levels of trips in areas with good public transport accessibility (or which have future planned transport infrastructure); to improve interchange between modes of transport; to increase the use of transport by water for passengers and freight; to facilitate the efficient distribution of freight and minimize its effects on the transport network; to support a shift to more sustainable modes through travel demand management; to promote greater use of low-carbon technology to reduce the overall impact of transport on global warming; and to promote an increase in walking by improving the quality of the urban realm.

Funding, mainly from the central government, has been secured in recent years to implement a range of new transport initiatives by 2031, including upgrading the Underground network, and building Crossrail, a new cross-London, high-speed and -capacity rail link (see page 199). The old and often disused rail network within London is being modernized and linked up to provide efficient orbital rail services. Sustainable (non–car based) access to airports, ports, and the international rail termini will also be improved.

Though the current mayor, Boris Johnson, recognizes the importance of air travel to London in maintaining its position in a global economy, he is opposed to further expansion of London's main airport, Heathrow, due to the adverse noise- and air-quality impacts on residents under the flight paths. He is also particularly supportive of cycling, and his target is to increase the percentage of journeys by cycle to 5% by 2026 (from the current level of 2%) by building a network of Cycle Superhighways (strategic cycle routes) and the London Cycle Hire (bike share) scheme. He also aims to significantly increase the number of journeys that are made on foot by ensuring that the quality of the urban realm and the street environment is conducive to walking, by implementing a network of strategic walking routes and expansion of the Legible London way-finding scheme (see page 201).

Mayor Johnson is also committed to tackling traffic congestion by "smoothing traffic" through a number of demand-management initiatives to reduce vehicle journeys and by evening out traffic flows. If these measures are not successful, however, he has not ruled out considering road-user charging as a management tool (more on page 198). The London Plan seeks to prevent excessive car parking within new development by setting maximum car parking standards, while ensuring parking for disabled people and the provision of charging points for electric vehicles and recommending car-free development in locations with high public transport accessibility.

The mayor is committed to improving freight distribution within London and limiting its impact on highway congestion. Much freight activity is not actually destined for London but simply passes through the city, and there is a commitment to develop corridors to bypass London, especially for rail freight. There will be an emphasis on managing local freight, establishing freight consolidation centers, and supporting a modal shift to rail.

Examples of Policy in Action

Decentralized Energy

To reduce the carbon load of the power sector, London has been exploring options for decentralizing its energy supply, such as generating energy closer to the point of use. Traditional energy sources waste energy in production (through excess heat) and delivery (through loss). Fossil fuel power plants are estimated to waste 70% of the primary energy in the fuel. The plan is to capture and use surplus energy, such as heat from advanced waste conversion technology, anaerobic digestion of organic waste and sewage, local energy production processes, and biomass boilers.

The former London Development Agency, in partnership with local authorities and other agencies, has developed a groundbreaking district heating project in the Thames Gateway, Europe's largest urban regeneration region. The London Thames Gateway Heat Network will be a hot water transmission network that will connect sources of low/zero-carbon heat to existing and new developments. The first phases of the heat network are being planned around the Royal Docks and are due to open in 2012. The pilot phase is to supply 4,500 MWh of heat in the first year from existing industrial energy sources. The follow-on phase, when complete in 2014, will supply an additional 16,500 MWh of heat each year to existing and future planned development.

The pilot and first stage will together save more than two thousand tons of CO_2 emissions each year. The vision is that ultimately many areas within London will be connected to local district heating networks, using low/zero-carbon heat from a number of differing sources.

Transport

Transport for London (TfL) was established in 2000 as part of the newly formed GLA. It was created as the single functional body responsible for all public transport and strategic highways in London, including taxi and river services.[9] All the public transport services were to be properly integrated into a seamless and coordinated network; that meant linking modes wherever possible through convenient interchanges to facilitate transfer from mode to mode, as well as considering easy access for walkers, cyclists, or those arriving by taxi. TfL is responsible for the strategic highway network but also oversees the road network as a whole, and the London Traffic Control Center is responsible for the six thousand traffic signals in London.[10] As many of the roads carry buses, ensuring that they can get through traffic is an essential aspect of improving bus journey reliability. TfL is also responsible for planning future transport to meet anticipated growth in demand.

TfL has had to consider both subtle and radical measures to ensure adequate capacity is provided on both public transport and roads. Central to this is ensuring a shift away from private car use to public transport, walking, and cycling. The focus is therefore on not only the provision of new public transport infrastructure, but also extensive travel demand management initiatives to encourage more sustainable travel options.

An important improvement made by TfL was to simplify fares and to have a standard means of paying for services across the network. TfL introduced the Oyster card (a smart card) that allows passengers to move from mode to mode with ease. Multiple journeys in a single day are automatically charged at the cheapest rate. The advantage is that this system significantly speeds up the boarding process, thus improving journey times.

ROAD TRAVEL

Despite the extensive public transport network in London, there are twenty-one million journeys on London's 18,500-mile road network every day. In 2000 the level of traffic in central London was so high that average speeds were reputed to be slower than in Victorian times, about 5 mph. Mayor Ken Livingstone decided that bold and decisive action had to be taken to reduce the number of cars traveling in central London. He believed there was only one way to achieve this—through pricing for the privilege of driving into the city center. In 2003 a zone was created within which all vehicles (with the exception of public transport, taxis, police and ambulance vehicles, and a few special categories) would have to pay a daily charge of five pounds. The scheme was based on identifying vehicles by cameras, using automatic number plate recognition. Though there was much initial opposition to the proposals, and a legal challenge mounted by the borough of Westminster, the scheme went ahead without any hitches and the benefits were quickly seen. In the first year there was a 21% reduction in traffic, 30% reduction of congestion, and a 43% increase in cycling in the city center. In addition, there was a reduction in accidents and key traffic-related pollutants, and £125 million was raised in revenue for public transport improvements. Contrary to fears, the public transport network absorbed displaced journeys, and property values were unaffected.

An extension to the original congestion charge area in 2007, known as the Western Extension, was removed by TfL in December 2010 following a public consultation, which highlighted that the majority of local residents and businesses were not in favor of the scheme. TfL's priority now is to work on smoothing traffic flows by rephrasing traffic lights, resolving issues at problematic junctions, and managing disruptive roadwork.

REDUCING VEHICLE EMISSIONS

In 2008 TfL introduced a Low Emission Zone (LEZ) across most of London to improve air quality by restricting the most polluting vehicles, and to encourage diesel vehicles in particular to become cleaner. Vehicles that do not meet the pollution standards set for the zone have to pay up to £200 a day to drive in the zone, with heavy fines if they fail to pay. To drive for free in the LEZ, the vehicle must meet certain emissions standards. All London buses under TfL contracts and all licensed taxis meet these standards, and by 2012 all London buses will be low-polluting. The LEZ operates twenty-four hours a day, every day of the year, and is enforced using automatic number plate recognition. The target for LEZ is to deliver a 16% reduction in pollution by 2012. Another aspect of improving vehicle emissions is the promotion of electric vehicles, and Mayor Johnson has made clear his commitment to make London the electric vehicle capital of Europe.

CROSSRAIL

It has long been recognized that London needs a service to complement the central London Underground network, which is near capacity. As a result, London has committed to build a major rail project, Crossrail, which will link rail services to the east and to the west of London via a high-speed tunnel, and provide interchange with the existing Underground network. It will connect major retail centers, the City and Canary Wharf financial services centers, and Heathrow Airport with a high-frequency, high-capacity, convenient, and accessible train service across the capital beginning in 2018. Crossrail will deliver a 10% increase in rail capacity and reduce crowding on the existing central Underground services.

The almost £16 billion project is being paid for by a number of funding streams, roughly one-third from the central government, borrowing against future fare receipts, a supplement on the London Business Rates, contributions from the main financial districts of the City of London and Canary Wharf, British Airport Authority, as well as from developments within central London, and a levy to be raised by the mayor.

Bus Travel

In the 1980s, Prime Minister Margaret Thatcher famously said that a man over twenty-six years of age who was still traveling by bus was a failure. Bus travel had a very poor image and was an unpopular mode of transport, mainly because bus journey times were highly unpredictable due to traffic congestion.

In the first years following the establishment of TfL, bus services were extensively improved and frequencies increased. Mayor Ken Livingstone made it one of his priorities to develop services and make journeys faster and more predictable by the introduction of almost two hundred miles of dedicated bus lanes, giving priority to buses over other traffic. Many new bus services were introduced, including real-time information about approaching services at bus stops, onboard information announcing next stops, and new diagrammatic bus maps based on all the services available at a given location. As a result of the modernization of bus services, bus passenger miles rose by almost 60% between 2001 and 2009.

Walking

Economists, urbanists, and retail experts realized in the 1980s and 1990s that walking is fundamental to a city's "health" in the broadest sense. Shops are more likely to be successful in areas of high foot traffic, businesses thrive where staff can meet colleagues easily, communities are more likely to be safe and cohesive where the people are out on the streets regularly, and, of course, the population will be physically healthier. It was recognized that a key to regeneration is making it easy and attractive for people to walk to and within an area. At that time, the areas in central London on the south side of the river had significantly lower land values and were rundown and unattractive, despite having many of London's famous cultural attractions located there. There was a clear sense that this area needed to be better connected to the area across the River Thames to the north, via pedestrian bridges. As a result, two new pedestrian bridges were created to mark the millennium, the Hungerford and Millennium Bridges

Figure 8.4 Before the Millennium Bridge was built, there was little pedestrian traffic between the north and the south of the Thames, and the South Bank was underdeveloped. Now there is a constant stream of both tourists and commuters using the bridge, and the South Bank has become a major tourist and leisure destination. Credit: Camilla Ween.

(figure 8.4). The impact was instantly evident. The South Bank immediately became an essential part of the tourist experience and now hosts an estimated twenty-five million visitors every year.[11] The bridges are in constant use by visitors and commuters alike, in all seasons and weather. In the 1980s and 1990s it was almost impossible to find a place to eat after the theater on the South Bank; it is now a mecca of restaurants and bars.

There was a real push to improve the walking experience by enhancing the streetscape. Sidewalks have been de-cluttered, pavements widened, a public realm created where people can dwell and meet, and trees planted. It was recognized that many more journeys could easily be done on foot, but people tend to resort to bus, Underground, or even taxis because of uncertainty about the route, distance, and journey time. TfL has developed an advanced walking tool, Legible London, to encourage walking and support way-finding. Based on the theory of "mental mapping," it helps people connect areas, regions, and transport systems. At strategic points such as street intersections, Tube station exits, bus stops, and key buildings, travelers will find coordinated street signs to help with the next stage of their journey by foot. Distinctive and elegant "totems" show the direction to walk, how long it will take, and notable landmarks along the way. What is unique to the concept is providing "heads-up" maps that face the way you are looking (as opposed to having north at the top), which identify all the key destinations and landmark features.[12]

CYCLING

Part of Mayor Boris Johnson's campaign manifesto was to deliver a cycle hire (bike sharing) scheme for London. A committed cyclist himself, he wanted to raise the profile of cycling in London and encourage more people to opt for cycling for short-hop journeys. He launched his *Cycle Revolution* in 2009 with a pledge to provide central London with a cycle hire scheme. The concept is that users only take out a cycle for the duration of the journey and then return it to a docking station. The aim is to keep the cycles in multiple circulation twenty-four hours a day, rather than users keeping a bike for the whole day. Hence the pricing encourages quick short trips, with the first half hour being free, but with long rentals rising exponentially in cost. The scheme was launched in the summer of 2010. The target is to have a docking station within a two-minute walk anywhere in central London. By 2012 the scheme will have been expanded to cover twenty-five square miles with eight thousand bikes and a target of forty thousand new cycle journeys every day. The first six months of the scheme saw over six million miles of cycle journeys, equivalent to traveling to the moon and back thirteen times. Boris Johnson has also introduced a number of strategic Cycle Superhighways—continuous bright blue cycle lanes to help commuters find their way from the residential suburbs to the central area.

GREEN TRAVEL PLANS

It is now required that all new developments being proposed in London have Green Travel Plans. These are plans and commitments made by the property owners to assist occupants in making smart travel choices. The whole package of how the scheme will be managed, monitored, and updated is secured as part of the planning conditions attached to the approval of the project. Even where redevelopment is not taking place, large employers, public-sector organizations, schools, and hospitals are being encouraged, through TfL's Smarter Travel Program, to develop plans that highlight sustainable travel options. A scheme for the Richmond area (2008–10) achieved a 6.4% reduction of car journeys to schools, a 13%

average decrease in car journeys overall, and a 16% increase in public transport use. The scheme involved providing sustainable travel advice to residents and businesses, holding roadshows and cycle training, encouraging walk-to-school programs, and introducing car clubs, cycle parking spaces, and Legible London walking information.

Waste Treatment and Recycling

London Plan policy requires London's local authorities, in line with UK national policy, to reduce the amount of waste sent to landfill. By 2020, 85% of all waste will have to be processed locally. There is a requirement to reduce the amount of waste generated, particularly in the building construction industry, and to increase reuse, recycling, and composting of waste. Further, the amount of energy used, and the transport impacts from the collection, treatment, and disposal of waste, must be minimized, in line with the target of reducing CO_2 emissions. The generation of renewable energy from waste is being promoted. By 2020 the target is to achieve recycling and composting levels for commercial and industrial waste of 70%, and recycling and reuse levels for construction, excavation, and demolition waste of 95%.

Where waste cannot be recycled, the generation of renewable energy and hydrogen from waste is being encouraged using new and emerging technologies, especially where the products of waste treatment could be used as fuels (e.g., biofuels and hydrogen). As a result, the perception of what "waste" is has changed and has led to a new approach: reduce, reuse, and recycle, with disposal as the last resort. The aspirational aim is to eventually send zero waste to landfill. In the longer term, it is hoped that waste plants will be integrated with decentralized energy heat networks, using waste heat for domestic and commercial heating.

London Waste's EcoPark in North London, the city's largest private-sector recycling and sustainable waste-management facility, handles about a quarter of London's waste. It has developed processes for recycling, composting, and recovery of energy. The EcoPark looks for "closed loop" solutions, such as turning kitchen and garden waste into quality compost and then returning the compost to residents for garden use. Untreated wood such as pallets, offcuts, some furniture, decking, and fencing is shredded into chips, which can be used for animal bedding, new wood-based products, or fuel. Waste that cannot be recycled is incinerated in the Energy

Center, where the heat generated is used to create electricity, which is fed into the National Grid. Currently it produces sufficient power for sixty-six thousand homes annually, as well as all its own needs. The EcoPark is also seeking to reduce the environmental impact of transport and is currently exploring making use of the adjacent canal for transport purposes.

A new development at Wembley City of 4,200 homes has planned to rationalize the way waste is disposed, using the Envac system. Though not new—started in Sweden some forty years ago—it is a complete departure from conventional waste collection using bins on streets and heavy waste carts for collections. The system is based on a network of underground pipes and a number of chutes, either within buildings or outside (figure 8.5). Residents sort waste within their apartments into separate containers for recyclable, organic, and nonrecyclable waste and then drop it in the appropriate chute. The waste is automatically transported through a fully enclosed system of underground vacuum pipes, at 50 mph, to a central station where it is compacted and stored for collection. The waste trucks make one single pit stop for collection, instead of having to cruise the entire estate making multiple pickups. The system is designed to stimulate high levels of recycling and keep the district clean by frequently removing waste and reducing refuse truck miles by up to 90%. At Wembley it is estimated that the system will reduce CO_2 emissions by four hundred tons a year compared with conventional refuse collection.

Enhancing Natural Habitat

Fundamental to our understanding of sustainability is our sense of being connected to our planet. It is therefore vital that people growing up in a city have access to growing plants, live animals, and wildlife so that they understand the vulnerability and balance of nature. London has been restoring and creating new wildlife habitats so that Londoners can experience the natural world at close hand.

Close to the center of London, on the banks of the Thames, is the 104-acre London Wetland Center, which opened in 2000. Unused concrete water reservoirs dating from the 1890s were transformed into a haven for wildlife and migrating birds. The River Thames acts as a wildlife corridor and "flyway" for many migrating bird species, which arrive by the thousands from around the globe. It attracts more than 180 different bird species each year, and supports a breeding colony of endangered water voles

1A The waste is thrown into a waste inlet.

1B The system can also be expanded with additional inlets for more fractions.

2 The computer-controlled evacuation takes 30 seconds. One fraction at a time.

3 All waste is sucked out through a network of pipes at a speed of 70km/h

4 Fans create the partial vacuum that sucks the waste through to the reception facility in the terminal station.

5 The waste is directed to the correct container.

6 The air is cleaned by filters before it is released.

Figure 8.5 The Envac automated underground waste system can reduce waste collection truck miles and the associated carbon emissions by up to 90%, cut traffic congestion, and increase recycling levels. Credit: Envac.

and more than half of all UK dragonfly and damselfly species. It has become the best urban spot in Europe to observe wildlife and is now deemed a Site of Special Scientific Interest. It is an important educational resource and provides Londoners with an opportunity to experience wildlife up close.

Trees process CO_2 and help to improve air quality. They also offer benefits such as attracting wildlife, acting as sound barriers, providing shade and cooling, and reducing flood risk. Not least, trees create beautiful urban spaces. Though London does have green lungs and parks, squares, and tree-lined streets, Mayor Boris Johnson believes that London does not have enough trees and has set a target to increase tree cover from the current 20% to 25% by 2025, which equates to about two million more trees. He has also pledged to fund ten thousand new street trees by 2012 in residential neighborhoods where few trees currently exist. He aims to deliver this with the help of his RE:LEAF London campaign, aimed at encouraging individuals, schoolchildren, businesses, and organizations to plant more trees. Ideas being considered include the development of community orchards and tree nurseries, mass tree planting events, and voluntary tree warden schemes.

Sustainable and Affordable Living

Housing need in London is critical. In 2007 there were 3.2 million housing units. Changes in social norms and age mean that by 2031 it is expected that London will need almost four million households. Meeting this demand with a changing mix of household types and sizes is a key challenge that the London Plan addresses.

Housing in London has historically been pigeonholed into either private-owner occupation or social-rented "council" housing. Council housing is almost always easy to identify; Victorian philanthropic social landlords developed typologies that were distinct and recognizable, and the glut of post–World War II housing blocks were often iconic architectural experiments that rarely considered aspects such as sense of place or community and quickly became drab as a result of neglect. Social problems have inevitably led to a stigma associated with the council estates. Current thinking is that residential developments should be "tenure-blind"—that is, it should not be possible to identify the type of housing by its appearance. Further, tenure should be mixed, so that the local community comprises a wide range of socioeconomic groups, and new developments are required to include the maximum reasonable amount of affordable housing. Providing "lifetime" homes, which cater for the needs of the elderly, is also a priority. Sustainability of construction practice, long-term energy consumption, transport servicing, and waste collection are all key factors that are taken into account through the planning system, to ensure minimum impact on the environment.

Another key aspect of sustainable housing is its performance in terms of carbon emissions, as well as the amount of carbon release involved in the manufacturing of the constituent materials. Part of London's green strategy has been the exploration of more sustainable approaches to housing. Prior to the establishment of the Greater London Authority, initiatives were emerging from groups such as Carbon Neutral, a consultancy helping clients to reduce CO_2, and BioRegional, an entrepreneurial nonprofit environmental organization. BioRegional built London's first experimental low-carbon housing development, BedZED (see below), and went on to develop (in partnership with the International World Wildlife Fund) the One Planet Living concept. One Planet Living is a global initiative based on ten principles of sustainability: zero carbon; zero waste; sustainable transport; local and sustainable materials; local and sustainable food; sustainable water; natural habitats and wildlife; culture and heritage; equity and fair trade; and health and happiness. It presents the choices and challenges we must address if we are to enjoy a high quality of life within the means of the planet's resources, such as reducing carbon emissions and waste; promoting sustainable transport, management of water, materials, and food; and enhancing biodiversity, cultural heritage, fair trade, and health and well-being.

BioRegional, with the Peabody Trust, developed the 2002 housing scheme BedZED (Beddington Zero Energy Development), designed by Bill Dunster Architects. It comprises one hundred homes, workspace for one hundred people, and a number of community facilities such as a healthy living center, a nursery, a café/telecommuting center, and shared renewable energy generation (photovoltaic) and composting. One of the key objectives was to show that eco-development and green lifestyles could be accessible and affordable.

The achievements at BedZED led to BioRegional producing the Toolkit for Carbon-Neutral Developments, which outlines how the construction industry can build desirable buildings that produce zero net carbon emissions and minimize environmental impact, without necessarily reducing profitability. It also describes measures to reduce environmental impact during occupation. The toolkit includes the BedZED Construction Materials Report, which puts into perspective the environmental impacts of extracting, processing, and transporting construction materials, and how to deal with construction waste in terms of the contribution to greenhouse gas emissions, toxic emissions, habitat destruction, and resource depletion.

A monitoring review of the scheme in 2007 carried out by BioRegional found many positive outcomes, despite the fact that the CHP plant is not working. Individual energy use is 45% of the local average, and water use is less than half the local average. The sense of community is strong, with most residents knowing twenty or more neighbors (compared to the local average of eight). The ecological footprint of the "average" BedZED resident is significantly lower than the UK average, though still not deemed sustainable; this is mainly due to their impact outside the development (e.g., workplaces, schools, goods purchased). Despite the high aspirations of the original project not having been met, it has nonetheless been an important step in the right direction and has challenged major developers and house builders to consider sustainability more seriously.

The principles of sustainability are now being pushed, developed, and embraced in a number of developments across London. The GLA actively encourages the development of low-carbon housing, and a number of large-scale housing schemes have been designed by the private sector that include a wide range of innovative sustainability measures.

An early example of a comprehensive approach to building a sustainable community is Greenwich Millennium Village, which is built on a formerly uninhabitable brownfield site (figure 8.6). The master plan was designed by architect Ralph Erskine, whose vision was to create a model urban village where pedestrians have priority over cars. This development comprises 2,700 mixed-tenure units and includes commercial space and social and community facilities, a school, a health center, restaurants, workshops, open space, and an ecology park. The buildings are being constructed from environmentally sustainable materials, using recycled and local materials wherever possible. Off-site prefabrication, and the segregating and recycling of materials, is considerably reducing construction waste. The buildings are oriented and designed to maximize the benefits

Figure 8.6 The Greenwich Millennium Village in East London is "tenure-blind," with privately owned apartments seamlessly mixed with affordable housing. Credit: Greenwich Millennium Village Ltd.

of solar gain, creating sheltered and tempered microclimates. A key design strategy was to ensure social integration by seamlessly mixing social rented housing with privately owned units.

Sustainable travel was central to the concept. Walking and cycling was made easy and attractive by ensuring that the whole site was pedestrian- and cycle-friendly. A comprehensive network of pedestrian and cycle routes provide interesting, attractive, safe, and direct routes within the village and beyond. Safe and secure cycle parking is provided throughout the development as well, as at public transport interchanges. Use of public transport was promoted (over personal car use) by having easy access to public transport services and by making the development virtually car-free. What traffic there is (e.g., servicing) is managed to reduce pollution.

New green open space has been created for informal use by adults and children, as has a fifty-acre "Eco-Park," which has boosted biodiversity and the return of many native species that had been lost. This area now acts as an educational and leisure facility.

The project set high targets for environmentally sustainable development over its projected lifetime (from 2000 averages): 80% reduction in primary energy consumption; 50% reduction in embodied energy; 50% reduction in construction waste; 30% reduction in water use; 30% reduction in construction costs; and 25% reduction in project construction time.

Food Production

Since the publication of the City Limits report (see above), there has been a growing urban agriculture movement in London, exploring ways to develop low-input organic agriculture that could reduce dependency on land beyond the city for food production. The London Plan encourages local authorities to protect agricultural land to meet the needs of farming. The aim is to create cultivated walls, roofs, balconies, and leftover space that can produce fruit and vegetables. It is thought that 60% of a city's food needs could be grown within the city by putting derelict open space, roofs, and balconies into food production.[13] There is a strong belief that local farms have an important role, as a place where people can experience firsthand growing food, and also because they bring communities together and can be a focus for overcoming alienation. Many experimental projects are springing up across London, some taking inspiration from Cuba, where large-scale urban farming projects were created in response to food shortages following the breakup of the Soviet Union. Abundance is a project established on neglected open space between 1930s housing in Brixton. With a small grant and help from University College London, this space has been turned into vegetable plots by local volunteers who are now growing a variety of crops. The plan is to extend the project to include the roofs. There are other similar projects such as the FARM:shop project in Dalston, which also has livestock such as chickens and a mini fish-farm, and is run by a team of forty volunteers. The project aims to educate about sustainable food production and encourage healthy eating.

How London Is Driving the Urban Sustainability Agenda

In 2000, when the GLA was established, London was a world city but there was an undercurrent of uncertainty about its future. Traffic congestion in the late 1990s was so bad that international organizations were looking to relocate. Transport was seen as one of the biggest problems facing the city's financial growth and needed to be addressed if London was to maintain its position as a world-class city. The availability of affordable housing was also a problem. A scheme introduced by the Thatcher regime in the 1980s that gave tenants the right to buy their social housing (without corresponding reprovision of these units) had created an overall loss of affordable housing. Further, environmental issues were beginning to receive greater attention. Londoners wanted change. Devolution of power to London from the UK government, the establishment of the GLA, and the ascendance of a strong mayor made it possible to bring sustainability to the forefront of decision making. London has been able to transform itself over the last ten years because it had comprehensive powers to drive an agenda of change and tackle the city's problems in a strategic and integrated way. Further, having a single authority has made it easier to force through challenging targets for climate change mitigation. The mayor of London leads the decision-making process and has the authority to do so.

Sustainability has been a strong driver among all the political parties that make up the assembly. There was an expectation from the beginning that sustainability had to be embedded in policy objectives, and both of London's mayors to date have taken up this challenge. As a result of this mayoral support and the creation of the London Plan, all policies interrelate, so that when considering, for example, transport solutions, other criteria such as social inclusion, health, and climate change mitigation are all brought together. Sustainable policy is ultimately policy that is all encompassing and links physical, social, economic, and cultural targets.

The London Plan obliges developers to integrate their developments with local communities; provide open space and a quality public realm; consider the public transport plans and enhance, where necessary, existing public transport provision; include sustainable design and, more recently, sustainable energy, water, and waste systems; and make provision for biodiversity and habitat renewal. The plan encourages development in appropriate places by identifying growth areas and creating Opportunity Area Planning Frameworks (high-level master planning policies) for these areas, setting out the level of growth and key social and transport infrastructure that must be delivered alongside development.

Lessons for the U.S.

One of the successes of London is its Greenbelt, which has contained the city's growth so that it is still surrounded by relatively undeveloped countryside. This has resulted in intensification around internal transport nodes and gradual expansion of the transport system within the city boundary to meet growing demand. There has also been strong policy for decades to preserve open space within the city. U.S. cities need to set growth boundaries and work toward higher density and a greater mix of land uses, so that people are able to work and enjoy recreation within relatively close proximity of where they live, and thus reduce the need to travel. The focus should be on creating city centers where people of all ages actually want to be, that are vibrant, livable, affordable, and attractive, as well as being civilized and safe. Transport solutions should focus on internal measures, including walking and cycling, rather than long-distance commuter transit to bring people into the city from ever farther afield.

Cities need a comprehensive vision with binding and enforceable policies. Radical and comprehensive change cannot realistically be achieved simply through persuasion or encouragement—developers are ultimately motivated by profit margins, not philanthropy.

An important factor in London was placing virtually all public transport and the strategic highway network into one administrative body, Transport for London, which the mayor controls. This made it possible to integrate public transport services properly and make the network more efficient by improving interchange between services. It also means that planning for future growth is done holistically, along with the promotion of softer measures such as the integration of walking and cycling and the encouragement of sustainable travel choices. An integrated transport authority is essential. Public transport has to be subsidized, and the only way to do this efficiently is to have all services under a central authority. But services can be franchised, as is the case in London with the bus network, which is run by private companies, but to the standards and fares set by Transport for London.

It will be impossible to chip away at urban sprawl in the U.S. without comprehensive and integrated policies and strong governance that can tackle and deliver the often costly and difficult changes needed. Governance of cities in the U.S. needs to change; there is an urgent need to lobby for cities to have strong and overarching local powers to coordinate spatial development with sustainability principles, to integrate transport, energy, and waste policies, and to be able to force through painful but necessary changes to reverse the tide and create civilized cities fit for people to live in.

Conclusion

London saw uncoordinated growth (albeit within its Greenbelt boundary), disparity between communities, and fragmented transport and highways networks throughout most of the 1980s and 1990s. The establishment of strong governance for London reversed this trend dramatically within a short time. Public transport has been enhanced and all travel modes have been better integrated, so that the network has become more efficient. Since 2000 there has been a 5% shift from private to public and sustainable transport in London.[14] London is the only major city in the world to record such a shift.

This has stimulated investment, halted the process of decay, and led to the creation of a city that now has greatly enhanced its public realm, calmed traffic, and is easier to walk and cycle in. The city's population is getting younger, indicating, among other things, that people are now choosing to stay in London and have families.

Is London a model sustainable city? Of course not. It is far from perfect, and changing a two-thousand-year-old city takes time. In fact, London was ranked only 11th in the Siemens European Green City Index in 2009, after (in order) Copenhagen, Stockholm, Oslo, Vienna, Amsterdam, Zurich, Helsinki, Berlin, Brussels, and Paris. What the establishment of the GLA, the mayor, and the London Plan has meant is that new development will have to be sustainable and that there are now policies to change, over time, the way we do things. Sustainability initiatives now run through all the policies and drive decision making. Having a strong mayor with the authority to act has made it possible to deliver some difficult schemes. Congestion charging would not have been accomplished without the determination of Ken Livingstone; London's bike hire scheme would not have happened (in just eighteen months) without Boris Johnson's unwavering commitment to deliver his Cycling Revolution in London. Major improvements have been delivered in transport and an improved public realm, which has made London a much more agreeable city. But London ranks poorly in terms of energy use, and its per capita energy consumption is high. Most of London's existing building stock is old, uninsulated, and energy-inefficient. This will have to be addressed. There are initiatives to promote more efficient-energy solutions such as combined heat and power, local heat networks, and energy from waste, and to improve the performance of existing buildings; in time these will make a difference, but London has a long way to go. Bringing down energy consumption is a priority. London has had the courage to set itself very high targets to reduce CO_2 emissions—60% (below 1990 levels) by 2025. By setting out a clear and challenging vision that is supported by strong policy in the London Plan, London has a strategy for change. The key to any adaptive change is to stop whining and get on with it, and that London has done. It has started with a blend of heavy-hitting and light-touch initiatives and by exploring new ways of doing things.

Notes

Some of the material in this chapter is an extension of a text written by Camilla Ween for a chapter in *Ecological Urbanism*, edited by Mohsen Mostafavi with Gareth Doherty (Cambridge, MA, and Baden, Switzerland: Harvard University Graduate School of Design and Lars Müller, 2010).

1. Global Cities exhibition, Tate Modern 2007.
2. City of London Report: A Capital Contribution—London's Place in the UK Economy 2007–2008.
3. Key Visitor Statistics 2009, VisitLondon.com.
4. Office of National Statistics 2010.
5. UK Census 2001 (33,929 people per square mile).
6. Demographia.com (26,517 people per square mile).
7. 2009 Travel in London Report.
8. By the consultants Best Foot Forward.
9. Excluding the national rail services that traverse or terminate in London.

10. Transport for London: Traffic Operations in London 2007.
11. South Bank Manifesto 2010.
12. For more information, see http://tfl.gov.uk/legiblelondon.
13. Robert Biel, Development Planning Unit, University College London.
14. Travel in London Report 2009.

9

Conclusion: Green Cities of Europe as Compelling Models

Timothy Beatley

There is a reason that Americans covet and anticipate trips to European cities like London, Paris, and Venice. They are beautiful cities that provide unparalleled urban and natural qualities, that permit us to relax, stroll, and eat outside, that allow us to get around easily by bicycle, foot, or train. Because we know and enjoy these places, hold them in high esteem, read books about them, and have such close historical and cultural connections, it is only natural that we would want to learn from and emulate them. At least for American cities, there is no more logical place in the world to look for useful and applicable ideas and innovations for making our own cities greener and more sustainable.

As these final pages are being written in the summer of 2011, there is an unprecedented urgency to the green cities agenda. The rising price of oil and fears about a decline in supply are roiling international markets. There is growing concern about the rising price and supply of food, and in many parts of the world, a shortage of water. The full effects of climate change are only beginning to unfold, but a growing consensus is developing that the window for effective action, at least the prevention of the most severe change scenarios, is narrow and closing fast. Confronting the environmental problems facing the nation and world will require a new urban agenda, a *green* urban agenda, and the models of green and sustainable cities that have evolved in northern and western Europe offer unusual hope and promise for what form this agenda should take.

As the preceding chapters of this book compellingly show, there are many lessons to learn from these exemplary cities. Perhaps the obvious first set of lessons relates to the physical layout and architectural design of a city. The key lesson is that design matters, and matters abundantly in shaping the social and environmental contexts in which people live. Having compact, mixed-use, transit-oriented urbanscapes, amenities within short distances of residences, interesting walking environments, and investments in the public realm leads to lifestyles that are better for human and environmental well-being. They are more interesting places to live—their urban design and streetscape qualities literally propel us to spend time walking, which is an important lessons for Americans facing severe impacts (and financial costs) associated with a highly sedentary populace. These communities have significantly lower per capita greenhouse gas emissions and greater resilience in the face of declining global oil supplies.

A serious commitment to investing in the creation and upkeep of the infrastructure—both gray and green—of a sustainable city is another important lesson. For gray infrastructure, transit is the best example and probably the most important—the basis for mobility and lifestyles that allow less (or no) reliance on private automobiles. European cities, together with national governments, have committed to the operation of reliable, extensive, fast, integrated transit. For example, in chapter 3, Medearis and Daseking describe Freiburg's extensive and interconnected network of trains, trams, and buses. Of course, this is partly a matter of culture and history—there is a strong expectation of the availability of good transit in European cities and many creative ways of funding it. In Stockholm, for instance, there is a dedicated portion of a county income tax that goes toward paying for transit. The continued expansion of high-speed rail throughout Europe (and its recent expansion in countries like Italy and Spain) is further testament to the commitment and value of these long-term infrastructural investments.

The European experience in continuously investing in and expanding its high-speed rail network stands in contrast to the more nascent and halfhearted efforts in the U.S. The difficulties of building high-speed rail were made clear in 2011 when Florida governor Rick Scott gave back $2 billion in federal funding for high-speed rail there, for a route that would have connected Orlando and Tampa, in that traffic-choked sunbelt state.[1] This decision came on the heels of similar rejections by Ohio and Wisconsin, a mix of conservative politics that resents federal programs, and suspicion about the benefits and societal value of this form of mobility. As a result, other states, notably California, will benefit from the extra funding, but these state actions show the still-precarious nature in the U.S. of such long-term investments in a green future. Nevertheless, Europe's high-speed rail can rightly claim much of the credit, even for these nascent efforts, serving as a positive beacon of a sensible, forward-looking mobility system (see figure 9.1).

European cities have also invested much in green infrastructure—parks, natural systems, urban agriculture, and greenery—to a degree rarely seen in U.S. cities. And the transformative benefits are equally evident. For example, Copenhagen's Finger Plan, discussed in chapter 4, has resulted in a regional growth pattern where relatively dense urban development follows not only investments in the rail system but also the protection of large green wedges near where large numbers of people live. Helsinki similarly has protected incredibly large blocks of green space, such as the Helsinki Central Park described by Jaakkola in chapter 5. These large green spaces serve as the framework within which many smaller green spaces can be found.

European green urbanism is admirably comprehensive in scope and holistic in vision, and this is another important lesson. Cities like Copenhagen, Freiburg, and Paris are not doing just one or two things, but have

Figure 9.1 The AVE, Spain's high-speed rail system. Countries such as Spain and Italy have made substantial investments in expanding high-speed rail in recent years. Credit: Timothy Beatley.

developed a long and impressive list of green urban programs, policies, and strategies, often highly integrated and usually mutually reinforcing. These include compact land use, investments in transit and bicycling, but also green building and renewable energy, urban agriculture, air- and water-quality improvements, and green governance, among others. Each city has its own special package of innovations, but the cases here show the value, indeed the necessity, of a full and comprehensive set of actions that together make up the green urban vision of a city.

The European approach to green governance is also exemplary, recognizing the importance of setting strident green targets and stringent minimum energy and environmental standards. And equally important, European cities and nations have in numerous ways changed the economic incentive structure to support and promote green outcomes. Adoption of carbon taxes at the national level, in addition to gasoline and auto taxes, has served to profoundly reinforce more sustainable outcomes. Europe's long-standing philosophy of taxing at the pump, and using these revenues to support public transit, has been sharply different from our practice in the U.S. And consider the value of Denmark's high tax on new autos (more than the actual price of the car) in discouraging car dependence and mobility. As a further example, Germany's national feed-in tariff legislation has done much to create financial incentives for the installation off solar energy there. There are equally important examples at the local and state levels, including many European cities that impose stormwater fees based on impervious surfaces (a practice that has begun to catch on in the U.S., in cities from Washington, D.C., to Greensboro, North Carolina), and that provide extensive financial incentives for the installation of green features (again, an idea beginning to find application in American cities like Chicago).

Overcoming Barriers to Implementation

My goal in assembling these experts to tell the stories of their cities is partly to inspire, partly to demonstrate what is indeed in the realm of possibility, and to offer up a rich assortment of green urban ideas, tools, and approaches. Despite their obvious virtues and values, there will nevertheless be many impediments and obstacles that must be faced in accelerating the uptake of European green-urban ideas and practices in the U.S. Some of these obstacles are financial and economic, others political and cultural. These include, for instance, the real or perceived additional up-front costs associated with green ideas and technologies (e.g., for green rooftops, green walls), even though most or all of these greening strategies are cost-effective over a relatively short time frame (e.g., green rooftops protect and extend the life of the underlying roof and thus economically justify the small up-front costs; green buildings save money in heating and cooling; the cost of tree planting and free tree distribution is more than paid for by reduced cooling and energy demands). The answer lies in part in the practical European approach of regulating and incentivizing green strategies. Pricing mechanisms in European cities and countries help to level the financial playing field and make green urban investments more attractive and feasible. Some North American cities are beginning to do this. For example, Toronto now mandates green roofs for certain kinds of structures, following the lead of many European cities, and cities like Portland, Oregon, provide density bonuses for eco-roofs.

Many of the benefits of urban greening are less easily quantified, of course (e.g., improvements in worker productivity, psychological benefits of trees and greenery), and may be public in nature (e.g., reducing GHG emissions and thus global warming, reduced strain on the electric grid).

Some of the obstacles are perceptual in nature, such as the inability to see and understand cities in profoundly new and different ways. Understanding cities as living systems and consisting of complex metabolisms and resource flows is an innovation in Europe. But we are still not used to viewing trees, day-lit streams, and green rooftops as essential *infrastructure* in the same way that we see roads, bridges, and utilities, though this is certainly changing.[2]

Cultural differences and sensibilities are important as well, and help to explain, for example, why children (and adults) are more likely in European cities to be outside, and more likely to be walking (or riding a bike). In the U.S., we have developed an indoor culture, confirmed by time-log studies that demonstrate that a typical American spends some 90% of his or her time indoors. While quality and accessibility of parks and natural areas, as well as inviting public spaces and biking and walking infrastructure, can help to pull Americans outdoors, an indoor cultural tendency may make this difficult. How to shift lifestyles and life patterns in the direction of outdoor activities, integrated into daily life, is a challenge to say the least. High visitation to the greenbelt in Vitoria-Gasteiz, Spain, is in part due to the tendency for the Spanish to spend much less time in their flats and houses and more time in the public realm. Climate can be a factor, but even in harsher winter climates, outdoor-oriented cultures prevail. In

Finland, schoolchildren spend an unusual amount of the day outside, with tremendous learning and pedagogical benefits. These may be difficult cultural conditions to emulate in American settings, but it is helpful to know (and see) that such patterns are indeed possible.

There are numerous other political, cultural, and legal obstacles that are often offered as reasons for why positive green ideas and projects move forward in Europe and not here, many quite valid. Europeans stroll and walk more often, it is noted, and have a culture that values time in the public realm. Parliamentary systems tend to provide a voice (and political power) to green political parties, while our two-party approach seems to eschew change and innovation. Our overly litigious society, it is true, tends to give credence to concerns about liability and emphasizes public risk-reduction. Fears of the other, higher crime rates and poorly funded public school systems that push Americans away from cities are all significant impediments to bringing about the kinds of European cities described in this book. Acknowledging these impediments should not serve as an excuse, however, for failing to tackle them, and to put into place the regulatory standards and incentives, to fund the transformational infrastructure, and to design and build the communities we wish our children and grandchildren to live in.

A final obstacle perhaps is the conventional sense that we have of buildings and urban neighborhoods, and the failure to fully imagine how profoundly green, sustainable, and connected to natural systems they could in fact be. That our current planning predicament in the U.S. is a failure of imagination as much as anything is worthy of repeating, and suggests the importance of restoring some of the efforts and programs in the past that took American delegations to see and experience firsthand the virtues of the European green model. There is even more to see today.

This is also a failure of imagining a more sensible, coherent, forward-looking planning system. The physical conditions and urban form of these European examples is made possible to a large degree by the kind of planning system in place there. Cities like Copenhagen demonstrate the compelling value and importance of regional planning, while other Scandinavian cities like Helsinki show the merits of using extensive public land acquisition. Almost all these cities show the value of integrated city planning frameworks (region framing city, city framing district and neighborhood). It is not likely that American cities will be able to emulate, at least in the short term, some of these strong planning systems, but it is true that some cities and regions of the U.S. have been able to form a stronger planning path (e.g., Portland, Oregon's Metropolitan Services District, or "Metro").

We lack the imagination to see our cities and communities in new and different ways, better suited to our contemporary environmental (and global) challenges. Progress in moving away from our fossil-fuel dependence will require serious localizing and local and regional sourcing of many of our urban needs and inputs (from food to building materials). This in turn provides tremendous new opportunities to build more sustainable place-economies. It is also about reforming lost connections and connectedness to place, to sustaining landscapes, and ultimately to human relationships and (at least partially) overcoming the stifling anonymity that characterizes our age. Americans, perhaps like the Swedish and the British, increasingly want to know where their food is grown, want to develop personal relationships, and projects in European cities (such as BedZED) help move us in the direction of becoming (more) native to place.

These European cities represent new and interesting ways of *reconceptualizing* what cities are. As the green architect William McDonough says, we should design buildings that function like trees, and cities that function like forests.[3] A house or an office building is reimagined as a power plant, as the source and producer of energy rather than just a consumer (as in the plus-energy homes in Freiburg). At the urban scale, Freiburg designs and manages its development with microclimate and prevailing wind patterns in mind: street patterns in Vauban are east-to-west to facilitate the movement of the prevailing evening winds (from the Black Forest) that cleanse and refresh the city.

These European cases show that a green urban agenda need not be about sacrifice or deprivation, but rather an opportunity for a more lively, livable, rich, and healthy lifestyle with a smaller ecological footprint. It is possible to design homes and businesses that use dramatically small amounts of energy yet provide delightful living and working spaces, as seen in the many examples in this book, from BedZED in London to Vauban in Freiburg.

A frequent response to European examples and best practice is, "That's nice, but it will never work here." Perhaps this is a function of the unique and deep feelings of American exceptionalism, but there is in fact a long history of American designers and planners visiting and learning from European projects and cities and applying these ideas back home, as stated in the introduction. For example, New York City mayor Michael Bloomberg brought a group of city officials to Copenhagen to see what the European capital has done to provide better biking and walking infrastructure and public spaces.

The former Chicago mayor Richard Daley, traveling in Europe, saw lush green rooftops and brought the idea back, initiating a dramatic retrofit of the rooftop of City Hall, and a program for encouraging and financially supporting the installation of green rooftops throughout the city. There are now more than 450 of them completed or in the planning stages there.

And there are countless other examples of European ideas applied and in short order mainstreamed: community-supported agriculture, slow food, shared or community bikes, ecological stormwater management, and energy-plus homes, among many others. In some cases it takes an unusually passionate expert or emissary to make the cross-Atlantic application possible (think Jan Gehl and the pedestrian projects in New York City); in other cases it is a matter of taking advantage of commercial opportunities (as in the case of car sharing); while in still other cases it may be more a matter of the advocacy and bridging work of sustainability organizations (such as the International Council for Local Environmental Initiatives). There are likely many avenues or conduits for innovation transfer, and we should explore them all.

The changing physical realities and environmental circumstances of the world necessitate more rapid transfer and community uptake of some of these ideas, especially low-energy housing, energy-plus and positive-energy development, and renewable energy and carbon-neutral design practice generally, and here again, European urban models are well suited to our times. There is growing consensus among the science community that we are on the verge of irreversible tipping points with climate change and that a relatively narrow temporal window exists for undertaking major societal action.[4] Exemplary green projects and programs will become the norm by necessity.

There will be some institutional and regulatory obstacles to overcome, but they can be and are being surmounted, both here and in Europe. The U.S. is a large and diverse nation, of course, and some European ideas may be best suited to certain regions and cities, with others to follow once the value and success of these innovations have been proved.

Shifting the American Dream in a European Direction?

The need to craft a new form or version of the American Dream has over the years been suggested by numerous organizations and individuals, and the imagined new dream is much closer to the European model. These have included the Center for the New American Dream, advocating, among other things, less-material lives and lifestyles, and shifts in the direction of community, family, and relationships.[5] The urbanist Chris Leinberger has recently suggested the need to "invest in a new American Dream," one where "walkable urbanism" is supported, where federal subsidies are shifted away from cars and highways, and where local zoning regulations are adjusted to permit these new, higher density forms of living.[6]

Arguably many Americans want to do more, want to do the right thing, to make a difference, but have little clue and few tangible avenues for expression of their latent environmental ethics. More to the point, perhaps, it is time to challenge Americans to live according to their self-proclaimed environmental values, to understand and take stock of the consequences of their lifestyle and consumption choices, and to give them tangible options and opportunities to demonstrate these commitments in the future.

The changing nature of U.S. politics and the unlikely new power of the conservative Tea Party movement bodes ill for many of these innovations, of course. In a divisive political climate in which a bike share program is described as a gateway to communism, or as a UN conspiracy designed to deprive Americans of their freedoms, it may be even harder to implement the green cities agenda, at least in particular parts of the nation. It may be necessary to spend as much time framing green urbanism in politically advantageous ways, and building coalitions and political partnerships, as ever before. And the importance of developing and utilizing networks of peer cities, able to help one another and to share critical knowledge about what works and what does not—another lesson from Europe—may also help. When it comes to political framing, it may be necessary to wrap some of the best European ideas in garb that emphasizes benefits that will especially resonate with this new political climate: measures to reduce use and dependence on private automobiles can, as some already argue, be defended on grounds of patriotism and national security, and the need to reduce our dependence on other countries and parts of the world. The health of the American family, and the educational attainment of children, will be fostered by neighborhoods and cities that provide abundant parks and green features. And, of course, the health and productivity of the American economy can and should be linked in new ways to these investments in green urbanism. Sprawling, energy-guzzling, carbon-spewing built environments jeopardize long-term economic vitality, and put nations at continued risk of environmental and economic calamity and instability.

We will need to better understand the processes by which green city innovations, indeed innovations generally, are embraced, adopted, and implemented. Successful adaptation of these innovative green practices requires effort on many levels—education, advocacy and political leadership, technical capability and financial incentives, and emerging markets where developers, builders, and housing and office consumers are able to see the economic and amenity values and are willing to pay a premium for them. In the American context, support and advocacy by green-minded mayors is one successful avenue. Examples include Richard Daley, and now Rahm Emanuel in Chicago, Michael Bloomberg in New York, and Antonio Villaraigosa in Los Angeles (who commonly cites the importance of "green urbanism"). Indeed, among European cities, much of the green success and innovation has been a function of proactive mayors (one thinks of Ken Livingston, former mayor of London, and Bertrand Delanoë in Paris), albeit working in more receptive social and political environments. Political leadership is essential, and if the idea is at its core a good and compelling one, the skepticism can be overcome. With strong political leadership, creative design, and a collaborative spirit, along with a real effort at nurturing the background conditions of a sustainable culture, similar green projects and progress can happen in the U.S—indeed, they must.

Notes

1. Patrick McGeehan, "Rail Money Rejected by Florida Heads to the Northeast," *New York Times*, May 10, 2011; Alex Leary, "Florida's Rail Money Doled Out," *St. Petersburg Times*, May 10, 2011.

2. In the words of one researcher, "These people [utility managers, engineers, planners] have not yet reconciled how a green living thing interacts with grey infrastructure. . . . There has not yet been a mind shift that says that trees are technology." Blaine Harden, "Tree-Planting Drive Seeks to Bring a New Urban Cool," *Washington Post*, September 4, 2006.

3. See William McDonough, "Buildings Like Trees, Cities Like Forests," 2002, accessed December 22, 2012, http://www.mcdonough.com/.

4. See, for example, Tim Flannery, *The Weather Makers*, New York: Grove Press, 2001; and Jim Hansen, *Storms of My Grandchildren*, New York: Bloomsbury, 2009.

5. See http://www.newdream.org/.

6. Chris Leinberger, *The Option of Urbanism: Investing in the New American Dream*, Washington, DC: Island Press, 2007.

Contributors

Luis Andrés Orive is General Manager of Environmental Affairs for the City of Vitoria-Gatseiz, the capital of the Basque Country of Spain. He was Director of the Environmental Studies Center of Vitoria-Gasteiz from 1989 to 2007.

Timothy Beatley is Teresa Heinz Professor of Sustainable Communities at the University of Virginia, where he has taught for the last twenty-five years.

Michaela Brüel is a senior architect and planner with the city of Copenhagen, where she has worked for more than thirty-five years.

Wulf Daseking is Head of Urban Planning for Freiburg, Germany, a position he has held since 1984. He is also Lecturer in City Planning at Freiburg University and at Darmstadt University of Architecture, City of Freiburg.

Rebeca Dios Lema is an architect in the Environmental Studies Center of Vitoria-Gasteiz. With a postgraduate specialization in Landscape Architecture and Environment, she is a PhD student in Urban and Landscape Planning, focusing her research on the Greenways Network of Alava and the Green Belt of Vitoria-Gasteiz.

Maria Jaakkola heads the Environmental Office in the Helsinki City Planning Department. She is trained as a landscape architect.

Lucie Laurian is Associate Professor in the School of Urban and Regional Planning at the University of Iowa. She holds a PhD in city and regional planning from UNC–Chapel Hill.

Dale Medearis is Senior Environmental Planner with the Northern Virginia Regional Commission. He is responsible for coleading the region's climate mitigation, energy, and international urban sustainability programs.

Marta Moretti is Deputy Director of the International Center Cities on Water in Venice. She studied contemporary history at the University of Venice and is also a freelance journalist.

Camilla Ween is an architect and urban planner. She worked for Transport for London (part of the Mayor's Office) for eleven years, and is now a partner in Goldstein Ween Architects, where she focuses on urban planning and transportation.

Index

Note: page numbers followed by an 'f', 't', 'b', or 'n' refer to figures, tables, boxes, and endnotes, respectively.

Aalborg Charter (EU), 3, 110, 133, 156
Aarhus Convention (EU), 186
Agenda 21 (UN), 97, 100–102, 110, 156
Agriculture
  London, 209–10
  pollution from, 35, 137
  Vienna, 22
  Vitoria-Gasteiz, 158–59, 167
Airflow (Freiburg), 14, 70
Air quality. *See also* Carbon and greenhouse
    gas (GHG) emissions
  Copenhagen, 86, 105
  Freiburg airflows and, 70
  London, 189–90, 199
  Paris, 29, 58
Air travel and London, 196
Akersleva River (Oslo), 14, 15f
Alava Province (Spain) Ecological Network,
    173–78, 176t, 177f
Albertslund, Denmark, 3
Alonso, Alfonso, 171
American Dream, 5, 6t, 222–24
Anchoring, 102
Aragon, Spain, 19
Austria, 16, 22, 23, 24
Autolib' car-sharing scheme (Paris), 10, 44
Automobiles and traffic planning. *See also*
    Transportation and transit
  Autolib' car-sharing scheme, Paris, 10, 44
  Copenhagen, 86, 90, 91–92
  Freiburg restrictions on cars, 71, 77
  Helsinki, 120–21, 123–24

London congestion pricing, 185, 196,
    198–99
  ownership rates, 10
  Paris, 33, 43
  sedentary lifestyle and, 6
  U.S., role of car in, 7

Baden Wuerttemberg Development Agency
    (LEG), 77
Barcelona, Spain, 18–19
Basque Country. *See* Vitoria-Gasteiz
Bassett, Edward, 4
BedZED (Beddington Zero Energy
    Development), 207
Bees and apiculture, 57–58, 59f
Bicycles
  Amersterdam, 10–11
  Copenhagen, 10, 11, 93–94, 95f, 105, 107
  Freiburg, 71, 72f
  Helsinki, 120–21, 123
  London, 10, 195, 196, 202, 209
  Paris, 11, 11f, 49–50
  shared, 10–11, 11f, 165, 196, 202
  Vitoria-Gasteiz, 164–67, 166f
Biocapacity, 167–68, 174f, 185
Biodiversity
  Helsinki, 115
  Paris, 53–58, 55t, 56f
  Vitoria-Gasteiz, 167–68, 174f
Biogas, 22
Biophilia, 12–17
BioRegional, 206–7

Black Forest (Germany), 70
Blanc, Patrick, 16–17
Bloomberg, Michael, 221, 224
Boeri, Stefano, 17
Bois de Vincennes (Paris), 50, 53, 58
Bosco Verticale residential towers (Milan,
    Italy), 17
Brownfield redevelopment
    Helsinki, 120, 122
    San Giuliano Park, Venice, 138–40
    Western Harbor district, Malmö, Sweden,
    17
Buildings and energy
    Copenhagen, 89, 103, 104f
    Freiburg, 75–76
    London, 193
    Paris and France, 35, 38, 39–41
Buses
    Helsinki, 120–21
    London, 185, 195, 199, 200, 212
    Paris, 44–45, 45f, 46, 63n18

CaixaForum Museum (Madrid), 17
Calatrava, Santiago, 141
Carbon and greenhouse gas (GHG)
    emissions. See also Energy and climate
    Copenhagen, 20, 102–3, 106
    EU 20-20-20 goals, 37
    Freiburg, 80
    Helsinki, 112–13
    Kyoto Protocol, 37
    London, 20, 192–93, 197, 199, 204,
    206–7
    Paris and France, 20, 37, 44
    Stockholm, 20
Carbon footprints, 35
Carbon taxes, 35, 62n6, 218
Cars. See Automobiles and traffic planning
Center for the New American Dream, 223
Chicago, 222
Children, 17, 152
Chirac, Jacques, 34, 54
Climate change adaptation. See also Energy
    and climate
    heat wave preparation (Paris), 20, 38–39
    Helsinki, 115
    London, 194
Compact urban form
    Freiburg, 7, 68f, 81f
    Helsinki, 123
    infill, 68, 69, 119–20

Oslo, 6–7
Vitoria-Gasteiz, 157–58
    walkability and, 12
Consorzio Venezia Nuova (CVN), 144–45,
    147–49
Copenhagen, Denmark
    Agenda 21 (UN) and, 97, 100–102
    background and profile, 83–85
    bicycle policy, 10, 11, 93–94, 95f, 105, 107
    bridge to Malmö, 91–92
    building standards, 89, 103, 104f
    car ownership in, 10
    climate plan, 20, 106
    Danish planning legislation, 85, 88–89,
    100–101, 103–4
    Eco-Metropole, 104–6
    "Environmental Accounts" and "green
    accounts," 24, 102–3
    Finger Plan, 85–88, 87f, 90–91
    green spaces and recreational areas, 13,
    94–98, 96f
    harbor and swimming, 13
    Metro, 92–93
    as model, 4
    municipal planning, 89
    pedestrian spaces, 98–99
    public participation, 103–4
    regional planning, 85
    traffic and transportation issues, 91
    urban development strategy, 90–91
    urban ecology and, 99–100
Council for Local Environmental Initiatives,
    222
Crossrail (London), 196, 199–200
Cruise ships, 150
Cuerda, José Ángel, 156
Culture, indoor- vs. outdoor-oriented,
    219–20
Cycle Superhighways (London), 10, 202
Cycling. See Bicycles

Daley, Richard, 222, 224
Delanoë, Bertrand, 34, 224
Denmark. See also Copenhagen, Denmark
    Albertslund, 3
    Dogme 2000 alliance, 101
    Øresund Bridge, 91–92
    planning legislation, 85, 88–89, 100–101,
    103–4
Di Mambro, Antonio, 139
District heating (Helsinki), 18, 112

Dogme 2000 alliance (Denmark), 101
Dongtan, China, 4
DTADDs (Directives territoriale
    d'aménagement et de développement
    durable, France), 36

Eco-budgeting (Heidelberg), 23–24
EcoBusiness Plan, Vienna, 24
Eco-cycles (Stockholm), 21
Ecological footprint, 23, 185–86, 207
Ecological Network (Alava Province, Spain),
    173–78, 176t, 177f
Ecological networks, corridors, and
    connectivity
    Green and Blue Networks in France, 35
    Nature Policy Plan (Netherlands), 13–14
    Vitoria-Gasteiz and, 160–61, 170–71
Ehrenström, Johan Albrect, 110
Elithis Tower, Dijon, France, 19–20, 20f
Emanuel, Rahm, 224
Energy, renewable. *See also* Solar energy
    biogas, 22
    EU 20-20-20 goals, 37
    Freiburg, 66, 74–76
    geothermal energy, 41
    Paris and France, 37, 41–43
    Stockholm transit and, 24
    from waste, in London, 203–4
    wind energy, 35, 42
Energy and climate, 197. *See also* Energy,
    renewable
    overview, 18–20
    airflow, breezes, and ventilation (Freiburg),
        14, 70
    Freiburg, 67, 73–74
    Heidelberg, 18
    Helsinki, 18, 112–13
    London, 193–94, 197, 213
    Paris and France, 35, 37–41
Envac waste system, 204, 205f
"Environmental Accounts" (Copenhagen),
    102–3
Erskine, Ralph, 208
European Commission, 3
The European Dream (Rifkin), 5, 6t
European Green Capital designation, 3, 155
European Sustainable City Award, 3, 111
European Union (EU)
    20-20-20 goals, 37
    Aalborg Charter, 3, 110, 133, 156
    Aarhus Convention, 186

Kyoto Protocol and, 37
Sustainable Cities and Towns Campaign
    and Aalborg Charter, 3, 110
UK planning legislation and, 186
Venice and, 137

Fair trade, 24
Feed-in tariffs, 20
Financing
    billing systems for water, in Freiburg, 71
    Rieselfeld, Freiburg, 80–81
    taxation, 35, 47, 62n6, 63n20, 107, 218
Finger Plan (Copenhagen), 85–88, 87f,
    90–91
Finland, 113–15. *See also* Helsinki, Finland
Flood mitigation. *See* Water, stormwater, and
    flood mitigation
Flow systems, 20–23
Food production and consumption. *See also*
    Agriculture
    community gardens and horticulture,
        117–18, 127n29, 167, 168f, 189
    Copenhagen, 105–6
    Europe as model for, 22–23
    urban agriculture in London, 209–10
Footprint, ecological, 23, 185–86, 207
France. *See also* Paris, France
    Charter for the Environment, 34
    Elithis Tower, Dijon, 19–20, 20f
    geographic, socioeconomic, and
        environmental-policy context of,
        30–32
    Grenelle de l'Environment, 34–37
    Regional Charter for Biodiversity, 54
Fraunhofer Institute for Solar Energy
    Systems, 74
Freiburg, Germany
    airflow and "clean air corridors," 14, 70
    background and profile, 65–67, 66t
    Charter for Sustainable Urbanism, 7, 8b
    compact urban form, 7, 68f, 81f
    energy and climate, 66, 73–76
    KIOSK, 80b
    landscape planning, 69–70
    planning context, 67–69
    Rieselfeld project, 76f, 78–81, 79f
    transportation, 71–73
    Vauban project, 17, 75f, 76–78
    water, 70–71
French Revolution, 34
Fresh cell therapy (Freiburg), 69

Gallagher, John, 4
Gardens and community gardens
   Helsinki, 117–18, 127n29
   London, 189
   Market Gardens, Vitoria-Gasteiz, 167,
      168f
   Paris, 52–53
Gehl, Jan, 99, 222
Gehry, Frank, 140
Geothermal energy, 41
Germany. *See also* Freiburg, Germany
   feed-in tariffs, 20
   Heidelberg, 18, 23–24
   planning and nature protection laws,
      69–70
   Stuttgart, 14
Girardet, Herbert, 26, 185
Glocalism, 24
Greater London Authority (GLA), 182, 186,
   210
"Green accounts" (Copenhagen), 24, 102–3
Green and Blue Networks (France), 35
Green audits, 23
Green Capital City program (European
   Commission), 3, 155
Green Cycle Routes program (Copenhagen),
   10, 93–94, 95f
Green fingers approach (Helsinki), 116f, 117
Greenhouse gas (GHG) emissions. *See*
   Carbon and greenhouse gas (GHG)
   emissions
Green spaces and greenbelts. *See also*
   Vitoria-Gasteiz (Basque Country, Spain)
      greenbelt
   Copenhagen, 13, 94–98, 96f
   Freiburg, 81f
   Helsinki, 13, 115–19, 116f, 118f, 119f, 122
   London, 183, 184f, 188, 209, 211
   Paris, 50–53
   Venice, 138–40
Greenwich Millennium Village (London), 17,
   208–9, 208f
Growth management. *See also* Compact
   urban form
   Copenhagen's Finger Plan, 85–88, 87f
   Freiburg, 67–69
   Helsinki, 123
   London, 191, 191f
   Vitoria-Gasteiz, 157–58, 170
Guerilla Gardening movement, 57

Hammarby Sjöstad (Stockholm), 9–10, 17, 22
Haussmann, Baron Georges Eugène, 32, 34, 52
Health and environment, 102
Heidelberg, Germany, 18, 23–24
Helsinki, Finland
   background and profile, 109–11, 110f
   climate and energy, 18, 112–13
   equity issues, 113
   as green city, 122–25
   green spaces, 13, 115–19, 116f, 118f, 119f,
      122
   infill and green city strategies, 119–20
   planning system, national, 113–15
   stormwater management and flood
      prevention, 113
   Sustainability Action Plan, 111–12
   transportation and mobility, 120–21
Home zones, 12, 49–50
Housing policy and developments. *See also*
   Buildings and energy
   Helsinki, 113
   London, 191–92, 206–9, 208f
   Rieselfeld project (Freiburg), 76f, 78–81,
      79f
   Vauban project (Freiburg), 17, 75f, 76–78
Human rights, 34

Imagination, failure of, 220–21
Immigration and immigrants (Paris), 30–31
INBIOS project (Spain), 167–68
Incentive programs
   European practices, 218, 219
   France, 39
   Freiburg, 70–71
   green rooftops and, 16
   Heidelberg, 18
Infill, 68, 69, 119–20. *See also* Compact
   urban form
International Union for Conservation of
   Nature, 177
Italy (Milan), 17. *See also* Venice, Italy

Johnson, Boris, 182, 187, 188, 192–96, 202,
   205, 213

KIOSK (Freiburg), 80b
Kyoto Accord and Protocol, 2, 37

Land use planning. *See also* Growth
   management

Copenhagen, 89
Freiburg, 67–69
Helsinki and Finland, 110f, 111, 113–14
Paris, 63n8
public transit and, 9
Vitoria-Gasteiz, 158
Leinberger, Chris, 223
Linz, Austria, 16
Livingstone, Ken, 182, 194, 198, 200, 213, 224
London, England
background and context, 181–82
bicycles, 10, 195, 196, 202
Blue Ribbon Network, 189
bus system development, 200
climate change, emissions, and energy, 20,
192–94, 197, 199
Crossrail project, 199–200
ecological footprint, 185–86, 207
economic diversity, 192
Green Travel Plans, 202–3
Greenwich Millennium Village, 17, 208–9,
208f
home zones, 12, 50
housing, 191–92, 206–9, 208f
London Plan, 186–92, 191f, 211
metabolism, 21–22
Metropolitan Open Land (MOL), 188
physical characteristics, 183–84
regional planning and neighborhoods,
190–91
road travel, 198–99
Transport for London (TfL), 197–202
transport issues, 185
transport strategy, 194–97
urban agriculture, 209–10
urban sustainability agenda, 210–11
walking, 195, 200–202, 201f
waste and recycling, 203–4, 205f
wildlife habitat and tree planting, 189f,
204–6
London Thames Gateway Heat Network, 197
Louis XIII, 32, 52
Louis XIV, 32
Louis XVI, 32
Louv, Richard, 13
Low Emission Zone (LEZ), London, 199
Luxembourg Garden (Paris), 52, 58, 59f

Madrid, Spain, 17
Mäenpää, Pasi, 123

Malmö, Sweden, 17, 18, 91–92
Market Gardens, Vitoria-Gasteiz, 167, 168f
Maroto, Javier, 173
Masdar City, Abu Dhabi, 4
Mayors Climate Change Agreement (U.S.), 2
McDonough, William, 221
Metabolism, sustainable, 20–23, 219
Metropolitan Open Land (MOL), London,
188
Metro systems, 33, 46–48, 63n20, 92–93, 185
Milan, Italy, 17
Mobilien rapid transit system (Paris), 45, 45f
Mobility. See Bicycles; Transportation and
transit; Walking and walkability
MOSE floodgate project (Venice), 144–47,
145f
Musée du Quai Branly (Paris), 16–17

Napoleon III, 32, 52
Nature and natural systems, 12–13, 118. See
also Green spaces and greenbelts
Nature Deficit Disorder, 13
Nature Policy Plan (Netherlands), 13–14
Netherlands, 10–11, 12, 13–14
New York City, 221–22
Nickels, Greg, 2
Norway (Oslo), 6–7, 14, 15f
Nuclear power, 74

Obesity, 6
Olarizu Botanical Garden of European
Threatened Woods (Spain), 168
One Planet Living initiative, 206–7
Open space. See Green spaces and greenbelts
Oslo, Norway, 6–7, 14, 15f

Paris, France
Autolib' car-sharing scheme, 10, 44
background and profile, 29–30
bicycles, 11, 11f, 49–50
biodiversity, 53–58, 55t, 56f
energy use, 39–41
geographic, socioeconomic, and
environmental-policy context of, 30–34
green spaces, 50–53
green walls, 16–17, 55, 56f
national environmental laws and planning
frameworks, 34–37
Paris Climate Plan, 20, 38–39, 41, 43, 52
Paris Transportation Plan (PDP), 43–44

Paris, France (*continued*)
  regional planning and Grand Paris project,
    46–48
  renewable energy, 41–43
  slow traffic zones, 49–50, 51f
  transit systems, urban and regional, 10,
    33, 44–48
  walking and walkability, 48–49
Paris Plages ("Paris Beach") operation, 49
Paris respire ("Paris Breathes") operation, 49
Parks. *See* Green spaces and greenbelts
Passive house concept, 18
Pedestrians. *See* Walking and walkability
People Mover (Venice), 141, 142f
PIG (Projet d'interet général) projects
    (France), 36
Planning. *See specific places and topics*
Population decline, 4, 151, 184
Population growth. *See* Growth
    management
Porto Marghera, Venice, Italy, 136–38, 138f,
    149
Positive-energy buildings, 19–20
Public participation
  Copenhagen, 103–4
  Freiburg, 77, 79
  London, 186
  Vitoria-Gasteiz, 173
Public transport. *See* Transportation and
    transit

Railways. *See* Train and rail systems
Recreation. *See also* Green spaces and
    greenbelts; Walking and walkability
  Copenhagen, 84, 94–98, 96f, 97f, 105
  Helsinki, 115, 117, 124, 124f
Regional planning
  Alava Province (Spain) Ecological
    Network, 173–78, 176t, 177f
  Copenhagen and Denmark, 85, 88
  DTADDs and SRCAEs (France), 36–37
  Freiburg, 74
  London, 190
  Paris, 46–48
Rieselfeld project (Freiburg), 76f, 78–81, 79f
Rifkin, Jeremy, 19
Rights, human, 34
Rivers. *See also* Water, stormwater, and flood
    mitigation
  biodiversity and the Seine, Paris, 54
  daylighting, in Oslo, 14

Paris Voguéo shuttle boat line, 46
  Thames (London), 183, 189, 201f, 204–5
  underwater turbines, Seine River, Paris, 42
  Vitoria-Gasteiz, 162
Roads. *See* Automobiles and traffic planning
Rooftops, green
  economics of, 219
  Linz, Austria, 16
  Paris, 54–55, 58
  U.S., 64n25, 219, 222

Salburua wetlands, Basque Country, 163–64,
    165f
Sarkozy, Nicolas, 34, 47
Schimmelpennink, Luud, 10–11
SCOTs (Schémas de cohérence territoriale,
    France), 36
Serge Gainsbourg Garden (Paris), 52
Solar City designation, 18
Solar energy
  Barcelona, Spain, 18–19
  Freiburg, 74–75
  Freiburg, Germany, 66
  Malmö, Sweden, 18
  Paris, 41–42
  passive, 18
Solar Region Freiburg, 74
Spain. *See also* Vitoria-Gasteiz (Basque
    Country, Spain) greenbelt
  Alava Province Ecological Network, 173–
    78, 176t, 177f
  CaixaForum Museum, Madrid, 17
  INBIOS project, 167–68
  Olarizu Botanical Garden of European
    Threatened Woods, 168
  positive-energy buildings in Aragon, 19
  solar energy in Barcelona, 18–19
SRCAE (Schéma régional climat air énergie,
    France), 36–37
Stockholm, Sweden
  carbon emissions, 20
  Hammarby Sjöstad, 9–10, 17, 22
  parks and nature reserve, 13
  transit energy sources, 24
  urban metabolism, 21, 22
Stormwater. *See* Water, stormwater, and
    flood mitigation
Stuttgart, Germany, 14
Subsidies
  Paris, 40–41
  for solar energy, Freiburg, 74–75

Suburban expansion and urban sprawl
  governance and, 212
  Mäenpää's "wide urbanism" concept,
    123
  in Paris, 33
  sedentary lifestyle and, 6
  in U.S., 212
Subways. *See* Metro systems
Sustainability. *See also specific topics*
  Copenhagen, 83, 90, 91, 99–102, 103,
    106–7
  Europe as pioneer and model in, 3–7,
    23–26
  Freiburg, 65, 81–82
  Helsinki, 111–12, 114–15, 122–23
  London, 186, 193, 210–11, 212–13
  need for models, 1
  Paris, 29–30, 34–37, 59
  Sustainable Cities Plan, France, 36
  United States, 2
  urban form and, 7
  urban metabolism and, 20–23
  Venice, 133–34, 137, 151–52
Sustainable Cities and Towns Campaign
  (EU), 3, 110–11
Sustainable Cities Plan (France), 36
Sweden. *See also* Stockholm, Sweden
  Envac waste system, 204
  Hammarby Sjöstad, Stockholm, 9–10, 17
  Malmö, 17, 18, 91–92

Taxation
  Copenhagen, 107
  European practices, 218
  France, 35, 47, 62n6, 63n20
Thatcher, Margaret, 182, 200
Thermal insulation programs, 40
Tibéri, Jean, 34
Tourism
  carbon emissions and (Paris), 38, 44
  London, 184
  Venice and, 133, 150
Train and rail systems
  Copenhagen, 85–86, 90–91, 92–93
  Freiburg, 71–73, 73f
  high-speed, 9, 196
  integration of regional and national with
    local, 9
  London, 185, 196, 199–200
  Paris RER network and Métro, 33, 46
  Venice, 140–43

Transportation and transit. *See also*
  Automobiles and traffic planning;
  Bicycles; Walking and walkability
  air travel, 196
  Copenhagen, 85–88, 90–94
  Freiburg, 71–73, 73f
  green fuels, Stockholm, 24
  Helsinki, 120–21
  integration of, 9
  land use decisions and, 9
  London, 185, 194–97, 209, 211–12
  Paris, 33, 38, 43–48
  Venice, 140–43
Tree planting. *See also* Green spaces and
  greenbelts
  London, 189f, 205–6
  Paris, 55–57
  Vitoria-Gasteiz, 168
Turner, Chris, 4
20-20-20 goals (EU), 37

UN Agenda 21 action plan, 97, 100–102, 110,
  156
United Kingdom, 186. *See also* London,
  England
United States
  American Dream, 5, 6t, 222–24
  automobile, role of, 7
  climate, energy, and emissions, 2
  European cities as model for, 3–4, 6–7,
    25–26
  implementation barriers, overcoming,
    218–22
  lesson from Europe for, 211–12, 215–18
  sustainability initiatives, 2
  urgency to green cities agenda, 215
Urban ecology and urban greening. *See
  also* Green spaces and greenbelts; Tree
  planting
  Copenhagen, 99–100
  European cities as pioneers in, 16
  London, 194
  Vitoria-Gasteiz, 168–69
Urbanization, 1, 170
Urban sprawl. *See* Suburban expansion and
  urban sprawl

Vauban project (Freiburg), 17, 75f, 76–78
VEGA (Venice Gateway for Science and
  Technology), 137
Vélib' shared bike system (Paris), 11, 11f, 50

Venice, Italy
 background and profile, 129–33, 130f, 132f
 "city on water" and "city on land," 134–35
 contradictions in, 151–53
 Giudecca transformation and city center,
  135–36
 MOSE floodgates project, 144–47, 145f
 pedestrian paths and new Ponte della
  Constituzione, 141, 141f
 People Mover, 141, 142f
 port activities, cruise traffic, and green
  policy, 149–51
 Porto Marghera, 136–38, 138f, 149
 San Giuliano Park, 138–40
 Strategic Plan, 134
 transportation and mobility, 140–43
 VEGA science and technology park, 137
 water protection and city maintenance,
  143–49, 144f
Venice Gateway Project, 140
Vienna, 22, 23, 24
Villaraigosa, Antonio, 224
Vitoria-Gasteiz (Basque Country, Spain)
 greenbelt
 agricultural activities and rural landscape
  preservation, 158–59, 167
 Alava Province Ecological Network, 173–
  78, 176t, 177f
 background and profile, 155–57, 156f, 161f
 biodiversity and biocapacity, 167–68
 ecological planning on urban fringe,
  159–60
 economic benefits of ecological planning,
  169
 greenbelt strategy, launching of, 160–61
 hydrological system regulation, 162–64,
  163f
 landscape characteristics, 157–59
 pedestrian and bicycle mobility, 12, 14,
  164–67, 175–76
 public use, integration of, 164
 threats and issues on hold, 169–72

urban green infrastructure system
  potential, 172–73
urban planning and design, 168–69

Walking and walkability
 overview, 11–12
 Copenhagen, 98–99, 105
 Freiburg, 71, 72f
 Helsinki, 120–21, 123
 London, 195, 200–202, 201f, 209
 Paris, 48–49
 Venice, 141, 141f, 151
 Vitoria-Gasteiz, 164–67, 166f, 175–76
Walls, green, 16–17, 55, 56f
Waste and recycling
 Copenhagen trash clean-up, 106
 energy from, 41, 203–4
 Envac system, 204, 205f
 London, 194, 203–4
 Paris, 41
 Venice canals and, 143
Water, stormwater, and flood mitigation. See
  also Rivers
 Copenhagen Harbor and swimming,
  96–97, 97f
 Freiburg, 70–71, 79
 Helsinki, 113, 118–19, 119f
 London, 183, 189, 194
 Paris, 39
 pond rehabilitation and construction
  (Paris), 54
 Venice, 131–32, 140, 143–50, 144f
 Vitoria-Gasteiz, 162–64, 163f
"Wide urbanism," 123
Wildlife habitat, London, 204–5
Wilson, E. O., 12
Wind energy (France), 35, 42
Woonerf (shared space), 12, 49–50
World War II, 33

ZAC (Zone d'aménagement concerté)
  projects (Paris), 42